JOURNAL FOR THE STUDY OF THE NEW TESTAMENT SUPPLEMENT SERIES
160

Sheffield Academic Press

Johannine Ecclesiology

Johan Ferreira

Journal for the Study of the New Testament
Supplement Series 160

To DeGuang

Hannah and David

ἵνα ἡ ἀγάπη ἣν ἠγάπησάς με ἐν αὐτοῖς ᾖ κἀγὼ ἐν αὐτοῖς

Copyright © 1998 Sheffield Academic Press

Published by Sheffield Academic Press Ltd
Mansion House
19 Kingfield Road
Sheffield S11 9AS
England

Printed on acid-free paper in Great Britain
by Bookcraft Ltd
Midsomer Norton, Bath

British Library Cataloguing in Publication Data

A catalogue record for this book is available
from the British Library

ISBN 1-85075-887-5

CONTENTS

ACKNOWLEDGMENTS

I am very pleased to acknowledge the guidance and encouragement of the following persons in the publication of this book which represents the results of my doctoral research carried out at the University of Queensland. Needless to say, without their generous assistance the appearance of this book would not have been possible.

The two persons to whom I owe the greatest gratitude are Professor J.H. Charlesworth, the George L. Collord Professor of New Testament Language and Literature at Princeton Theological Seminary; and Professor M.S. Lattke, Professor of New Testament and Early Christianity Studies at the University of Queensland. These two scholars were most influential in my development as a student at Princeton and at the University of Queensland. I thank Professor Charlesworth, one of my thesis examiners, for his encouragement to publish this study in the Supplement series of the *Journal for the Study of the New Testament*.

My deepest appreciation also goes to Professor Lattke for acting as my *Doktorvator* at the University of Queensland. Professor Lattke provided exceptional supervision throughout my research program, and also showed an interest in my own academic development that was more than his duties required. I learned tremendously from his meticulous scholarship and immense knowledge.

In addition, I would like to thank Professor P. Allen, Dr R.E. Strelan, Dr A. Stimpfle and Dr M. Harding. Professor Allen of the Australian Catholic University provided encouragement through most of my doctoral studies while I was working as her research assistant. Dr Strelan read the final manuscript of my thesis and made valuable suggestions for improving it. Dr Stimpfle of Augsburg University and Dr Harding, Dean of the Australian College of Theology, not only acted as examiners of the thesis but also gave constructive advice towards its publication. Of course, any weakness remaining in this

Johannine Ecclesiology

book is due to myself alone, and in no way reflects on the expertise of these excellent scholars.

Finally, I would like the thank the staff at Sheffield Academic Press for their expertise in preparing my manuscript for publication.

Johan Ferreira
Brisbane, 1998

ABBREVIATIONS

AJBA	*Australian Journal of Biblical Archaeology*
AJBI	*Annual of the Japanese Biblical Institute*
AnBoll	Analecta Bollandiana
BA	*Biblical Archaeologist*
BAGD	Walter Bauer, William F. Arndt, F. William Gingrich and Frederick W. Danker, *A Greek–English Lexicon of the New Testament and Other Early Christian Literature* (Chicago: University of Chicago Press, 2nd edn, 1958)
BETL	Bibliotheca ephemeridum theologicarum lovaniensium
BFCT	Beiträge zur Förderung christlicher Theologie
Bib	*Biblica*
BIFAO	*Bulletin de l'Institut français d'archéologie orientale*
BiKi	*Bibel und Kirche*
BJRL	*Bulletin of the John Rylands University Library of Manchester*
BTB	*Biblical Theology Bulletin*
BZ	*Biblische Zeitschrift*
BZNW	Beihefte zur ZNW
CBQ	*Catholic Biblical Quarterly*
CJT	*Canadian Journal of Theology*
ClerR	*Clergy Review*
CNT	Commentaire du Nouveau Testament
Com(US)	Communio, Spokane, Washington
CTA	A. Herdner (ed.), *Corpus des tablettes en cunéiformes alphabétiques découvertes à Ras Shamra–Ugarit de 1929 à 1939* (Paris: Imprimerie nationale Geuthner, 1963)
CurTM	*Currents in Theology and Mission*
EBib	Etudes bibliques
EDNT	*Exegetical Dictionary of the New Testament*
EstBíb	*Estudios bíblicos*
ETL	*Ephemerides theologicae lovanienses*
EvQ	*Evangelical Quarterly*
Exc.	Excerpt (in the *Anthologium* of Sobaeus)
ExpTim	*Expository Times*
FRLANT	Forschungen zur Religion und Literatur des Alten und Neuen Testaments
HSM	Harvard Semitic Monographs
HTR	*Harvard Theological Review*
*IDB*Sup	*IDB*, Supplementary Volume

IEJ	*Israel Exploration Journal*
IJT	*Indian Journal of Theology*
IKaZ	*Internationale Katholische Zeitschrift*
Int	*Interpretation*
ITQ	*Irish Theological Quarterly*
ITS	*Indian Theological Studies*
ISBE	Geoffrey Bromiley (ed.), *The International Standard Bible Encyclopedia* (4 vols.; Grand Rapids: Eerdmans, rev. edn, 1979–88)
JA	*Journal asiatique*
JBL	*Journal of Biblical Literature*
JETS	*Journal of the Evangelical Theological Society*
JTC	*Journal for Theology and the Church*
JTS	*Journal of Theological Studies*
KAI	H. Donner and W. Röllig, *Kanaanäische und aramäische Inschriften* (3 vols.; Wiesbaden: Harrassowitz, 1962–64)
Lib.	Libellus (of the Corpus Hermeticum)
MScRel	*Mélanges de science religieuse*
MTZ	*Münchener theologische Zeitschrift*
Neot	*Neotestamentica*
NGWG	*Nachrichten (von) der Gesellschaft der Wissenschaften (zu) in Göttingen*
NHC	*Nag Hammadi Codex*
NTG	New Testament Guides
NThS	*Nieuwe theologiske Studien*
NTS	*New Testament Studies*
RB	*Revue biblique*
RevistB	*Revista biblica*
ResQ	*Restoration Quarterly*
RHPR	*Revue d'histoire et de philosophie religieuses*
RSR	*Recherches de science religieuse*
SBL	Society of Biblical Literature
SBLDS	SBL Dissertation Series
SE	*Studia Evangelica I, II, III* (= TU 73 [1959], 87 [1964], 88 [1964], etc.)
SER	Sheffield Excavation Reports
SHR	*Studies in the History of Religions*
SNTSMS	Society for New Testament Studies Monograph Series
STÅ	*Svensk teologisk årsskrift*
StANT	*Studia zum Alten und Neuen Testament*
STDJ	Studies on the Texts of the Desert of Judah
SVTP	Studia in Veteris Testamenti pseudepigrapha
SVTQ	*St Vladimir's Theological Quarterly*
TDNT	Gerhard Kittel and Gerhard Friedrich (eds.), *Theological Dictionary of the New Testament* (trans. Geoffrey W. Bromiley; 10 vols.; Grand Rapids: Eerdmans, 1964–)
Theol.	*Theology*, London
THKNT	Theologischer Handkommentar zum Neuen Testament

ThViat	*Theology Viatorum*
ThWAT	G.J. Botterweck and H. Ringgren (eds.), *Theologisches Wörterbuch zum Alten Testament* (Stuttgart: W. Kohlhammer, 1970–)
TLZ	*Theologische Literaturzeitung*
TRE	*Theologische Realenzyklopädie*
TRu	*Theologische Rundschau*
TWOT	R. Laird Harris, Gleason L. Archer, Jr and Bruce K. Waltke (eds.), *Theological Wordbook of the Old Testament* (2 vols.; Chicago: Moody Press, 1980)
TZ	*Theologische Zeitschrift*
VSpir	*Vie spirituelle*
VSVD	Verbum Societatis Verbi divini
WMANT	Wissenschaftliche Monographien zum Alten und Neuen Testament
WUNT	Wissenschaftliche Untersuchungen zum Neuen Testament
ZAW	*Zeitschrift für die alttestamentliche Wissenschaft*
ZNW	*Zeitschrift für die neutestamentliche Wissenschaft*
ZST	*Zeitschrift für systematische Theologie*
ZTK	*Zeitschrift für Theologie und Kirche*

Chapter 1

INTRODUCTION

1. *Justification and Purpose of the Research*

Despite a tremendous amount of scholarship over the past 100 years
the Fourth Gospel remains 'the most marvellous enigma' of the New
Testament (Harnack 1905: I, 96). More than a century of critical
research has seen opinions shifted from one end of the spectrum to the
other.[1] And according to a prominent commentator on the Fourth
Gospel 'a solution of the "Johannine question",[2] agreement on the
complicated network of particular questions which it contains, cannot
be foreseen' (Schnackenburg 1990: I, 11). Therefore, any proposal to
wrestle with the Johannine question does not need much justification.
The present study is particularly relevant as it attempts to focus on an
under-researched,[3] and increasingly important, area of Johannine
theology.[4] The purpose of this research is to examine a question that
continues to be debated, in the words of Brown, 'a burning issue in
Johannine studies' (1966: I, cv), namely, Johannine ecclesiology. In
this study the term 'ecclesiology' refers to the theology of the church,
or the concept of the community of believers, which is found in the

1.   Thorough discussion on Johannine research is provided by Kysar (1975),
Ashton (1991), and in the major commentaries by R.E. Brown (1966) and Schnackenburg (1990).

2.   I shall discuss the so-called 'Johannine question' in Chapter 2.

3.   Although many studies have dealt indirectly with Johannine ecclesiology, major
studies have been few. Consult the bibliography for a list of studies dealing indirectly
with Johannine ecclesiology. Major studies on the subject are that of Domínguez
(1967–68) and Miller (1976). Articles dealing with Johannine ecclesiology are that of
R.E. Brown (1966: I, cv-cxi), Edanad (1985), Grayston (1967), Haacker (1973),
Kysar (1977), O'Grady (1977), Minear (1982), and Schnackenburg (1974; 1977;
1990: III, 203-217) *et al.*

4.   I am using the word 'theology' in its broad sense.

Fourth Gospel. Though the term ἐκκλησία does not occur in the Fourth Gospel, the Gospel does have a prominent and defined concept of a community of believers who are bounded together by their belief in the Revealer. Therefore, we use the term 'ecclesiology' in the title of this study because there is not another term available that better expresses the subject nature of the present study. Furthermore, the occurrence of the term ἐκκλησία in 3 John shows that the Johannine community would not necessarily have objected to its usage.[5] By the expression 'Johannine ecclesiology' this study is referring to the Fourth Gospel's *theology* of the church. Therefore, this study attempts to make a contribution to the discussion of Johannine theology (*Gemeindetheologie*) and not the social history (*Sitz im Leben*) of the community.[6] However, the historical situation of the community will be important as it throws light on the theological concept.[7]

In past research, Christology has enjoyed, and rightly so, the place of privilege; John[8] is a christological document. However, the emphasis on Christology should not prevent us from appreciating other Johannine themes. This study will argue that ecclesiology is a major Johannine concern and not just an incidental thought.[9] It will also argue that ecclesiology is part of the centre of Johannine theology, and played an important role in the formation of John's theological construct.

In the present study, Johannine ecclesiology will be examined on the basis of an exegetical and terminological study of John 17. Therefore, though John 17 is the Gospel's most significant statement on ecclesiology, the study is by no means an exhaustive treatment of the subject.

5.   The term occurs three times at 3 Jn 6, 9 and 10.

6.   R.E. Brown's *The Community of the Beloved Disciple* (1979) is largely an attempt to reconstruct the history and the *Sitz im Leben* of the Johannine community and does not deal with the theological concept that the community had of itself.

7.   The studies of Onuki (1984) and Stimpfle (1990) are good examples of how the historical situation influences the theological formulation of the Fourth Gospel. For example, for Stimpfle the split in the Johannine community and the death of the Beloved Disciple effected the Gospel's realized eschatology (1990: 247-72). Also see Meeks's article, 'The Man from Heaven in Johannine Sectarianism' (1972), for the way theological motifs serve social functions.

8.   By 'John' I simply mean the Fourth Gospel without making any comment on the authorship of the Gospel.

9.   For Käsemann, John 'does not seem to develop an explicit ecclesiology' (1978: 27). Likewise, Berger considers that a specific ecclesiology is absent from the Gospel of John (1989: 202-203).

Among other things, I shall argue that the prominence of the place of the community in John 17 underscores the importance of ecclesiology in the construct of Johannine theology. John 17 presents Jesus' last words to his disciples and serves as a kind of overview of the entire Gospel.[10]

This study will attempt to show that previous studies on Johannine ecclesiology have suffered under the influence of the categories of Pauline or 'orthodox' ecclesiology. Scholars have often approached John with theological categories that are alien to the Gospel itself. They have looked at the Fourth Gospel for evidence it can provide on church order, government and the sacraments.[11] However, these Pauline or 'orthodox' characteristics of the church are not the major concern of the Johannine community's ecclesiology. Of course, that does not mean that John has no interest in church order or the sacraments; nevertheless, its concern lies elsewhere. John is more concerned about the origin, nature, and especially the function of the believing community than about matters of liturgy or church order. Therefore, the research of the present study is needed to highlight the real nature and purpose of John's concept of the community. This study will argue that John develops a 'christological ecclesiology' in the sense that the Johannine community is *Christus prolongatus*. It will also argue that this 'christological ecclesiology' has its origins in the unique *Sitz im Leben* of the Johannine community, and serves to defend, sustain, and encourage the community, which was in conflict with a synagogue (or synagogues) during the latter part of the first century.

2. *Methodology Used and Plan of the Research*

This study will approach the Gospel of John from a historical perspective, and will therefore employ the methods of historical and

10. Appold has noted that Jn 17 'has all the distinct markings of a summary of the Fourth Gospel's total concern' (1978: 365). Käsemann says, '... it is unmistakable that this chapter is a summary of the Johannine discourses and in this respect is a counterpart to the prologue' (1978: 3). Also, Onuki writes, 'Beide, Prolog und Gebet, bilden die Pfeiler am Anfang und Ende von Jesu Wirken, auf denen der gewaltige Bogen aufruht, der in Gottes Offenbarung besteht. Deshalb enthalten Prolog und Gebet auch je für sich das Summarium der johanneischen Theologie' (1984: 173).

11. For example, see R.E. Brown's discussion (1966: I, cv-cxi).

literary criticism. The research will work closely with several documents of early Judaism, Christianity and Gnosticism. Therefore, the
present study will by and large ignore the more recent developments
in narrative or reader–response criticism.[12] This does not mean, however, that a narrative approach to the Gospel of John is flawed or that
it has produced insignificant results.

The study will focus on John 17 as it will serve the purpose of our
investigation well. This passage contains many major terms and concepts of the Gospel arranged in close proximity. I shall highlight the
important terms and concepts of the passage and try to point out their
significance for Johannine ecclesiology. Since the focus will be on
John 17, the study will only refer to 1 John for supporting evidence
or to illustrate a point. As such, the study will not deal with the
Johannine epistles, though the epistles would be important for a full
treatment of Johannine ecclesiology (Brown 1966: cvii). Therefore,
this study is not an exhaustive treatment of Johannine ecclesiology. I
shall not spend time discussing Johannine church order or the Johannine view of the sacraments. As has been mentioned above, these factors are not central in John's concept of the community. The study
will also attempt to relate sociology, or the historical condition of the
Johannine community, to the Gospel's ecclesiology.

In the following chapter, I shall deal with the history of research
and shall give a brief overview of the major issues in Johannine
studies. This overview will provide the scholarly context in which the
research is to be read. The chapter will also attempt to draw some
conclusions which will serve as the presuppositions of the research.

The research will then consist of two parts, first, an exegetical part,
and secondly, a terminological part. The exegetical part will consist of
two chapters, one dealing with the context and structure of Jesus'
prayer, and the other dealing with the exegesis of the prayer. The exegesis will especially focus on the ecclesiological aspects of the prayer,
and as such may be regarded as an ecclesiological exegesis. The terminological part will contain two concept studies dealing with major
theological terms of the prayer, namely, glory and sending. Documents from different religious traditions will be examined to see how
these terms were used in John's religious milieu, and how they may
have influenced John. The purpose is to relate these terms to John's

12. One of the best examples of this approach to the Gospel of John is that of
Culpepper (1983).

concept of the community, as well as to understand John's own *relig-ionsgeschichtliche* context. The sociological setting (*Sitz im Leben*) of the Johannine community will be a very important factor to be considered. In the conclusion, I shall present a summary of my findings and attempt to give a description of the essence of Johannine ecclesiology. In view of the results of the present study, I shall also briefly explore the *religionsgeschichtliche* setting of the Gospel, and further areas of research for Johannine ecclesiology.

Chapter 2

HISTORY OF RESEARCH

1. *Context of Present Research*

a. *The Johannine Question*

The research contained in this study should be seen in the context of the discussion concerning the 'Johannine question' which was first clearly articulated by Harnack.[1] Harnack appreciated the marked differences, first highlighted by Baur, between John and the Synoptics in style, form, and content. At first Harnack drew attention to the problem of the religious milieu of the Gospel (1905: 96), but later applied himself to questions of authorship and date (1958: 651-80). Since Harnack's important contribution some vagueness has arisen on the exact nature of the Johannine question. Consequently, scholarship has focused on various problems as a key to unravel the Johannine riddle, including authorship, sources, religious milieu, Christology and purpose.

b. *Authorship*

Earlier in the history of Johannine research, scholars occupied most of their time with questions regarding the Gospel's historical reliability[2] and the related question of authorship (Ashton 1991: 15). The traditional view that the apostle John wrote the Gospel was largely rejected. In the words of Käsemann, 'Historical criticism has demolished the traditional opinion that the Fourth Gospel was written by John, the son of Zebedee' (1978: 1). However, Käsemann went on to say that '...historical criticism has not offered us an acceptable substitute for that outdated view' (1978: 1). The question is complicated for several reasons: (1) the Gospel itself does not identify the author, and when the Gospel does refer to the author it is vague and inconsistent;

---

1. See Harnack (1923: 36-43; 1905: 96; and 1958: 656-80).
2. Baur rejected the historical reliability of the Fourth Gospel which was unquestioned until his time.

(2) the matter is complicated by the fact that more than one 'John' has been associated with the Gospel in early church tradition;[3] and (3) the problem of authorship is further confused by the recognition that there are a mingling of different sources and several layers of redaction in the Gospel. The four most common modern alternatives to the problem have been listed by Kysar as follows:

> (a) John, son of Zebedee, is directly responsible for the present gospel;
> (b) John, son of Zebedee, is indirectly responsible for the gospel, since he was the originator of the tradition which another put in the form of the present gospel; (c) John Mark is indirectly responsible for the gospel and was the originator of the tradition embedded in the gospel. (d) An anonymous person is responsible for the present gospel and the source of his tradition is equally unknown (1975: 88).

There is no majority view as to these four alternatives.[4] The most recent consideration of the question of authorship is Charlesworth's *The Beloved Disciple: Whose Witness Validates the Gospel of John?* (1995). As the title indicates, the book does not deal directly with the question of authorship but seeks to assertain the identity of the Beloved Disciple. Charlesworth's close reading of the text and impressive mastery of secondary literature will no doubt convince many that Thomas Didymus is the Beloved Disciple.

c. Sources, Redactions and Editions
Related to the problem of authorship is that of sources, redactions, and editions. Gardner-Smith's little volume *Saint John and the Synoptic Gospels* (1938) argued persuasively that John is independent from the Synoptic Gospels. His thesis has gained widespread approval with some qualifications,[5] and has led to the question, 'If John did not use the Synoptics, from where did his material originate?' Bultmann,

---

3.   John the Presbyter, mentioned by Papias, enjoyed considerable consideration.
4.   Hengel, *The Johannine Question* (1989), argues that 'John the Elder' mentioned by Papias is the principal figure behind the Gospel.
5.   Bultmann, Noack and Dodd all follow Gardner-Smith's thesis. Hengel holds that John knows at least one of the Synoptics but is critical of them (it) and does not use them (it) as sources (1989: 75-77, 91-92, 127-30). According to Painter, John uses Synoptic material like other traditions (1993: 78). Consequently, Smith writes that '...it is now possible to speak of a loose, but real, consensus regarding a Johannine tradition relatively independent of the synoptics...' (1984: 60).

following the lead of earlier critics,[6] expended much effort in his commentary attempting to isolate several sources and layers of redaction. According to Bultmann John used three sources: (1) a signs or *semeia* source; (2) a revelatory-discourse source (*Offenbarungsreden*); (3) and a passion and resurrection narrative.[7] Ever since his commentary Bultmann's three sources have enjoyed considerable discussion. However, only the signs source has received widespread acceptance among source critics.[8] Fortna produced the most detailed reconstruction of the signs source based on his criterion of aporias. He postulated that the signs source had been compiled in the context of the early Christian mission to the Jews (Fortna 1970: 223-25). Another prominent Johannine scholar, D.M. Smith, also argues for the existence of a signs source and possibly a narrative source (1984: 39-93). And more recently, Cope has argued that the 'Signs Gospel' may have been the earliest Gospel (1987). Therefore, it appears that most Johannine scholars affirm that the author of John used a source that described Jesus' miracles as signs revealing his glory (Käsemann 1978: 21-22).

The reconstruction of a signs source, however, has not been without its critics. Among the critics are Lindars, Carson and Meeks. Though Lindars concludes that the Gospel is 'the product of a literary process' (1971: 14) and concedes the probability of a signs source, he criticizes attempts to reconstruct an extended signs source (1971: 43).[9] Carson does not deny the existence of a signs source but concludes with 'a gentle plea for probing agnosticism in this matter' (1978: 411). Meeks also criticized rearrangement hypotheses by the failure of scholars to note 'one of the most striking characteristics of the evangelist's literary procedure: the elucidation of themes by progressive repetition' (1972: 55).

Apart from these cautions, the general opinion of current scholarship is that the Gospel is built upon a *Grundschrift*, which included a

6. A 'signs source' was already suggested by Schwartz (1907) and Faure (1922).

7. For a systematic presentation and criticism of Bultmann's source hypothesis see Smith (1965).

8. Käsemann levelled the most severe criticism against Bultmann's *Offenbarungsreden* in his article 'Ketzer und Zeuge: Zum johanneischen Verfasserproblem' (1951). H. Becker is one of the few scholars to argue with Bultmann for an *Offenbarungsreden* (1956). Scholars arguing for the existence of a *semeia* source include J. Becker, Schnackenburg, Nicol, Teeple, Temple and Smith.

9. My only problem with Lindars's book is that after he rejects the possibility of reconstructing the signs source, he gives a theology of the signs source!

signs source, and had been expanded, redacted and edited over a long period (Schnackenburg 1990: I, 49). Lindars suggests that the Gospel was completed over a 'lengthy process, beginning in the 80s and not complete until the 90s' (1971: 14). M.-E. Boismard (1962) even suggests that the Gospel was produced over a period of two generations (c. CE 50-110). He also holds that it was first written in Aramaic.[10]

Related to the question of sources is that of redactions and editions. The present form of the Gospel seems to suggest that there must have been different editions of the Gospel.[11] R.E. Brown suggests a five-stage process in the composition of the Gospel (1966: I, xxxiv-xxxix). It is not necessary to provide a detailed examination of these suggestions for the present study. Nevertheless, the present study is based on the recognition that the Gospel represents a complicated and lengthy process of composition, which (1) included a miracle or signs source, (2) underwent a number of redactions, (3) and also went through a number of additions.[12]

d. *Religious Milieu*

Another focus of scholars attempting to answer the Johannine question, which is crucial for interpretation, concerns the original spiritual or religious setting of the Gospel. Schnackenburg even says, 'The spiritual background, the world of thought in which it is situated, is of supreme importance for the *whole* understanding of John' (1990: I, 119).[13] And, 'Our chief task today is to determine what were the most insistent, effective and dominating influences to which the fourth evangelist was subject' (1990: I, 119). This approach was indeed the

10. On the Aramaic question see Burney (1922), Torrey (1923), de Zwaan (1938), and M. Black (1967).

11. W. Wilkens proposed three editions of the Gospel all written by the Beloved Disciple (1958). Parker proposed two editions of the Gospel (1956). Boismard proposed that John the son of Zebedee either wrote or controlled the writing of at least two editions, and that the final redactor was Luke (1962).

12. Jn 1.1-18 and Jn 21 are later additions to the Gospel. This process of adding material to the Gospel can clearly be seen by the late second-century addition of the Jn 7.53-8.11 pericope. It is also probable that the Farewell discourses were not a part of the Gospel initially. Then, there is the odd numbering that occurs at Jn 2.11 and Jn 4.54, the strange order of chs. 5 to 7, the apparent contradiction at Jn 4.2 (cf. Jn 3.26), the illogical transition between chs. 14 to 15 (cf. Jn 14.31), and the first conclusion at Jn 20.30-31.

13. The emphasis is mine.

driving force behind the *Religionsgeschichtliche Schule* started by Otto Pfleiderer.[14] As for Johannine scholarship, it is argued that a source or sources should be sought to account for all the religious ideas expressed in the Gospel. The differences of opinion in this matter have been most dramatic.

The history of research has occupied itself with examining three major influences on the Gospel, namely, Hellenism, Gnosticism and Judaism (Brodie 1993: 7).[15] Under the influence of German critical scholarship the prevailing opinion until Bultmann's commentary is expressed in Barrett's sentiment that John was 'the gospel of the Hellenists; it was written by a Greek thinker for the Greeks; it marks a decisive point in the hellenization of the Christian faith' (1955: 3). This view found its greatest exponent in the writings of C.H. Dodd, who believed that the high Hellenistic religion expressed in the Hermetica provided the best background for understanding John. Later, W.D. Davies followed up Dodd's suggestion by providing many comparisons between John and the *Hermetica* (1966: 398-408). However, Bultmann changed the direction of Barrett and Dodd's influence in arguing for a Gnostic setting. Bultmann's critical article in the mid 1920s, 'Die Bedeutung der neuerschlossenen mandäischen und manichäischen Quellen für das Verständnis des Johannesevangeliums', argued strongly for a Gnostic influence on John by citing many parallels between it and later Mandaean and Manichaean writings. In his commentary that appeared about 30 years later, Bultmann consistently applied his theory of a Gnostic Redeemer myth to the Gospel. Bultmann's suggestion has had a considerable influence on the debate of Johannine scholarship, and though his theory has largely been rejected by most scholars it is still maintained by some.[16] Though support for a

14. The central idea of this school of scholarship is summed up by Pfleiderer's statement quoted by Kümmel, 'Christianity as a historical phenomenon is to be investigated by the same methods as all other history, and that in particular its origin is to be studied as the normal outcome of the manifold factors in the religious and ethical life of the time' (1973: 210).

15. Concerning the origin of John's thought Ashton has suggested six possibilities (1991: 23-26): (1) the Synoptics; (2) Paul (advocated by Harnack, Goguel, Bousset *et al.*); (3) Judaism (advocated by Schlatter, Odeberg, J.A.T. Robinson, Brown, Charlesworth, Hengel *et al.*); (4) Hellenistic Judaism; (5) Hellenistic religion (advocated by C. H. Dodd); and (6) Gnosticism (advocated by Menoud, Bultmann, Käsemann, R.M. Grant *et al.*).

16. Bultmann's proposal was that John was written in a context of oriental

Gnostic trajectory behind John is declining, Kysar's statement should be noted, 'One caution must be mentioned: Recent scholarship has seen notice given that the Coptic gnostic materials must be studied and compared carefully with regard to their bearing on the issue' (1975: 145).[17] This is arguably one of the most important questions that faces Johannine scholars today.[18]

After the discovery of the Dead Sea Scrolls in 1947 another paradigm shift occurred in Johannine studies. Many scholars came to believe that John's thought had a Palestinian or Jewish origin. This view gained great popularity among American scholars. J.A.T. Robinson's article, 'The New Look on the Fourth Gospel' (1959), which argues that the Gospel could have arisen in Palestine in the mid-first century, was the first major assessment of this new trend (MacRae 1970: 14).[19] The Jewish milieu of the Fourth Gospel is now taken for granted by many scholars.[20] In concluding his discussion on the setting of the Gospel, Kysar says that '...contemporary research favors a Palestinian, Old Testament, Jewish setting for the thought of the gospel' (1975: 144). Though I agree with this contemporary assessment of research, some qualifications need to be made. In the first place a Jewish setting does not exclude the influence of a Gnostic

Gnosticism. His thesis is followed by E. Käsemann, J. M. Robinson, L. Schottroff, R. M. Grant *et al.*

17. Hengel's statement is therefore immature, 'The rather later writings from Nag Hammadi have not contributed much that is new to the understanding of the Fourth Gospel' (1989: 113).

18. Whether John is influenced by Gnosticism depends to a large extend on the definition of Gnosticism used (van Baaren 1970). If Gnosticism refers to the highly developed metaphysical system of thought as is expressed in the second-century writings of Valentinus, then John is not influenced by Gnosticism. However, if our definition of Gnosticism includes the Gnostic thought expressed in the more simple systems of Simon Magus and Menander, then John is probably influenced by Gnostic thought in some respect. For Bultmann, the central idea of John, which is akin to Gnosticism, is that Jesus is the emissary of God; Jesus has been sent as the Revealer and brings revelation (1925: 57).

19. Also see Cribbs (1970) who argues that John is an early (pre-70 CE) Palestinian Gospel.

20. See, for example, R.E. Brown's comment, 'A large number of scholars are coming to agree that the principal background for Johannine thought was the Palestinian Judaism of Jesus' time. This Judaism was far from monolithic, and its very diversity helps to explain different aspects of Johannine thought' (1966: I, lix). Also see Quispel's article 'John and Jewish Christianity' (1975).

trajectory on John, even as J.A.T. Robinson's statement implies, 'He stood, I believe, much more in what has aptly been called the "pre-gnostic" stream of Jewish wisdom-mysticism' (1959–60: 130). And secondly, in the words of MacRae:

> In the end, John's message is that Jesus can be approached in many ways, but can only be understood on Christian terms, not Jewish or Greek or Gnostic. That is why the Fourth Gospel was accepted as a Christian book: not, as Käsemann suggests, because its gnosticizing trend was misunderstood, but because despite its gnosticising trend it is the Christian gospel it proclaims (1970: 24).[21]

The past hundred years of scholarship have done us a great service in exposing false and one-sided presuppositions regarding the religious milieu of John. The task remains now to return to the text itself with the confidence that we are less likely to make the same mistakes. In the words of Schnackenburg, '...the last word must always lie with one's verdict on the text of John itself, with the analysis of its thought and language' (1990: I, 119).

Another important point that should be made about the religious milieu of the Gospel is that New Testament scholars have become more precise in the use of categories and *termini technici*. For example, many scholars prefer not to use the term 'background' (*Entwicklungslinie*) in New Testament studies anymore (Lattke 1975: 41-45). Robinson suggested replacing the term 'background', which implies a rather static state of affairs, with that of 'trajectory', which is more dynamic and conveys the historic process at work in every tradition (Koester and Robinson 1971: 8-9). Robinson says that 'the religious world through which early Christianity moved has been conceptualized as strangely immobile. Rabbinic Judaism, Gnosticism, an

---

21. Bultmann asked which background best serves to explain all the elements of John. Bultmann knew that many of the Gospel's themes are found in Judaism. However, Jewish thought alone cannot account for the full range of the Gospel's thought. Käsemann is equally insistent upon the need to ascertain the one decisive influence on John. John must 'point to a specific sector of primitive Christianity and, conversely, we must be able to deduce it from them' (1978: 3). Bühner deals with the Johannine question in a similar way: 'It is a matter of the correct placing of the Johannine community in the history of early Christianity, the placing of its literary work in the genesis of the New Testament, the question concerning the origin of the christological outline of the journey of the Son of God who is sent into the world and then returns to his heavenly home' (1977: 1).

oriental cult, a given mystery religion—each was presented as a single position' (Koester and Robinson 1971: 12). On the following page Robinson further expands his thesis:

> The Jewish, Greek, or gnostic 'background' or 'environment' cannot be mastered by reducing it to a mass of disorganized parallels to the New Testament; it must be reconceptualized in terms of movements, 'trajectories' through the Hellenistic world (Koester and Robinson 1971: 13).

These observations are important for assessing the religious milieu of the Gospel and for understanding specific Johannine terminology.

e. *Christology*

Probably the greatest point of unanimity among Johannine scholars is that the Gospel has a 'basic Christological interest' (Schnackenburg 1990: I, 154). The Gospel is diffused with traditional christological titles, and the emphasis is no longer as in the Synoptics on the kingdom Jesus preached but on the person of Jesus himself. However, the exact function of Johannine Christology is being debated.[22] Indeed, some scholars have seen the decisive Johannine question as whether the Gospel presents a Docetic or an incarnational Christology (Smith and Spivey 1989: 285).[23] Käsemann's short but influential study, *The Testament of Jesus: A Study of the Gospel of John in the Light of Chapter 17*,[24] argues consistently that the Johannine Jesus is the glorified Jesus, that is, there is no real concept of Jesus' humiliation and suffering. Even the cross represents the glorification of the Son. Käsemann has therefore described Johannine Christology as incipiently Docetic. Jesus is '...God walking on the face of the earth...' (1978: 75; cf. 1966: 132). Käsemann's reconstruction, however, has received widespread criticism. Richter strongly argues that the Fourth Gospel's purpose is in fact to counter Docetic interpretations of the incarnation.[25] Certainly, the Johannine Jesus is the Jesus of glory, but

---

22. See Cullmann (1959), Fascher (1968), Hahn (1969), Pollard (1970), Fortna (1973), Ellis (1988), Loader (1989) and Anderson (1993).

23. See Kysar, 'It is clear that one of the points of indecision in the present state of Fourth Gospel criticism is the history of the relationship of a theology of glory and a theology of the cross' (1977: 361).

24. Translated from the German *Jesu letzter Wille nach Johannes 17* published in 1966. A second and third German edition was published in 1967 and 1971 respectively.

25. At the conclusion of his article, 'Die Fleischwerdung des Logos im

then, the immediate question is what does that 'glory' mean in the Gospel? Chapter 5 of this study will attempt to answer this question.

f. *Readers and Purpose*

The question concerning the purpose of the Fourth Gospel is another crucial issue in Johannine research. The distinctive character of the Gospel in contrast to the Synoptics, and the explicit statement regarding its purpose (Jn 20.31), immediately invite the reflection of the scholar. The most influential voices of the early church considered that the Fourth Gospel was only written to supplement the Synoptics, and that it does not add anything that is substantially different (Torm 1931: 30, 130; Hendriksen 1961: 21-22). In more recent times, traditional scholarship has regarded the Gospel as a missionary document to evangelize either Jews or Greeks (Carson 1987: 639-51). During the last half of this century, however, the discussion has become much more sophisticated with the recognition that the Gospel has been composed from a variety of sources which reflect different aims: missionary, pastoral, and apologetic concerns can be identified in the Gospel (Schnackenburg 1990: I, 48-52; and R.E. Brown 1966: I, lxvii-lxxvii). More and more scholars are shifting away from the opinion that John is a missionary document, emphasizing the pastoral, and especially apologetic concerns. The question concerning the readers for whom the Gospel was written, and the purpose for which the Gospel was written, is closely related. Ashton sums up the possibilities:

> There are, broadly speaking, three questions that may be asked concerning John's audience or readership: was it (a) universal or particular; (2) Jewish or Gentile (or possibly Samaritan—somewhere in between the two); (c) Christian or non-Christian? If a non-Christian audience is intended then the writer's aim could be either polemic (attack) or apologetic (defence) or kerygmatic (missionary); if, on the other hand, the audience is Christian then the purpose could be either hortatory (to warn or to encourage) or catechetic (to teach or remind). These possibilities are not

Johannesevangelium', Richter writes that the incarnation, '... ist nur real zu verstehen, im Sinne des vollen Menschseins Jesu; denn sie ist ja Antwort auf die doketistische Behauptung, dass Jesus keinen wirklichen menschlichen Leib hatte, nicht in Wahrheit Mensch war' (1977: 196). And again, 'Der vierte Evangelist war mit Sicherheit kein Doketist' (1977: 197). Other scholars arguing against Käsemann's view include Hoskyns, J. Becker and Thompson.

mutually exclusive, since a writer may have more than one purpose in writing and more than one audience in mind. Besides, if it be allowed that the work may have gone through successive stages, then it must also be allowed that the purpose of each may be different (1991: 102).

Probably the most ancient opinion is that the purpose of the Gospel is to refute the heretics and to complement the Synoptic Gospels (Ashton 1991: 11). The source of this idea can be traced back to Clement who said that John 'wrote a spiritual Gospel',[26] and to the statement of Irenaeus who says that John wrote his Gospel to refute the error of Cerinthus (*Haer.* 3.11.1). If this is the case the Gospel would have a Christian audience and serve apologetic and catechetic purposes. As already mentioned above, Richter (1977: 149-98) and Hoskyns (1940) see the purpose of the Gospel to counter the tendency of a Docetic view of Jesus. Others have seen John as an apologetic document against the followers of John the Baptist (Baldensperger 1898). John 4.2 is clearly directed against some baptist group. Also the Baptist's statement that Jesus is more important than he, can be an apologetic statement against those who regarded John as the Messiah (cf. Jn 1.27; 3.28-30). For Kysar, following J.L. Martyn and W. Meeks, the specific purpose of the Gospel is Christian–Jewish dialogue (1975: 165). In all these instances a Christian audience, whether Jewish or non-Jewish, is implied.

Another popular opinion has been that the Gospel is a missionary document written to evangelize either Jews or non-Jews to the Christian faith (Bornhäuser 1928; Oehler 1936; van Unnik 1959). Some have suggested that the mission was to Samaria (Buchanan 1970; and Freed 1968), which seems to be the case in John 4. The missionary character of the Gospel has enjoyed greater consideration in the last ten years with the appearance of many important studies that highlighted the missionary themes of the Gospel (Ruiz 1987; Okure 1988). Smith concurs that 'there is a strong missionary thrust in the Fourth Gospel', but he gives this qualification, 'That the present form of the Gospel is solely or even primarily evangelical in purpose is, however, questionable' (1986: 83). Smith gives two reasons to prove his point. First, the

---

26. Clement's view is recorded in Eusebius, *Hist. Eccl.* 6.14.7: τὸν μέντοι Ἰωάννην ἔσχατον, συνιδόντα ὅτι τὰ σωματικὰ ἐν τοῖς εὐαγγελίοις δεδήλωται, προτραπέντα ὑπὸ τῶν γνωρίμων, πνεύματι θεοφορηθέντα πνευματικὸν ποιῆσαι εὐαγγέλιον.

Farewell discourses and the prayer addressed issues that pertain only to Christians, and, secondly, the conclusion of the Gospel (ch. 20) can pertain to either Christians or non-Christians, whereas ch. 21 pertains exclusively to Christians (1986: 83). At this point, however, a question may be raised, Does a document always need to call non-Christians to believe before it can be characterized as a missionary document? A missionary document's purpose may be broader than the call to believe, and may include other important issues relating to its evangelical purpose. If the Gospel's purpose is to encourage a beleaguered Christian community to continue its mission in the world it could still be called a missionary document. Onuki, for example, sees the function of John as enabling the community to reflect theologically on the rejection of its message, and so to return to its task of proclamation in the world (1984: 217-18).

g. *Conclusion*

It should be clear from this short survey that the Johannine question is a complex of related questions. Questions of historicity, authorship, sources, religious milieu, and theology cannot be separated from one another but are all interrelated. Though it is rooted in Jewish soil, Johannine theology is drawn from a variety of sources.[27] The Gospel presents a compilation of material that reflects the concerns of different situations and times. It is the product of the birth, history, conflicts, struggles and experiences of a small Christian-Jewish group. Therefore, in approaching the Fourth Gospel the scholar deals with an interrelated set of questions as he or she studies the Gospel. The task of the interpreter then is to isolate Johannine motifs in their particular *religionsgeschichtliche* context. This task is not easy, and, in some cases may be impossible to achieve. Nevertheless, though a satisfactory solution to the Johannine question will probably never be found, the present research is conducted with the confidence that we are approaching a clearer solution to the problem.

---

27. Kysar is of the same opinion, 'The question of the intellectual milieu of the gospel is perhaps confused by the fact that the evangelist's background was a mixture of religious motifs and movements characteristic of his day, and what scholars were once labelling as gnostic are simply syncretistic expressions of the evangelist and his milieu' (1975: 146).

2. *Major Advances in Scholarship*

Schnackenburg's statement nearly 30 years ago, which was quoted above, that 'a solution of the 'Johannine question', agreement on the complicated network of particular questions which it contains, cannot be foreseen' (1990: I, 11), still describes the current state of Johannine studies. Nevertheless, although it is probably naive to expect agreement on all the questions that John presents, major advances are being made in solving the Johannine riddle. About this Kysar has isolated six accomplishments of recent Johannine scholarship:

> A. The efforts of critical study have shown quite decisively that the fourth gospel incorporates a body of traditional material and was composed over a period of years in what might have been a rather complex process.
>
> B. Contemporary Johannine criticism has confirmed that the gospel is a community's document.
>
> C. It is the accomplishment of current Johannine scholarship that the evidence for the syncretistic, heterodox Jewish milieu of the gospel has become irresistible.
>
> D. That the dialogue between the church and the synagogue comprises the major element in the concrete situation of the fourth evangelist appears to be the emerging consensus of the critics.
>
> E. Research on the religious thought of the gospel demonstrates that it is an innovative and sophisticated mode of Christian thought radically christocentric in all its expressions.
>
> F. Finally, the recent criticism of the gospel attests fully to the fact that the johannine community is a distinctive form of early Christian life and thought (1975: 267-76).

Of these six 'advances' three are of special significance for the present research, namely, the Johannine School hypothesis, the history of the community, and the Gospel's heterogeneous-Jewish setting.

a. *The Johannine School*

As mentioned above, the traditional view that the apostle John wrote the Gospel in Ephesus has largely been rejected in critical research.[28]

---

28. Some conservative scholars still hold to the traditional view that the apostle John wrote the Gospel. Their insistence has to do with the historical reliability of the Gospel; since the author is an eyewitness it must be the apostle John. See Hendriksen (1961).

Recently, however, the idea of a single author has also been rejected by an increasingly larger number of scholars. Instead, it is proposed that a 'school' or a 'community' produced the Gospel. This does not mean, however, that the traditional view has totally faded from the horizon. Many scholars still believe that a certain John, probably the apostle, in some way stands behind the Gospel. Braun (1959) affirms that the Gospel does not come directly from John, though the main tradition goes back to him. Schnackenburg also recognizes the weight of the early evidence that John the son of Zebedee lived until old age in Ephesus and was the author of the Gospel (1990: I, 102). And more recently Hengel has argued that the Gospel is the basic work of 'John the Elder' that grew 'over quite a long time' in the teaching of the school (1989: 102).

Though many critics have recognized the problem the aporias in the text present, there have always been those emphasizing the unity of the Gospel. Many scholars working on John have acknowledged that the Gospel has a uniform style (Schweizer 1939; Ruckstuhl 1951). The best solution to this problem to date is found in the proposal that the Gospel is the collective product of a school.

The idea that the Gospel is a 'community's document' became prominent with the publication of Culpepper's doctoral dissertation *The Johannine School* (1975). After having examined the characteristics of schools in the Hellenistic world, Culpepper concluded that the Johannine community shares nine characteristics with ancient schools.[29] Culpepper's thesis has achieved widespread acceptance. Around the same time Cullmann's study *The Johannine Circle* reached

---

29. According to Culpepper these characteristics are: (1) The Johannine community was a fellowship of disciples; (2) The community gathered around, and traced its origins to, a founder—the Beloved Disciple; (3) The community valued the teachings of its founder and the traditions about him; (4) Members of the community were disciples or students of the founder—the Beloved Disciple; (5) Teaching, learning, studying and writing were common activities in the community; (6) The community observed a communal meal; (7) The community had rules or practices regulating admission and retention of membership; (8) The community maintained some distance from the rest of the society; (9) The community developed organizational means of ensuring its perpetuity (1975: 287-89). Though one might question the existence of some of the last mentioned organizational characteristics in the Johannine community, the basic thesis appears to be substantiated by the nature and content of the Fourth Gospel.

similar conclusions.[30] It is now commonly recognized that the Gospel of John is the result of a particular community's experiences and theological reflection.

The research of this study is based on the recognition that there is a compositional history behind the Fourth Gospel.[31] Though there is a wide range of opinions regarding the precise details of this history, there is increasingly a scholarly consensus on the following points: (1) the Gospel has been based on, or incorporated, a signs source; (2) it underwent redaction, (3) and though it reflects the influence of a powerful individual, (4) it is the product of a school. From this consensus the present research has adopted the following working hypothesis: a distinguished disciple, an influential figure in a specific region, constructed the Gospel on the basis of a signs source which had a definite missionary purpose. The writing of the Gospel was occasioned by a crisis that the Christians in his region faced, namely, conflict with a synagogue (or several synagogues). Later, a group of disciples gathered around this individual to form a community or school. After he passed away the community was faced with other needs or crises (Collins 1979), internal ones, which occasioned the need to make additions to the community's Gospel.

b. *The History of the Johannine Community*
J.L. Martyn has made a major contribution with his *History and Theology in the Fourth Gospel* first published in 1968. Martyn sees the crucial factor of the Gospel in a synagogue–church drama or conflict. The history of the Johannine community's conflict is played out by Jesus' conflict with the 'Jews'. In other words, what we have in the Gospel is a double history, the history and the experiences of the community are read back into the life of Jesus. Therefore, the text should be interpreted on two levels: first, it refers to 'an *einmalig* event during Jesus' earthly lifetime', and secondly, it also refers to 'actual events experienced by the Johannine church' (1979: 30). 'Where the

---

30. The German title *Der johanneische Kreis: Zum Ursprung des Johannesevangeliums* appeared in 1975, and the English translation, *The Johannine Circle: Its Place in Judaism, among the Disciples of Jesus and in Early Christianity: A Study in the Origin of the Gospel of John*, appeared a year later in 1976.

31. Meeks says that 'the Johannine literature is the product not of a lone genius but of a community or group of communities that evidently persisted with some consistent identity over a considerable span of time' (1972: 49).

two levels of witness overlie one another...one does not hope to distinguish them with absolute clarity' (1979: 30). It is in this sense that we should interpret the occasional transition between the first singular pronoun and third plural pronoun.[32]

Martyn further finds an exact historical occasion for this conflict, namely, the conflict between Johannine community and synagogue became acute after the Jewish council at Jamnia when the *Birkat-ha-minim* (*The Benediction Against Heretics*) were inserted in the Benedictions that were recited in the synagogue.[33] The Eighteen Benedictions were revised so that the twelfth benediction became a malediction against the *minim*, which can include Christians. The expression ἀποσυνάγωγος occurs three times in the Gospel and refers to Christians being excommunicated from the synagogue because of their belief in Jesus.[34]

Martyn reconstructs three stages in the development of the community's history. In the first stage (c. CE 40-85), the early period, the Jewish Christians existed harmoniously with the Jewish synagogue. In the second stage, the middle period, the community began to elevate the status of Jesus no longer as just the Messiah but as the divine son of God. This led to severe debate and conflict within the synagogue and eventual excommunication of those who persisted in their high view of Jesus. The third stage, the late period, was reached when the community focused on those who still had a high view of Jesus but remained in the synagogue.

Martyn's thesis has been adopted and adapted by many scholars after his seminal work.[35] Brown has proposed a much more detailed

32. Smith has a similar view when he says that '...John merges the history of Jesus into the history of his church, so that Jesus himself becomes the chief protagonist of his disciples and the gospel they preach. To make a rough comparison and generalization, Luke writes his Gospel and puts the Book of Acts alongside or after it; John writes his Gospel and overlays it with an account of his Christian community, particularly its struggles' (1986: 108-109). In an earlier article Smith writes, 'The presentation of Jesus in the Fourth Gospel is multidimensional. He is still the Jewish man of Galilee. But he is also the spiritual presence with, and head of, the community of disciples which we may safely call his church. He has been with the church in its past struggles and will continue with it into the foreseeable future' (1977: 376).

33. See Carroll (1957) and Horbury (1982) for further discussion on this subject.

34. Cf. Jn 9.22; 12.42; and 16.2.

35. Richter (1977) sees the community dividing into four groups emphasizing

hypothesis of the community's history by suggesting a five-stage history in the composition of the Gospel (1979). Wengst on the other hand proposed a Jewish-Christian community in Gaulanitis, Batanea, and Trachonitus (1981). Though the details should not be pressed there appears to be validity to the argument of the Christian–Jewish dialogue as an important factor reconstructing the history of the Johannine community. It is important for the present study to ask how the *Sitz im Leben* of the community shaped its theology. If we understand some of the concerns and struggles the community faced, we are in a better position to understand and appreciate the Gospel's intentions (Rensberger 1988: 14-15). Because of these efforts Käsemann's statement that, 'Historically, the Gospel as a whole remains an enigma, in spite of the elucidation of individual details' (1978: 2), is probably not true anymore.

Building on the work of Martyn, Onuki has produced a significant study on the dualism of the Fourth Gospel, entitled *Gemeinde und Welt im Johannesevangelium: Ein Beitrag zur Frage nach der theologischen und pragmatischen Funktion des johanneischen 'Dualismus'* (1984). Onuki uses the idea of *Horizontverschmelzung* between the tradition of Jesus and the historical situation of the community. John interprets a tradition about Jesus for his readers in light of their situation. In other words, according to Onuki, the historical situation of the earthly Jesus has been merged with the present situation of the evangelist and his community in the narrative of his Gospel (1984: 34). Therefore, Onuki makes the important observation that the prayer of John 17 should be understood from the standpoint of the community's historical situation (1984: 172).

c. *The Heterogeneous-Jewish Setting*
The discovery of the Dead Sea Scrolls has revolutionized the way in which scholars have approached the Fourth Gospel. First, the Dead

---

different beliefs: (1) Jesus as a prophet like Moses (Mosaic-prophet Christians); (2) Jesus as the son of God (Son-of-God Christians); (3) Jesus as the son of God in a Docetic way (Docetist Christians) and (4) Jesus as the son of God made flesh (Revisionist Christians). Cullmann (1976) suggests that the Johannine community were on the margin between Judaism and Hellenism similar to the Hellenists of Acts 6. Boismard (1962) proposed a long period of evolution in the community from CE 50 to 110, while Wengst (1981) postulated that the community consisted of various small groups among synagogues in the Transjordan region, etc.

Sea Scrolls have corrected the mistaken view of first-century Judaism as a rigid and monolithic movement similar to later Rabbinic Judaism (Boccaccini 1991; Sandmel 1978: 9-18).[36] Before the discovery of the Scrolls, scholars used late and 'biased' sources to reconstruct the Judaism of the first century, which resulted in a very strict and narrow form of Judaism. The Dead Sea Scrolls have clearly shown that the Judaism of the first century was much more diverse than at first thought. Pharisaic Judaism was only one expression of first-century Judaism. The Dead Sea Scrolls also showed that Judaism was open to syncretism and other non-Jewish religious ideas. Therefore, the definition of Judaism has broadened to include a wide variety of teaching and worship. Secondly, the Dead Sea Scrolls have been particularly important for Johannine scholars as there are many parallels between the Scrolls and John in matters of theology, style and expression. Charlesworth argues that 'John is influenced by Essene thought' (1990: 107) on the basis of a comparison of the dualism, many expressions, and theology between the Dead Sea Scrolls and John.[37]

The emphasis on Judaism in Johannine research after the discovery of the Dead Sea Scrolls was not without earlier anticipation, however. An interesting comment was made by Israel Abrahams in 1923 or 1924, 'To us Jews the Fourth Gospel is the most Jewish of the four' (Neill and Wright 1987: 315). Also the conservative English scholar Westcott emphasized the Old Testament and Jewish traditions in the Gospel. Similarly, in his thought-provoking commentary of 1929 Odeberg places the Gospel thoroughly in the context of early Jewish mysticism.[38]

The shift from a Hellenistic setting to a Jewish one is a dramatic breakthrough in Johannine research. The research of the present study is conducted with the presupposition that the Gospel is firmly rooted in Jewish soil. However, the picture of the Gospel's milieu is more complicated than simply choosing between two or three alternatives. Judaism is to be regarded as the primary religious milieu of the Gospel, but that assertion does not help us very much, for it is now recognized, as stated above, that Judaism was as diverse as the religious

---

36. Of course, Josephus referred to three 'sects' of the Jews, namely the Pharisees, Sadducees and Essenes.

37. Also see Gryglewicz (1959) and Brownlee (1990).

38. It is a pity for the present study that Odeberg was never able to fulfil his promise to follow up his first commentary with a study of Jn 13–20.

milieu of the rest of the Hellenistic world. Some scholars are dis-
covering Gnostic tendencies in the Dead Sea Scrolls.[39] Therefore, it is
possible that though John should be understood against a Jewish trajectory, it could still be very much indebted for instance to early Gnostic
thought. In other words, the working hypothesis of this study is that
though the Fourth Gospel is to be understood in a Jewish setting, there
are many other influences exerting themselves on the Gospel's thought,
especially from baptist, Essene, Samaritan and Gnostic movements.

3. *Research on Johannine Ecclesiology*

As has already been mentioned, there is a debate as to whether or not
ecclesiology is a central Johannine theme. Scholars have approached
the question in different ways. Usually the presence of, or allusion to,
an ecclesiological phenomenon, like the sacraments, is used to demon-
strate the importance of ecclesiology in the Fourth Gospel. However,
this approach tends to obscure the real concerns of Johannine ecclesiology.[40] The debate whether ecclesiology is important is only a pre-
liminary question. Once it is established that ecclesiology is an
important Johannine theme, the next question concerns the essence of
Johannine ecclesiology. And only after we have ascertained the central
concern of Johannine ecclesiology will we be able to give an adequate
description of Johannine ecclesiology. It is important to highlight this
question since scholarship has often occupied itself with matters that
lie outside the concern of John.[41]

The subject of Johannine ecclesiology covers a large area of Johannine scholarship, and includes questions of church order and offices,[42]

39. See Reicke (1954–55); also see Fischel (1946), Frye (1962), Percy (1939),
Schubert (1963) and Schoeps (1970).

40. Käsemann made a crucial point when he said that '... the raising of the right
questions ... is the necessary beginning of scholarship and frequently its most important result' (1978: 3).

41. Kysar has listed five themes on which studies on Johannine ecclesiology
have focused: (1) the dualistic view of the church in the world; (2) the unity of the
church; (3) the mission of the church; (4) the polemic nature of the church; and
(5) church order (1975: 241). This survey suggests that research on Johannine ecclesiology has followed different avenues, and that it is therefore important to isolate the
major concern of Johannine ecclesiology. Only then can we be confident to give a
statement of Johannine ecclesiology.

42. See Schweizer (1961) and Klauck (1985).

the sacraments,[43] the relationship between the community and the individual,[44] the relationship between the community and Jesus, the relationship between church and world,[45] and the relationship between church and Old Testament Israel.[46] Other Johannine themes like dualism,[47] eschatology, discipleship[48] and mission[49] also come into the picture. It is of course impossible to cover all these aspects. Therefore, this section will only survey the major approaches to Johannine ecclesiology by the most prominent Johannine scholars.

The earliest studies on the church in John were done by Gaugler (1924) and Faulhaber (1938), but these studies were very general with no exegetical foundation (Miller 1976: 16). Bultmann again was the one who determined the genesis and direction for the debate on this aspect of Johannine theology. Bultmann denied the existence of any real ecclesiology in John and devoted only three pages to the Johannine concept of the church in his *Theology of the New Testament* (1951–55: II, 8-9, 91-92). Since John does not have a history-of-salvation concept it is understandable that prophetic proof is not important and that the term for the church (ἐκκλησία) does not occur (1951–55: II, 8). When there is an implied reference to the sacraments Bultmann's answer is that the 'sacraments were subsequently introduced into the text by editorial process' (1951–55: II, 9). Similarly, *kyrios* (κύριος), a title employed by the early congregation for Jesus, only occurs in redactional glosses (1951–55: II, 9). Later in his *Theology*, Bultmann tells us that he has not treated the Johannine view of the church as a topic by itself because 'John himself never takes the concept "Church" for a theme as Paul does' (1951–55: II, 91), and 'no specifically ecclesiological interest can be detected' (1951–55: II, 91). When the Gospel does touch on ecclesiological themes, Bultmann

43. See Bornkamm (1956).
44. See O'Grady (1975; 1977).
45. See Baumbach (1972), Wiefel (1979), Lindemann (1980), Onuki (1984) *et al.*
46. See Barrett (1947), Allen (1955), Dahl (1962), Pancaro (1970; 1974–75), Painter (1978) *et al.*
47. See Onuki (1984).
48. See Beinert (1979), Vellanickal (1980), Pazdan (1982), Ray (1983), Segovia (1985a) *et al.*
49. Studies dealing with the missiology of the Fourth Gospel frequently include ecclesiological issues. See Kuhl (1967; 1971), McPolin (1969), Miranda (1977), Popkes (1978), Winn (1981), Schneider (1982), Schnackenburg (1984), Viviano (1984), Ruiz (1987), Okure (1988), Waldstein (1990) *et al.*

believes that the terms come from Gnostic thought and not from Jewish or Christian sources (1951–55: II, 91). Lastly, according to Bultmann, we can speak of the concept of an 'invisible Church in John, which is gradually realized in the visible Church of the disciples' (1951–55: II, 92).

Though Bultmann's student, Käsemann, shares his teacher's opinion that John does not develop an explicit ecclesiology (1978: 27), he has surprisingly much more to say about the church. In fact, later Käsemann appears to contradict his earlier statement when he says, 'It would be foolish to deny that obviously John also sets out an ecclesiology' (1978: 40). Käsemann also believes that John's concept of the church has been influenced by Gnosticism. But, whereas Bultmann interpreted Gnostic influence on John negatively, that is, John has Christianized (demythologized) his Gnostic tradition, Käsemann interpreted it positively, that is, John stands within the Gnostic movement. According to Käsemann John represents a stage in the development from the enthusiasts in Paul's time at Corinth to the elaborate Gnostic systems of the second century (1978: 75; 1969: 255). Therefore, John stands on the periphery of earliest Christianity and is at odds with the developing of early Catholicism at the end of the first century (1978: 39). In Käsemann's words:

> The Fourth Gospel (again!) mounts a remarkable counter-offensive against this development; it contains no explicit idea of the Church, no doctrine of ministerial office, no developed sacramental theology. Correspondingly, there is a strange compression of preaching, the effect of which is to bring 'Christ alone' into strong relief as the one thing necessary and to play this idea off even against the fathers who represent holy tradition... 'Church' denotes here the company of those living under this Word and determined by it alone (1969: 255).

In his significant contribution to New Testament scholarship *The Testament of Jesus* (*Jesu letzter Wille nach Johannes 17*) Käsemann devoted one chapter on the Johannine concept of the church under the heading *The Community under the Word* (*Die Gemeinde unter dem Wort*). John's ecclesiology is different from the rest of early Christianity. And Käsemann criticizes scholars who try to harmonize John's view of the church with that of wider Christendom. Käsemann sees a much more open or pneumatic view of the church in John. There is no strong sense of an apostleship in the Gospel, instead, 'The disciples who receive commission, Spirit and authority from the risen Christ

are simply the representatives of the Christian community' (1978: 29).
John is therefore critical of tradition because it can so easily replace
the presence of Christ himself (*Christus praesens*). Therefore:

> The community which knows itself to be governed by the Spirit can let the
> apostolate, the ministry and its organization melt into the background and
> understand itself in the manner of a conventicle which is constituted
> through its individual members and which designates itself as the circle of
> friends and brothers. This community may take up and use the oldest self-
> designations and traditions of primitive Christianity, traditions which at
> the end of the first century appear outdated and obsolete, and thus come
> into conflict with developing early Catholicism. In short, John stands
> within an area of tensions in the Church (1978: 31-32) ... For John, the
> Church is basically and exclusively the fellowship of people who hear
> Jesus' word and believe in him; in short, it is the community under the
> Word. All other ecclesiological definitions are orientated on this one and
> significant only in so far as they give expression to it (1978: 40).

Käsemann has been quoted at length here not only because of his
prominence as an interpreter of John's thought, but also because he
gives a valid and helpful description of the character of the Johannine
community. Similarly, Onuki, though he disagrees with Käsemann as
to the role of Christology in the theological formulation of the community, highlighted the spiritual and charismatic character of the
Johannine community (1984: 84).

E. Schweizer follows Bultmann in the view that John does not have
any concept of salvation history as Paul and Luke. For Schweizer the
church is not determined on the basis of a single act of God as Israel
was in the event of the Exodus. Rather, the church is only understood
as a distinct people if she stands under the daily rule, protection and
command of her Lord. In Schweizer's words, 'She is only a church in
so far as she lives "in" the Son and he in her (Jn 16.7, 13)' (1959:
378).[50] This emphasis on the intimate union between Christ and the
believer accounts for the strong emphasis on the individual in the
Gospel. Again, tradition is not important because it becomes sub-
ordinate to the believer's direct relationship with Christ. The believer
depends totally on Christ. Consequently, the need for special ministries
is minimized, and as such the Gospel is anti-institutional. There is
certainly some truth in what Schweizer says, but one feels that his case

50. The English translation of this article appeared in A.J.B. Higgins (ed.), *New*
Testament Essays: Studies in Memory of Thomas Walter Manson 1893–1958 (1959).

is weakened by his continual recourse to the argument from silence.

However, there are also many scholars who have argued that ecclesiological themes do occupy an important place in John. Barrett was among the first commentators to pay attention to the church in John (1955: 78-82). According to Barrett, 'John does...show, more clearly than any other evangelist, an awareness of the existence of the Church' (1955: 78). Barrett also sees in John a depreciation of the apostleship:

> The only meaning John will allow to apostleship is a strictly theological meaning. If the apostle ceases to be in as completely obedient a subjection to Jesus as Jesus was to the Father, if his own personality rather than the Spirit of God assumes dominance, he at once forfeits his position and, like Judas, goes out into the night (1955: 80).

A prominent Catholic interpreter, R.E. Brown, in his commentary challenges the view that John has no concept of the church. He first shows that the argument from silence—if something is not mentioned it does not exist or is rejected—can be turned around, that is, '...certain things are not mentioned in John, not because the evangelist disagrees with them but because he presupposes them' (1966: I, cvii). Brown goes on to list three 'disputed points in Johannine ecclesiology' (1966: I, cviii-cxi): (1) The Question of Community. Does the stress in John on an individual relationship with Jesus obviate the concept of community that is essential to ecclesiology? Brown answers this question in the negative. For John there can be no Christian life outside the community; (2) The Question of Church Order. This question too has often been answered by the argument from silence. Actually some passages in the Gospel would imply some sort of structure or order within the community, though it is difficult to provide a detailed statement on church order from the Gospel;[51] (3) The Question of the Kingdom of God. Brown explains the lack of the formula *basileia tou theou* in John in terms of a different emphasis in John. Whereas the Synoptics stress the presence of the *basileia* John stresses the *basileus*, the king of the *basileia*. Brown also points out that the church cannot be equated with the *basileia tou theou*, and therefore that the rarity of the phrase in John does not mean that the evangelist depreciates the church. In conclusion Brown states that:

---

51. Similarly, Edanad discusses 'certain figures that are ecclesial in signification', namely the figures of the flock and vine (1985: 136).

...there are passages in John which give a picture of a community of believers gathered by those whom Jesus sent out. This community is structured, for some are shepherds (at least Peter according to xxi 15-17) and others are sheep. That such ecclesiology does not receive major stress in the Gospel is quite intelligible if the evangelist was taking for granted the existence of the Church, its life and institutions, and attempting to relate this life directly to Jesus. That this was the case and that the evangelist was not opposed to an organized Church is suggested by other Johannine works. In 1 John we find an orthodox and righteous community from which heretics are excluded; in Revelation we find a strong sense of the continuity between the Christian Church organized upon the Twelve Apostles and the Israel of the Old Testament stemming from the twelve tribes (1966: I, cx-cxi).

Brown has given a useful summary of scholarship on this 'burning issue in Johannine studies' (1966: I, cv) up to the mid-sixties. The emphasis of subsequent scholarship has continued to concentrate on the role of the sacraments in John. The discussion on these matters has clarified many issues and provided helpful insights into the church of the Johannine community. However, none of these questions raised by Brown lie at the heart of John's ecclesiology. Again these questions were decided by the concerns of other communities and not by the concerns of the Johannine community.[52]

Schnackenburg is one of the most important scholars who have made a contribution to an understanding of the concept of the church in the Johannine writings. Schnackenburg holds that ecclesiology is deeply rooted, and even indispensable, for Johannine thought (1974: 103-104). According to Schnackenburg the church 'is assigned a quite definite position in the work of salvation' (1974: 104). It is through the church that the Spirit applies the salvation obtained by Christ to the world. John's interest in the church is further illustrated by the metaphors defining Jesus' work, namely that of the flock, and that of the vine and the branches (1974: 107-110). The true nature of the church is especially seen in the image of the vine and the branches, the union of believers with Christ. Schnackenburg goes on to say that

> Only in the Church is the abiding in Christ and the promise of Christ's abiding in them possible; the disciples and the later believers could not have understood this in any other way... in it [the church] the most profound communion with Christ is accomplished and that this alone permits

52. R.E. Brown has made valuable contributions to the discussion of the history of the Johannine community (1977a; 1978; and 1979).

any fruit to be borne... This idea of unity is hardly derived merely from
topical reasons of polemic through the danger of heretics, but belongs to a
profound Johannine grasp of the essence of the Church (1974: 110-11).

Mission was also a major concern of the Johannine church (1974:
112). It appears that Schnackenburg is closer to the essence of Johannine ecclesiology than Brown.

A number of scholarly articles deal specifically with the relationship
between Israel and the church in John. In an article examining the
relationship between the church and the Jews, Dahl states that John is
not a 'theologian of *Heilsgeschichte*' (1962: 140). Rather, in John the
Old Testament witnesses to Jesus. Dahl observes, 'The Qumran idea of
the more or less predestined 'children of light' who are gathered into
a community of the true Israel in some respects comes rather close to
the Johannine conception of the church' (1962: 141). Baumbach also
holds that John does not follow the Old Testament concept of the
people of God (1972: 125). This is in contrast to Paul who sees the
church as the continuation of the covenant people. In other words,
John is not interested in *Heilsgeschichte* (1972: 125). Instead, John
shows a tendency towards spiritualization. The Johannine community
has no institutional character and has no office or order. Baumbach
therefore, like Bultmann and Käsemann, favours a Gnostic influence
on John (1972: 134). The origin of John's ecclesiology lies in Christology (1972: 126). In connection with the two Johannine parables he
says:

> The images which John chose to describe the community, viz. the
> branches belonging to the vine and the sheep standing under the shepherd,
> show that his ecclesiology is 'derived from his Christology'. The church
> had its 'origin' in Christology (1972: 126).

Pancaro is another scholar who considered the relationship between
Israel and the church in John. He argues that λαός and τέκνα τοῦ
Θεοῦ are technical terms for the church (1970: 114-29): they refer to
either Jews or Gentiles who believe in Jesus. Similarly, 'Israel' is a
term that encompasses all believers (1970: 125). These conclusions,
according to Pancaro, 'go against the opinion that John avoids 'ecclesiastical' terms...' (1970: 129). In another article Pancaro says that
'John is not at all concerned with the Gentiles or the manner in which
they may be said to have replaced the Jews in God's salvific plan'
(1974–75: 405). His conclusion is, 'Although John does not use the
term "church", he is aware of the fact that Jewish-Christians form a

new community and he does reflect upon the relationship of the new community to the old. The Church is the new Israel' (1974–75: 405). Pancaro's two articles were, however, severely criticized by Painter. Contrary to Pancaro, Painter says, 'John never identifies believing Jews with the true Israel nor is there any self-conscious ecclesiology in the Gospel' (1978: 112). According to Painter, 'Ecclesiology is not explicitly treated but appears only in relation to Christology' (1978: 112). These scholars primarily considered the relationship of the church in John with Israel.

Haacker is another scholar who argued strongly for a distinct concept of the church in John. He isolated several expressions and *Bildworte* that refer to the church (1973: 180-88). According to Haacker, Jesus is the historical founder of the church (1973: 189). The Gospel does not recognize the apostleship or Pentecost. Rather, Jesus himself is the primary missionary and he carries out all the functions usually associated with the apostles (1973: 189). In the Gospel the historical origin of the church is in the Word and works of Jesus (1973: 201). In conclusion, Haacker emphasized two characteristics of the church in John. First, the antithesis between the church and the world, and secondly, the unity of Word, Spirit and history in the tradition (1973: 200).

J.W. Miller produced a PhD dissertation at Princeton entitled *The Concept of the Church in the Gospel according to John* (1976). At the conclusion, his dissertation highlights the Gospel's individualistic emphasis and the primacy of the individual's relationship to Christ above that of the community (1976: 233-35). However, the horizontal dimension of community life is not absent. This is seen particularly in the love command and the need for unity (1976: 235-38). Lastly, Miller also highlights the egalitarian and sectarian nature of the Johannine community (1976: 241-44). Miller's dissertation has highlighted some aspects of Johannine ecclesiology, but has failed, I believe, to adequately describe the essence of Johannine ecclesiology.

Nereparampil has written a short but perceptive article on the church in the Johannine writings. He states that, 'the whole outlook of the Johannine writings is saturated with the idea of the Church' (1979: 169). And he contends that John's ecclesiology is trying to explain the origin, nature, and function of the community. The 'origin of the new community is from above, from the saving activity of the Word become Flesh and the Holy Spirit' (1979: 173). The nature of the community, in contrast with the Jews and the world, is one of true worship, loving obedience and brotherly service. And, 'the function of this new community is to continue Jesus' mission in this world' (1979: 177).

Minear also challenged the conviction that John is unconcerned with ecclesiology (1982: 95). For Minear ecclesiology and Christology are interdependent, and he goes so far as to say, 'John's ecclesiology conditions his thinking about the Messiah' (1982: 95). Minear thus interprets Johannine ecclesiology in terms of the *logos* and talks of a 'logos ecclesiology'. John 1.14 is interpreted in terms of ecclesiology and not Christology (1982: 108). 'Within the Johannine perspective, the doctrine concerning incarnation is a doctrine concerning the church; to understand the life of the church is required before an interpreter can grasp many nuances in John's thinking about Christ' (1982: 110). In *John: The Martyr's Gospel* (1984) Minear argues that the Gospel was written to instruct the community about the likelihood of suffering and martyrdom as they engage in mission. More recently, Schnelle (1991) has also challenged the view that ecclesiology is only a minor theme in the Gospel. Ecclesiology is closely related and flows out of Christology. 'Doubtless, the Gospel of John bases all ecclesiological statements on its Christology...' (1991: 50).[53]

The most recent study on ecclesiology in the New Testament has been provided by Roloff (1993). Roloff discusses Johannine ecclesiology under the heading *Die Gemeinschaft der Freunde Jesu* (1993: 290-309). He agrees with Käsemann that John does not contain an explicit ecclesiology, but only develops an *indirekte Ekklesiologie*. The reasons given why John only develops an *indirekte Ekklesiologie* reveal that Roloff defines ecclesiology in Pauline terms, that is, the word ἐκκλησία does not occur in the Gospel, there is no concept of an apostleship, ecclesiological metaphors such as the 'body of Christ', 'house' and 'temple' are not mentioned, and there is also no interest in church constitution and organization (1993: 290-91). In his discussion of Johannine ecclesiology, Roloff highlights the role of the Spirit in the formation of the community. It is only through the Spirit that Jesus can be known, therefore, 'For them only the Paraklete is the genuine teacher: "He will teach you all things"' (1993: 296). Roloff

---

53. Likewise, Gnilka writes, 'Die Ekklesiologie ist von der Christologie bestimmt' (1994: 306).

also notes that the existence of the church is only the function of the fellowship of the individual believers and is not directly related to salvation history (1993: 299-301). As I hope to point out in this study, this statement does not appreciate the crucial soteriological role that the Johannine community plays in the continuation of the Son's sending.

This brief survey of scholarship on Johannine ecclesiology has shown that an increasing number of scholars are beginning to affirm that John has a definite ecclesiology. Though there are different understandings of, and approaches to, the question of the church in John, there appears to be a consensus developing that ecclesiology is a major theme in the Gospel. Another general agreement among scholars is that ecclesiology is closely related to Christology. Yet, this survey also shows that the question as to the essence of Johannine ecclesiology has not yet achieved adequate consideration.

The consideration of Johannine ecclesiology has suffered under the influence of Pauline or 'orthodox' views of the church. Often scholars have approached Johannine ecclesiology through 'orthodox' glasses. As such they have looked for forms of church government and attitudes towards the sacraments in the Gospel.[54] The present study argues that the Johannine community functioned differently from the later Pauline church (reflected in the Pastoral Epistles) with its officers, liturgy and sacraments. It was a much more loosely organized and spontaneous group. Neither the sacraments nor the concept of church structure lie at the heart of the Johannine community's concept of itself. As the community was initially a group within the Jewish synagogue, it is doubtful whether it had a developed system of officers and sacraments.

In conclusion, the problem that this study seeks to address can be formulated in the following way: Does John have an ecclesiology? And if so, what is the essence of this ecclesiology? Though other questions touched upon in the survey will be dealt with, these will be the major questions of the present investigation.

---

54. Käsemann has correctly pointed out that 'Worship and sacraments do not play a dominant role in our Gospel' (1978: 32), and that John's 'ecclesiology is not designed on the basis of the forms of church organizations' (1978: 40).

4. *Clarification of Terms*

A crucial question for current New Testament research is that of the definitions of *termini technici* (Koester and Robinson 1971: 20, 114-19; Charlesworth 1985: 58-62). For example, what do we mean by the adjectives 'Jewish', 'Gnostic', 'Greek', and even 'Christian'? Indeed all these adjectives could be used to describe some aspect of the Gospel of John! How many 'Jewish' elements must a document contain before it could be described as 'Jewish'? And under which category should we classify documents such as the *Gospel of Thomas* and *Odes of Solomon*? This study does not attempt to provide satisfactory answers to these problems, but since some handles are needed to deal with the material, some general definitions of how these and other terms are used in this study will be given below.

Christology: When I refer to 'Christology' in this study I mean the specific Johannine view of Christology. John used the traditional christological titles but they are reinterpreted according to Johannine theology. In Johannine Christology the teaching concerning Christ is closely connected with other Johannine themes such as the pre-existence and exaltation of the Redeemer, and especially soteriology. Indeed, in this study I also want to point out that there is a close relationship between Johannine Christology and ecclesiology.

Community: The study will refer to the historical Johannine 'church' as the 'Johannine community'. The word church is used in inverted commas because it carries too many modern Western theological connotations. The study does not prefer to use Culpepper's term 'school', because, though it is accurate in describing the immediate organization that produced the Gospel, it does not convey the wider influence and concern of the school. The term 'disciples' (μαθηταί), is a Johannine term but it implies a loosely organized group of believers. It would appear that there was some form of structure within the Johannine group of disciples. The word 'community' implies a more defined group of people within a wider society but it is less formal than church or school. The expression 'Johannine community' would then include the Johannine school as a smaller, yet controlling, group within it.

Ecclesiology: By 'ecclesiology' I refer to the concept that the Fourth Gospel has of the community of those who believe in Jesus as a distinct entity. In this sense 'ecclesiology' deals with the theological understanding the Johannine community had of itself, and not with the history of the community.

Gnosticism, *Gnostic*: The term 'Gnosticism' in the study refers to the second-century metaphysical system involving the idea of a divine spark in a person that needs to be awakened and saved through a secret revelation of knowledge, that is, *gnosis* (Bianchi 1970: xxvi-xxix). The adjective 'Gnostic' will be used in a broader sense, and does not only go with Gnosticism but also with what has been called Pre-Gnostic (what immediately precedes Gnosticism) and Proto-Gnosticism (what runs into Gnosticism).

Jewish, *Judaism*: By 'Jewish' this study refers to the literature, culture, religion, and writings produced by the Jews until the second century CE. By the term 'Judaism' it understands the system of culture and religion produced by the Jews from the third century BCE to the end of the second century CE. For the purposes of this study we do not need to distinguish between the different stages in the development of Judaism. Therefore, the study will not use terms like 'Formative Judaism' (Neusner 1983), 'Early Judaism' (Charlesworth 1985: 59) or 'Middle Judaism' (Boccaccini 1991). Of course, the study will not be using the misleading term 'Normative Judaism' (Charlesworth 1985: 61)

Johannine: By the adjective 'Johannine' I refer to the views expressed by the author(s) of the Fourth Gospel, which may also be the views of his (their) community. In this sense, the term 'Johannine' does not necessarily include 1 and 2 John.

John: The study will refer to the Fourth Gospel as simply the 'Gospel' or 'John'. By using 'John' I do not make any reflection on the authorship or compositional history of the Fourth Gospel.

Chapter 3

THE CONTEXT AND STRUCTURE OF JESUS' PRAYER

1. *Introduction*

This chapter will examine the genre, literary context, and structure of John 17 to provide the necessary foundation of our exegesis. Several questions have to be dealt with in detail. First, since John is primarily to be understood in the trajectory of first-century Judaism, as has been argued in Chapter 1, the nature and function of ancient Jewish prayer needs to be examined. An understanding of Jewish prayer and the way it functioned in literature is crucial for determining the purpose, and consequently for the interpretation, of the prayer of the Johannine Jesus in John 17. An important question in the scholarly literature is whether John 17 is a strict prayer[1] or presents some other literary genre.[2] Secondly, John 17 must also be examined in terms of its literary

---

1. By a 'strict prayer' we mean a prayer that was prayed historically, as for example the Lord's Prayer in Mt. 6.9-13 and Lk. 11.2-4 or Jesus' prayer in Gethsemane (Mk 14.36).

2. A number of theories have been proposed regarding the literary genre of the prayer. With the exception of Bultmann who sees Jn 17 as part of the Gnostic Revelatory Discourse Source, most scholars have understood the prayer in terms of Jewish tradition. Feuillet interprets the prayer on the basis of the pattern of atonement in Lev. 16 (1975). Agourides also sees the prayer in terms of an atonement motif by comparing it with the eucharistic prayer in the *Didache* (1968), though the similarities are at best remote. A larger number of scholars understand Jn 17 in terms of the genre of a testament that occurs in Jewish literature, e.g. Kolenkow (1975). Lacomara sees the Farewell discourse of Jn 13–17 as a new Torah and consequently divides it into five sections (1974). Marzotto sees the prayer in terms of the tradition of the giving of the law in Exod. 19 and 20 that is preserved in the Targums (1977). More recently, Manns also has seen Jn 17 against the tradition preserved in the Targum of Deut. 32–33 which relates Moses' prayer before his death (1991). Manns sees the origin of this Targum tradition in the liturgy of the synagogue, and therefore also sees Jn 17 as functioning in the liturgy of the church. Another group of scholars

context in the Gospel of John. In the present position John 17 is part of the Revealer's farewell to his disciples. This chapter will look therefore at the genre of the Farewell discourse in Jewish literature. It will be pointed out that a distinction has to be made between the original setting or social context of the prayer (*Sitz im Leben*) and its present literary context (*Sitz im Text*).[3] Lastly, this chapter will also need to examine the structure of the Johannine Jesus' prayer. Questions that must be asked include: Is John 17 a coherent unit of text? And, what is the theme and thought pattern of the text? The main purpose of these investigations will be to determine the overall purpose of the prayer in John 17. It will be proposed that John 17 is the most important text in the Gospel for understanding Johannine ecclesiology.

2. *Jewish Prayer and the Prayer of John 17*

What do we know of Jewish prayer in the first century? What kind of prayers do we find? How did prayer function in the community and synagogue? And does the prayer of John 17 belong to a specific genre of Jewish prayer? These are some of the important questions that must be asked before we can turn to the exegetical study of John 17. A number of studies on Jewish prayer have appeared which shed significant light on the customs, patterns, and functions of prayer during the first century.[4]

Prayer was an important part of Jewish religious life in the first century.[5] Schürer's description of Jewish prayers as being rigid and

sees Jn 17 as a eucharistic prayer: they include Hoskyns, Cullmann, Bornkamm and Wilkens. However, it is doubtful whether Jn 17 has any sacrificial intent, e.g. see Appold (1978: 366) and Barrett (1955: 417), who regard the title 'high priestly prayer' as a misnomer for Jn 17. I may also mention Walker who interprets Jn 17 as an expanded commentary on the Lord's Prayer (1982). However, such central elements as praise and the forgiveness of sins are absent from the Johannine prayer.

3.   This distinction is the concern of form criticism which attempts to go behind the written text to examine the social situation that shaped the tradition recorded in the text.

4.   See Charlesworth (1982; 1992), Flusser (1984), F.C. Grant (1953), Greenberg (1989), Heinemann (1977), Henrix (1979), Jeremias (1967), Kirby (1968), Kirzner (1991) and Martin (1968). For an excellent bibliography on prayer during the Graeco-Roman era consult Mark Harding's bibliography in J.H. Charlesworth (ed.), *The Lord's Prayer and Other Prayer Texts from the Greco-Roman Era* (1994).

5.   The student of early Jewish prayer has a rich variety of sources. These

lifeless has been discarded by modern research (Charlesworth 1992: 36). Jewish prayer in this period was vibrant and highly developed. Basically, Jewish prayer during the first century can be divided into two categories: prescribed statutory prayers and private or spontaneous prayers. The prescribed statutory prayers were at set times three times a day (Jeremias 1967: 69), that is, the morning, afternoon and evening.[6] Benedictions were also said before and after meals (Jeremias 1967: 72). The pattern of the three set daily prayers consisted of the *Shema*[7] and the *Tephilla*.[8] The *Shema* was recited in the morning and in the evening with the addition of the *Tephilla*. The afternoon prayer was set at the time of the afternoon sacrifice, when the *Tephilla* was prayed (Jeremias 1967: 70-72).

a. *The 'Law-court' Prayer and John 17*
Probably the most important contribution to our understanding of Jewish prayer is the work of Heinemann, *Prayer in the Talmud: Forms and Patterns* (1977). Heinemann identified several genres of Jewish prayer.[9] Of special significance for us is the identification of a 'law-court' pattern in some Jewish prayers. According to Heinemann, building on the studies of Gemser (1955), S.H. Blank (1948) and H. Schmidt (1928), three distinct parts can be identified in this kind of prayer (1977: 194): (1) the address; (2) the plea or justification; and (3) the request or petition.[10] The second part, the plea, is usually the

include: (1) the Old Testament Hebrew Scriptures; (2) the Old Testament Apocrypha; (3) the numerous documents of the Pseudepigrapha; (4) the Dead Sea Scrolls, especially the Thanksgiving Scroll; (5) the New Testament; (6) the Eighteen Benedictions; and (7) the Talmudim which may contain early traditions. For a description of the material of early Jewish psalms, hymns and prayers, see Flusser (1984).

6.   This custom of praying three times a day is already attested in Dan. 6.11.

7.   The term *Shema* is the transcription of the Hebrew word שמע and refers to the command and creed of Deut. 6.4-7.

8.   The term *Tephilla* is the transcription of the Hebrew word תפלה and refers to the prayer consisting of the so-called 'Eighteen Benedictions' that was standardized at the end of the first century. It is also known as the *Amidah*, because they were said standing, or as the *Shemoneh 'Esreh* (the Eighteen) (Kirby 1968: 84).

9.   Among the forms of prayer that Heinemann identified are statutory prayers, *Piyyût*-forms of prayer, private and non-statutory prayers, and prayers of *Bêt Midrash* origin.

10.   As an appendix Heinemann listed 36 examples of this kind of prayer from the Talmud (1977: 208-17).

longest, and includes the basis and justification of the request, and as such it often contains a recitation of past historical facts. This 'law-court' or judicial pattern of prayer is an outgrowth of the prayers of biblical sages, for example, Abraham's prayer for Sodom, Moses' intercession for the Israelites, Hannah's prayer at the temple, and so on (Heinemann 1977: 199-200). In the numerous examples Heinemann produced from the Talmud the petitioner pleas before God for intervention in nature, for justice regarding the petitioner's adversary and for the forgiveness of sins (1977: 208-17).

In addition to the examples produced from the Talmud by Heinemann, we have identified similar 'law-court' prayers in the Old Testament Pseudepigrapha and Apocrypha, and the Dead Sea Scrolls. In the prayer of Ezra in *4 Ezra* 8.20-36, which in its present form dates from the second half of the first century CE (Charlesworth 1993: 781), the three elements of the 'law-court' prayer are clearly evident. The *Prayer of Jacob* also reflects the 'law-court' pattern, though a clearly defined justification of the requests is absent (Charlesworth 1983: II, 720-23). Examples of the 'law-court' prayer from the Dead Sea Scrolls are located in 4Q504 (VI)[11], 4Q508 (fragment 2),[12] and in the *Psalm of Joseph* (4Q372 I 1632).[13] These examples show that the genre of the 'law-court' prayer identified by Heinemann in the Talmud was already current in the first century CE.

On examination, it appears that the prayer of the Johannine Jesus in John 17 corresponds closely with this 'law-court' pattern in Jewish prayer. In John 17 we have clear forms of address, numerous

11. The prayer reads, 'We pray Thee O Lord, since Thou workest marvels from everlasting to everlasting, to let Thine anger and wrath retreat from us' (Vermes 1990: 219). The address is 'O Lord'; the request is 'let Thine anger and wrath retreat from us'; and the justification is 'since Thou workest marvels from everlasting to everlasting'.

12. The prayer reads, 'Remember O Lord, the feast of mercies and the time of return... Thou hast established it for us as a feast of fasting, and everlas[ting] precept... Thou knowest the hidden things and the things reveal[ed]...' (Vermes 1990: 232). The address is 'O Lord'; the request is 'Remember... the feast of mercies and the time of return'; and the justification is 'Thou has established it for us as a feast, and everlas[ting] precept... Thou knowest the hidden things and the reveal[ed]...'

13. The psalm is too long to quote here in full, but I may briefly point out that the address is 'My father and my God'; one of the requests is 'do not abandon me in the hands of the nations'; and one of the justifications is 'For you select the truth, and in your hand there is no violence' (Chazon 1993: 771-72).

requests, and the recitation of facts justifying the requests. John 17 may be the compilation of a number of prayers that follow the pattern of the 'law-court' prayers. Further investigation seems to support this proposal.

An analysis of John 17 shows that thanksgiving and confession, two important features of Jewish prayer, are totally absent from the prayer. Instead, the prayer contains numerous petitions of the Revealer to the Father. Petitions are expressed with the imperative, a direct petition, and with the ἵνα plus subjunctive construction expressing a wish of the petitioner. John 17 contains four direct petitions with the imperative,[14] and twenty petitions with the ἵνα plus subjunctive construction.[15] Therefore, we may describe the prayer of John 17 as a petitionary prayer, which supports our suggestion that John 17 reflects or anticipates the pattern of a 'law-court' prayer.

Furthermore, when we examine John 17 we are able to isolate the three distinct parts that are associated with the 'law-court' pattern that I have identified above. We notice that the Johannine Jesus addresses God as πάτερ (vv. 1, 5, 21, 24), πάτερ ἅγιε (v. 11), and πάτερ δίκαιε (v. 25).[16] This usage is a specifically Christian form of addressing God in prayer, though there are some instances of its usage in non-Christian Jewish sources,[17] and reflects the address of the Lord's Prayer in Matthew and Luke. The requests are to glorify the Father; to glorify the Son; that the disciples may be one; that the disciples may be kept from the world; that the disciples may be sanctified; that the disciples may have joy; that the world may believe; that the love of the Father may be in the disciples; and that the disciples may be with Jesus and see his glory. We are also able to notice that the requests of Jesus are justified by numerous facts based on his work accomplished on earth. This may be demonstrated by dividing John 17 into several petitionary prayers. It must be pointed out that my division does not presume to be an accurate reconstruction of an earlier stage in the literary history of John 17, but just to show that the prayer follows the 'law-court' pattern identified in Jewish prayer. Though there are a

14. Cf. Jn 17.1, 5, 11 and 17.

15. Cf. Jn 17.1, 2, 3, 5, 11, 12, 13, 15 (twice), 19, 21 (three times), 22, 23 (twice), 24 (twice), and 26 (twice).

16. I shall deal with the textual variations concerning the grammatical case of πατήρ in the exegesis.

17. For example, it occurs in the Dead Sea Scrolls (cf. 4Q372).

number of ways in which the prayer can be divided, the three elements of the 'law-court' pattern are always conspicuous:

Petition 1, a petition for glory (verses 1-8):[18]

(a) The address: πάτερ (vv. 1 and 5)

(b) The justification: ἐλήλυθεν ἡ ὥρα (v. 1)...καθὼς ἔδωκας αὐτῷ ἐξουσίαν πάσης σαρκός, ἵνα πᾶν ὃ δέδωκας αὐτῷ δώσῃ αὐτοῖς ζωὴν αἰώνιον (v. 2)...ἐγώ σε ἐδόξασα ἐπὶ τῆς γῆς τὸ ἔργον τελειώσας ὃ δέδωκάς μοι ἵνα ποιήσω (v. 4)...ἐφανέρωσά σου τὸ ὄνομα τοῖς ἀνθρώποις οὓς ἔδωκάς μοι ἐκ τοῦ κόσμου. σοὶ ἦσαν κἀμοὶ αὐτοὺς ἔδωκας καὶ τὸν λόγον σου τετήρηκαν. νῦν ἔγνωκαν ὅτι πάντα ὅσα δέδωκάς μοι παρὰ σοῦ εἰσιν· ὅτι τὰ ῥήματα ἃ ἔδωκάς μοι δέδωκα αὐτοῖς, καὶ αὐτοὶ ἔλαβον καὶ ἔγνωσαν ἀληθῶς ὅτι παρὰ σοῦ ἐξῆλθον, καὶ ἐπίστευσαν ὅτι σύ με ἀπέστειλας (vv. 6-8).

(c) The petition: δόξασόν σου τὸν υἱόν, ἵνα ὁ υἱὸς δοξάσῃ σέ (v. 1)...καὶ νῦν δόξασόν με σύ, πάτερ, παρὰ σεαυτῷ τῇ δόξῃ ᾗ εἶχον πρὸ τοῦ τὸν κόσμον εἶναι παρὰ σοί (v. 5)

Petition 2, a petition for protection, unity, joy and consecration (verses 9-19):

(a) The address: πάτερ ἅγιε (v. 11)

(b) The justification: ἐγὼ περὶ αὐτῶν ἐρωτῶ, οὐ περὶ τοῦ κόσμου ἐρωτῶ ἀλλὰ περὶ ὧν δέδωκάς μοι, ὅτι σοί εἰσιν, καὶ τὰ ἐμὰ πάντα σά ἐστιν καὶ τὰ σὰ ἐμά, καὶ δεδόξασμαι ἐν αὐτοῖς. καὶ οὐκέτι εἰμὶ ἐν τῷ κόσμῳ, καὶ αὐτοὶ ἐν τῷ κόσμῳ εἰσίν, κἀγὼ πρὸς σὲ ἔρχομαι...(vv. 9-11a)

(c) The petition: τήρησον αὐτοὺς ἐν τῷ ὀνόματί σου ᾧ δέδωκάς μοι, ἵνα ὦσιν ἓν καθὼς ἡμεῖς (v. 11b)

18. See pp. 71-77 for a translation of John 17.

(b¹) The justification: ὅτε ἤμην μετ᾽ αὐτῶν ἐγὼ ἐτήρουν αὐτοὺς ἐν τῷ ὀνόματί σου ᾧ δέδωκάς μοι, καὶ ἐφύλαξα, καὶ οὐδεὶς ἐξ αὐτῶν ἀπώλετο εἰ μὴ ὁ υἱὸς τῆς ἀπωλείας, ἵνα ἡ γραφὴ πληρωθῇ (v. 12)

(c¹) The petition: νῦν δὲ πρὸς σὲ ἔρχομαι καὶ ταῦτα λαλῶ ἐν τῷ κόσμῳ ἵνα ἔχωσιν τὴν χαρὰν τὴν ἐμὴν πεπληρωμένην ἐν ἑαυτοῖς (v. 13)

(b²) The justification: ἐγὼ δέδωκα αὐτοῖς τὸν λόγον σου καὶ ὁ κόσμος ἐμίσησεν αὐτούς, ὅτι οὐκ εἰσὶν ἐκ τοῦ κόσμου καθὼς ἐγὼ οὐκ εἰμὶ ἐκ τοῦ κόσμου (v. 14)...ἐκ τοῦ κόσμου οὐκ εἰσὶν καθὼς ἐγὼ οὐκ εἰμὶ ἐκ τοῦ κόσμου (v. 16)

(c²) The petition: οὐκ ἐρωτῶ ἵνα ἄρῃς αὐτοὺς ἐκ τοῦ κόσμου, ἀλλ᾽ ἵνα τηρήσῃς αὐτοὺς ἐκ τοῦ πονηροῦ (v. 15)

(b³) The justification: ὁ λόγος ὁ σὸς ἀλήθειά ἐστιν. καθὼς ἐμὲ ἀπέστειλας εἰς τὸν κόσμον, κἀγὼ ἀπέστειλα αὐτοὺς εἰς τὸν κόσμον· καὶ ὑπὲρ αὐτῶν ἐγὼ ἁγιάζω ἐμαυτόν, ἵνα ὦσιν καὶ αὐτοὶ ἡγιασμένοι ἐν ἀληθείᾳ (vv. 17b-19)

(c³) The petition: ἁγίασον αὐτοὺς ἐν τῇ ἀληθείᾳ (v. 17a)

Petition 3, a petition for unity (verses 20-24):

(a) The address: πάτερ (v. 24)

(b) The justification: οὐ περὶ τούτων δὲ ἐρωτῶ μόνον, ἀλλὰ καὶ περὶ τῶν πιστευόντων διὰ τοῦ λόγου αὐτῶν εἰς ἐμέ (v. 20)

(c) The petition: ἵνα πάντες ἓν ὦσιν, καθὼς σύ, πάτερ, ἐν ἐμοὶ κἀγὼ ἐν σοί, ἵνα καὶ αὐτοὶ ἐν ἡμῖν ὦσιν, ἵνα ὁ κόσμος πιστεύῃ ὅτι σύ με ἀπέστειλας (v. 21)

(b¹) The justification: κἀγὼ τὴν δόξαν ἣν δέδωκάς μοι δέδωκα αὐτοῖς (v. 22a)

(c¹) The petition: ἵνα ὦσιν ἓν καθὼς ἡμεῖς ἕν (v. 22b)

(b²) The justification: ἐγὼ ἐν αὐτοῖς καὶ σὺ ἐν ἐμοί (v. 23a) (c²) The petition: ἵνα ὦσιν τετελειωμένοι εἰς ἕν, ἵνα γινώσκῃ ὁ κόσμος ὅτι σύ με ἀπέστειλας καὶ ἠγάπησας αὐτοὺς καθὼς ἐμὲ ἠγάπησας (v. 23b)

(b³) The justification: ὅτι ἠγάπησάς με πρὸ καταβολῆς κόσμου (v. 24b)

(c³) The petition: ὃ δέδωκάς μοι, θέλω ἵνα ὅπου εἰμὶ ἐγὼ κἀκεῖνοι ὦσιν μετ᾽ ἐμοῦ, ἵνα θεωρῶσιν τὴν δόξαν τὴν ἐμήν, ἣν δέδωκάς μοι (v. 24a)

Petition 4, a petition for love (verses 25-26):

(a) The address: πάτερ δίκαιε (v. 25)

(b) The justification: καὶ ὁ κόσμος σε οὐκ ἔγνω, ἐγὼ δέ σε ἔγνων, καὶ οὗτοι ἔγνωσαν ὅτι σύ με ἀπέστειλας· καὶ ἐγνώρισα αὐτοῖς τὸ ὄνομά σου καὶ γνωρίσω (vv. 25-26a)

(c) The petition: ἵνα ἡ ἀγάπη ἣν ἠγάπησάς με ἐν αὐτοῖς ᾖ κἀγὼ ἐν αὐτοῖς (v. 26b)

The above analysis is one way in which to divide the prayer of John 17. The divisions are arbitrary and there are other possibilities, for example, the prayer can be broken up into smaller sections. Nevertheless, the three aspects of the 'law-court' prayer are clearly evident. In petition 1 (vv. 1-8), God is directly addressed with the term πάτερ, the petition is for the glorification of the Son, and the justification runs throughout the section, that is, because the Son may then glorify the Father, may give life to those the Father has given him; and because the Son has glorified the Father on earth; has completed his work, and has revealed the Father's name to the disciples. In petition 2 (vv. 9-19), the direct address πάτερ ἅγιε occurs, the petitions are for the protection and consecration of the disciples, and the justification is given in terms of the election of the disciples and their reception of the Son's revelation. In petition 3 (vv. 20-24), the address πάτερ occurs, the petition is for the unity of the disciples and that the world may believe, and the justification is because the Son has given his glory to the disciples, because the Son and the Father are a unity, and because the Father has loved the Son. Lastly, in petition 4, the direct address is πάτερ δίκαιε, the petition is that the love of the Father for the Son may be in the disciples, and the justification is that the disciples, in contrast to the world, have known that the Father sent the Son.

I want to suggest, then, that the prayer of John 17 reflects the 'law-court' genre of Jewish prayer. Moreover, it seems that the *Sitz im Leben* of the Johannine community corroborates this suggestion. It was a community in severe conflict with the synagogue over their christological beliefs. As the community was being ostracized for their faith we may well imagine their requests to God for justice. Indeed, many petitions are concerned with the request for protection from the world. Furthermore, the conflict that the community later experienced within itself provides the background for the petitions requesting unity within the community.

Identifying the origin of John 17 as a number of 'law-court' petitions is significant in two respects. First, it helps us to determine the structure of the prayer, and secondly, it helps us to ascertain the function or purpose of the prayer. If the prayer of John 17 does have its origin in 'law-court' petitionary prayers, it follows that the prayer originally had an apologetic purpose.[19] In the 'law-court' prayer the petitioner pleads his or her cause for justice against an adversary. In other words, it is a means of defence. Therefore, John 17 may then be regarded as an apologia of the Johannine community for their existence. This fits in well with Martyn and R.E. Brown's reconstruction of the history of the Johannine community which I have discussed in Chapter 2. We may well envisage that the prayer of John 17 originated in the petitionary prayers of the Johannine community in their struggle with the synagogue. Therefore, I disagree with Brown who says that 'This is more a prayer of the union or communion of the Son and the Father than it is a prayer of petition' (1966: II, 748).

b. *The Function of Prayer in Jewish Literature and John 17*
We now need to consider the function of Jewish prayer in literature. An important characteristic of prayer in Jewish literature that has

---

19. Incidentally, this judicial or legal character of prayer is also highlighted by the meaning of the Hebrew word for prayer, תפלה, which is derived from the verbal root פלל meaning to intervene or to judge (F. Brown 1952: 313; Harris 1980: II, 725-26). Thus תפלה has often been defined as the 'invocation of God as judge' (Martin 1968: 12). We may note that the English word, to pray, and the German, *beten*, have different connotations where the idea of justice is absent, namely that of entreaty or supplication.

affinities with John 17 is that it often serves autobiographical and didactic purposes. Flusser has highlighted this genre of Jewish prayer in his article 'Psalms, Hymns and Prayers' (1984: 561-62). As examples Flusser sites the Syriac psalms 1, 4, and 5, which have the events in the life of David as their theme, and the prayer for wisdom in the Wisdom of Solomon (9.1-18) (1984: 562-63). Flusser states:

> Thus we are able to recognize in ancient Judaism a special autobiographical poetical genre. The natural place of such autobiographical poetry is in a book which narrates the pertinent deeds and events. This is so in the Hebrew Bible, e.g. Moses' song at the Reed Sea; the song of Deborah; the song of Hannah, and other psalms in the Book of Samuel; so also in the Book of Tobit, in the additions to the Greek books of Esther and Daniel, in the prayer of Manasseh, in the Aramaic prayer of Nabonidus and in the psalm of encouragement in the apocryphal book of Baruch (1984: 562).

Furthermore, the didactic purpose of some Jewish prayers is seen in a number of documents. The hymns of the *Thanksgiving Scroll* may have been written for study. Indeed, for Flusser 'it seems probable that both the *Thanksgiving Scroll* and the *Canticles of the Instructor* were composed for study rather than for use as prayer' (1984: 566). In this connection, Hanson has provided an interesting article entitled 'Hodayoth xv and John 17: A Comparison of Content and Form' (1974). Hanson points out that 'Each is intended, we may be sure, not for purely personal use but for the edification of the community also' (1974: 51-52). Other examples of prayer serving autobiographical and didactic purposes include the prayers of Mordecai and Esther in the additions to the Greek book of Esther (Flusser 1984: 552), the *Psalms of Solomon* (Flusser 1984: 573), and the prayers in the book of Tobit.[20]

John 17 certainly reflects autobiographical and didactic concerns. The prayer is autobiographical when the Revealer reiterates his deeds on earth (vv. 4, 6, 12, 14, 18, 22), and also when it describes the experience and action of the disciples (vv. 6, 7, 8, 10, 11, 12, 13, 14, 21, 26). It is also clear that the prayer has a didactic purpose as v. 13 is directed to be heard by the disciples. This is also born out when we look at the function of the other two prayers of Jesus in the Gospel, in

---

20. See Flusser's comment, 'Like most of the prayers in the Apocrypha and the Pseudepigrapha, the prayers in the Book of Tobit are not independent compositions but serve to express the feelings of the personages of the book' (1984: 556).

Jn 11.41-42 and Jn 12.27-28. In both instances his prayer is to teach something. In Jn 11.41-42 the Johannine Jesus explicitly says, 'I have said (prayed) this for the sake of the crowd standing here, so that they may believe that you sent me.' Schnackenburg's comment is to the point:

> Jesus did not make the prayer for his own sake, but for the sake of the people standing around, so that they should understand the miracle as God's testimony to his mission. The bystanders are meant to hear his words and, like Mary (v. 40), be exhorted to faith. This function makes Jesus' prayer not a demonstration. It is a stylistic device of the evangelist's, who is thinking more of his readers than of the crowd in Bethany (1990: II, 339).

And again the didactic purpose of the prayer in Jn 12.27-28 is clear when the Johannine Jesus prays, 'And what should I say, "Father, save me from this hour"? No, it is for this reason that I have come to this hour.' Again, in Schnackenburg's words, 'It is unlikely that the evangelist means to describe a psychological process rather than to explain the significance of "this hour"' (1990: II, 387). In this connection, Morrison has pointed out that prayer was often used as a medium of instruction in ancient times (1965: 259-60). It is not without reason, then, that Holtzmann regards John 17 as a *Lehrschrift* (Ritt 1979: 94).

I suggest, therefore, that several influences and functions can be detected in the prayer of John 17. The prayer cannot be interpreted in terms of a single literary genre, instead several literary traditions exert an influence on the prayer. Nevertheless, the traditions that flow into the prayer are solely Jewish. In my discussion I have proposed that the 'law-court' pattern of prayer reflects the original *Sitz im Leben*, and provides the general underlying structure of the prayer in John 17. I have also highlighted the autobiographical and didactic functions of prayer in Jewish literature, functions that can also be detected in John 17. Therefore, I agree with Käsemann that John 17 is not a strict prayer that was prayed on a particular occasion (1978: 5), and, like Käsemann, I have found no strong evidence for a eucharistic or liturgical setting for the prayer.[21] John 17 does not open with the common liturgical formula 'blessed' or 'thank you', and there are no

---

21. More recently Rosenblatt has considered the problem of the historicity of Jn 17 in her article 'The Voice of the One Who Prays in John 17' (1988). She correctly states that, 'John 17 is to be distinguished from other instances in the Gospels when the actual prayer of Jesus to his Father is reproduced' (1988: 131).

first-person plural pronouns, nor any indication that it was used in a liturgy. The suggestion that John 17 depends on the Lord's Prayer does not seem very strong. If John reacts against formalism, there may also be a reaction against set prayers like the Lord's Prayer. Instead it appears that the *Sitz im Leben* of the prayer is the struggle of the Johannine community with the synagogue. The prayer has didactic and apologetic purposes; it serves to strengthen the faith of the Johannine community in the face of opposition.

3. *The Literary Context of Jesus' Prayer*

This section needs to discuss the present literary context of the prayer, and related with that the genre of the Farewell discourse. At this point, a distinction has to be made between the original setting of the prayer (*Sitz im Leben*) and its current literary setting in the Gospel (*Sitz im Text*). The original setting of the development of the prayer is to be seen in the reflection of the Johannine community regarding its struggle with the synagogue and the threat of internal dissolution. In the prayer of Jesus for himself and the community we can hear the echo of the community's petitionary prayers to God for justice in their early struggle with the synagogue. However, as the prayer now stands it is in the literary context of the Gospel of John, and more particularly at the end of the section of the Revealer's farewell to his disciples. Both contexts must be appreciated for an understanding of the prayer. I shall first analyse the literary structure of the Gospel of John, and then discuss the tradition of the Farewell genre, especially in Jewish literature.

a. *The Context of the Prayer in the Gospel*
A close reading of the Gospel reveals that it is basically divided into two parts. The first part recounts the ministry of Jesus in the world and presents his conflict with the Jewish leaders (1.19–12.50). In the second part of the Gospel the focus is more towards the disciples and their relationship with Jesus (chs. 13–17). To these two parts must be added the Prologue (1.1-18), the Passion and Resurrection narratives (chs. 18–20), and the secondary conclusion of ch. 21. Most scholars, with some minor variation, have seen these sections as constituting the basic divisions of the Gospel.[22]

22. The following are some of the structural divisions that have been suggested:

Though all major commentators are in agreement that the second part of the Gospel deals particularly with the disciples, the implications of this fact for ecclesiology have not been adequately explored. Ecclesiological concerns play a major role in the second part of the Gospel. When we look closely at chs. 13–17, we discover that the emphasis is not only on Christology but also on ecclesiology. The opening scene of the Farewell presents Jesus' washing of the disciples' feet. Jesus' action is to serve as a model of how the disciples are to treat one another; as Jesus has served them they must serve one another (Jn 13.1-17). Here the concern is for mutual service within the believing community. And in the Farewell discourses themselves we find several ecclesiological themes. The commandment of love between the disciples is repeated several times (Jn 13.34-35; 15.9-10, 12, 17).[23] Also the departure of the Revealer serves to focus attention on the community that will be left behind (Jn 13.1, 33, 36; 14.3, 12, 18, 25-30; 16.7, 16-23, 28). The parable of the vine also has definite ecclesiological implications (Jn 15.1-11). The parable pictures the relationship between believers and Christ in terms of abiding or remaining (μένω), which is interpreted as abiding in Jesus' word (v. 7) and love (v. 10). Therefore, the parable of the vine does have a communal dimension.[24] Lastly, the concept of election (Jn 15.16, 18-19)

Bultmann (1971) divides the Gospel as (1) 1.1-18, The Prologue; (2) 1.19-51, The Witness of the Baptist; (3) chs. 2–12, The Revelation of the Glory to the World; (4) chs. 13–20, The Revelation of the Glory before the Community; and (5) ch. 21, Postscript. Barrett's (1955: 11) division is as follows: (1) 1.1-18, Prologue; (2) 1.19–12.50, Narratives, Conversations, and Discourses; (3) 13.1–17.26, Jesus alone with his Disciples; (4) 18.1–20.31, The Passion and Resurrection; and (6) 21.1-25, Appendix. Kysar's (1993: 18) outline is: (1) 1.1-18, Prologue; (2) 1.19–12.50, Jesus Reveals God's Glory; (3) 13.1–19.42, Jesus Receives God's Glory; and (4) 20.1–21.25, Resurrection. Smith and Spivey (1989: 162) proposed the following outline: (1) 1.1-51, Introduction; (2) 2.1–12.50, The Revelation of Christ's Glory before the World; (3) 13.1–21.25, The Revelation of Christ's Glory before the Community. The structure that Schnelle (1994: 548) gives is: (1) 1.1-18, Prolog: Jesus der Logos; (2) 1.19–12.50, Das Wirken des Offenbarers in der Welt; (3) 13.1–20.29, Jesu Offenbarung vor den Seinen, Passion, Erhöhung und Erscheinungen des Auferstandenen; (4) 20.30-31, Epilog: Vom Verstehen des Evangeliums; and (5) 21.1-25, Nachträge.

23. See Lattke (1975), Segovia (1982), and Augenstein (1993) for extensive treatments on the Johannine concept of love.

24. This has also been pointed out by R.E. Brown, 'One of the lessons of the symbol of the vine and the branches is that if one is to remain as a branch on the

and of God's indwelling of the believers (Jn 14.16-20, 23; 16.13) requires the existence of a community distinct from the 'world'. Likewise, these ecclesiological themes appear prominently in the prayer of John 17; namely, the concept of election (vv. 2, 6-9, 12, 14-16), of unity (vv. 11, 20-23) and of love (v. 26). This brief survey shows that ecclesiology features prominently in the content of the Farewell section.

The question concerning the literary structure of the Farewell section, however, is much more difficult. As I have already mentioned in the first chapter there is a major disjunction in the text at Jn 14.31. It seems that Jn 18.1 needs to follow directly on from Jn 14.31. This has led some scholars to reconstruct chs. 13 to 17. Bultmann thinks that John 17 should be placed after Jn 13.30, and that Jn 13.31 follows on immediately after the prayer (1971: 461). For Bultmann the prayer takes the place of the Last Supper. Jn 14.25-31 forms the conclusion of the Farewell discourses (1971: 459). Consequently, Bultmann reconstructs the order of chs. 13 to 17 as follows: Jn 13.1-30; 17.1-26; 13.31-35; 15.1–16.33; 13.36–14.31. However, though Bultmann seriously tries to wrestle with a major problem in the text his division is highly speculative. In criticizing his reconstruction we may say that the words of Jn 17.1a, 'after Jesus had spoken these words', seems better to follow directly after a conversation, and it breaks the sequence between Jn 13.30 and 31. Moreover, logically there should be no figure of speech or a lack of understanding by the disciples after Jn 16.29-30, but Jn 13.36–14.31 still contains figures of speech and confusion among the disciples. The prayer of John 17 appears to be the climax of the Gospel before the passion, and is therefore out of place at the beginning of the Farewell discourses. Lattke's reconstruction, on the other hand, recognizes these problems and is more plausible on literary grounds. His reconstruction is as follows: Jn 13.1-31a; 15–17; 13.31b–14.31 (1975a: 135).

Other scholars have preferred to deal with the Farewell discourses as they stand in the present order. Ukpong divides the last discourse into three sections: the first section deals with the departure of Jesus and the future of the disciples (Jn 13.31–14.31); the second section

---

vine, one must remain in the love of Jesus (xv 9). Yet this love must be expressed in love for one's fellow believer (xv 12). No Gospel stresses as much as John does, the point that Christian love is a love of one's fellow disciples of Jesus, and thus a love within the Christian community' (1966: I, cviii-cix).

deals with the life of the disciples and their encounter with the world after Jesus' departure (Jn 15–16); and the last section contains the concluding prayer of Jesus (Jn 17) (1989: 50). Boyle, on the other hand, proposed a division of two corresponding sections: Jn 13.31–15.10 and Jn 15.12–16.33 respectively, with Jn 15.11 as the centre (1975: 210). Boyle regards Jesus' origin and goal as the general theme of this section (1975: 217). And, according to Boyle, John 17 follows the same structure as the Farewell discourses with joy at the centre (1975: 222). However, Boyle's analysis is arbitrary and not very convincing.

Another school of thought sees Jn 13.31–17.26 as a collection of Farewell discourses. Barrett suggests two versions of the discourse, John 14 and John 15–17 respectively (1955). Schnackenburg also speaks of a collection of Farewell discourses (1990: I, 46). More detailed analysis of the Farewell discourses has been provided by Woll, Kurz and Painter. Woll suggested that Jn 13.31–14.31 is the first Farewell discourse of the Gospel.[25] In particular Woll has pointed out the importance that is placed on the role of the disciples as Jesus' successors:

> What has been overlooked in most analyses of the farewell discourse is the high status accorded to the *disciples*, as successor-agents of the works of the Son, and as bearers of the presence of Father and Son (1980: 234)... Furthermore, what the author has to say in addressing the issue of succession is not simply that Jesus continues to be present (the *praesentia Christi* of Becker), as his own successor, so to speak, but rather that Jesus continues to be *pre-eminent*. The issue is the rank of Jesus in relation to the successor-disciples, not simply his presence or absence (1980: 235).[26]

Woll goes on to say that the first Farewell discourse may have been directed against a threat 'such as would have been posed by the Christian prophets of Mark 13' (1980: 237). These prophets blurred the distinction between Jesus and his successors. Therefore, 'The farewell

25. This article presents the work of Woll's dissertation *Johannine Christianity in Conflict: Authority, Rank, and Succession in the First Farewell Discourse*, completed in 1978 and published by Scholars Press in 1981.

26. In chs. 13–17 the disciples as a whole are the successors of Jesus. Chapter 21, therefore, where Peter is appointed, probably represents a non-Johannine ecclesiological perspective, or a later development in the Johannine community (or communities).

discourse serves the function of legitimating the authoritative tradition of that event which is contained in the life-giving book of the gospel' (1980: 239). Woll's thesis regarding the threat of Spirit-enthusiasts is important and will again be referred to later.

Segovia is another scholar who has paid attention to the Farewell discourse. According to him the first two versions of the discourse are Jn 13.31–14.31 and Jn 15.18–16.4a respectively. The issue that the first discourse seeks to address is not a futuristic eschatology (J. Becker 1970) but 'the presence of outsiders who refuse to believe in Jesus, namely, the Jews' (1985: 488-89). The *Sitz im Leben* of the first Farewell discourse, then, is the bitter conflict between the Johannine community and the synagogue (1985: 490). Jn 13.34-35 is a later addition to the discourse as it reflects intrachurch concerns (1985: 491-92). Jn 15.1-17, 13.1b-3, 12-20 and 1 John also reflect this same situation. In an earlier article Segovia argues that Jn 15.18–16.4a is the first addition to the original Farewell discourse, and reflects the situation presupposed by the Gospel, that is, the conflict between the Christian community and the synagogue and is far removed from the intrachurch concerns of 1 John (1983: 225-26). 'Thus, at one time, 15.18–16.4a was added directly to 13.31–14.31; it was only at a later time that 15.1-17—and other related passages—was also incorporated' (1983: 228). More recently Segovia has shifted in his approach by adopting the narrative-critical method in analysing the text.[27]

Painter's hypothesis is that the evangelist composed three versions of the Farewell discourse on three different occasions, presenting the evangelist's response to three distinct crises that the community faced. In Painter's words, 'Each version of the discourse reflects a particular crisis to which the evangelist responded with a reformulation of the teaching about the Paraclete/Spirit of Truth' (1993: 421). In chronological order these discourses are: (1) 13.31–14.31; (2) 15.1–16.4a; and (3) 16.4b-33 (1993: 417). The first version of the Farewell discourse reflects on the crisis presented by the departure of Jesus (1993: 425). Painter suggests that it dates no later than the 50s (1993: 425). The second version reflects the bitter conflict with the synagogue. John 15.1-10 is addressed against the 'secret believers' who do not abide in Jesus (1993: 425-26). Lastly, the third version was written after the complete separation of the Johannine community from the synagogue when the community again experienced the abandonment

---

27. See *The Farewell of the Word: The Johannine Call to Abide* (1991).

by Jesus with increased intensity. This version is directed against an inward-looking attitude and isolationism (1993: 428). Chapter 17 presents new material and is not another version of the discourse (1993: 432). It was written later than the last discourse but before 1 John (1993: 417).

Painter's explanation, in general terms, appears the most convincing. The recurring themes and dislocations of the Farewell discourses do suggest that there was a repeated redaction of the discourse. However, the present study's main concern lies with ch. 17 and its relationship with the whole section. But before I am able to discuss the role of ch. 17 we need to look at the literary tradition that lies behind the Farewell discourses of John.

b. *The Jewish Farewell Genre*

It is important to understand chs. 14 (or beginning at 13.31) to 17 in terms of the Jewish Farewell genre that has been identified by scholars. Many interpreters of John have postulated that these chapters belong to the literary pattern of the Farewell genre. Stauffer was one of the first scholars to draw attention to this genre found in the ancient world both in Greco-Roman literature and Jewish literature. Stauffer also noted a distinction between the Greek farewell speech and the biblical, namely, that the subject of the Jewish (biblical) farewell speech is not the noble hero (*vir praeclarus*), but the man of God, the office-bearer and middleman of God, who speaks on behalf of God (1950: 31). Stauffer also gave a list of the parallels between the Farewell speeches of Jesus in the Gospels (also of the disciples in Acts) and the Old Testament tradition (1955: 344-47). According to Stauffer the form and style of these farewell discourses stem from the ancient biblical tradition (1950: 32). This observation is important since I have already argued that John's Jewish context is to be be appreciated. Munck's 'Discours d'adieu dans le Nouveau Testament et dans la littérature biblique' (1950) is another important article that appeared at the same time as Stauffer's work. In the article Munck discusses a number of Farewell speeches in the New Testament against the background of Jewish literature. The Farewell discourse in Jewish tradition contains four elements: (1) a person gives his farewell either because he will be raised to heaven or because he is about to die; (2) the person then gives exhortations or predicts what will happen; (3) less frequently, the person giving the farewell recounts his life which is to serve as a model; and (4) also rarely, the discourse contains a prophecy concerning the destination of the people in the last day (1950: 159). Munck then analyses the speech of Paul to the Ephesian elders (Acts 20.17-38), 1 Timothy 1.12-17, and 2 Timothy 4.6-8, and concludes that these New Testament passages were influenced by the Farewell discourse in Jewish tradition (1950: 163). Finally, Munck considers other passages in the New Testament, including the Farewell discourse in John 13–17. However, the discourse in John is distinct from the rest of the New Testament in that it has lost its apocalyptic character (1950: 167).

Following on from Stauffer and Munck, R.E. Brown has listed 13 features that are common to the biblical and postbiblical Farewell speeches and John's last discourses (1966: II, 598-601). These are: (1) the announcement of imminence of death; (2) sorrow and reassurance; (3) recalling past history; (4) directives to keep the commandments; (5) the command to love one another; (6) insistence on unity; (7) prophecy concerning the successors; (8) cursing of those who persecute the just; (9) the bestowal of peace; (10) the promise of God's faithfulness; (11) the endurance of the name of the departing person; (12) the appointment of a successor; and (13) prayer for those left behind. R.E. Brown is certain that the last discourses of John belong to the literary genre of the Farewell discourse (1966: II, 600-601).

Other studies dealing with the genre of the Farewell discourse have been provided by Michel, Di Lella, and Kurz.[28] Michel gave a good overview of the Jewish (biblical and postbiblical) Farewell *Gattung* in the middle section of his dissertation. He finds 13 elements that characterize this biblical genre (1973: 48-54). These are: (1) confirmation of approaching death; (2) address to a specific audience; (3) paraenetic expressions; (4) prophetic statements; (5) self-resignation; (6) the destiny of the followers; (7) the blessing; (8) the prayer; (9) the last command; (10) funeral directions; (11) promises and oaths; (12) further farewell gestures; and (13) the end. He concluded that the Farewell discourse is a definite literary genre (1973: 54). Another important question that Michel deals with is the function and *Sitz im Leben* of the Farewell discourse. According to Michel this genre served a paraenetic function. 'We are convinced that the Farewell discourse had its origin in paraenesis, which, on the basis of a

---

28. Also see the treatments of Schneider (1982a: II, 290-300) and Pesch (1986: II, 196-208) on Paul's Farewell to the elders of Ephesus, Acts 20.17-38.

defined understanding of history, points out the relationship between the past, present and future' (1973: 57). In his analysis of biblical and postbiblical material paraeneses are an essential part of the Farewell in all cases (1973: 49). The question concerning the *Sitz im Leben* of the Farewell discourse must be seen in relation to the particular theology of the Farewell. Michel also makes the point that the discourses were created *ex eventu*, and that they reflect the present situation of the author (1973: 54).

In his article, 'The Deuteronomic Background of the Farewell Discourse in Tob 14.3-11', Di Lella (1979) has isolated nine 'major correspondences' between Deuteronomy and Tobit's Farewell discourse (14.3-11) (1979: 380).[29] These are: (1) long life in the land; (2) the offer of mercy; (3) rest and security in the land; (4) the blessing of joy; (5) the fear and love of God; (6) the command to praise God; (7) a theology of remembering; (8) the centralization of the cult; and (9) a final exhortation. I should point out that a number of these elements are present not only in John's Farewell speeches but also in John 17, for example, the themes of life, security, joy, the theology of remembering, and exhortations. The only important elements that are absent from John 17 are the atonement motif and the concept of sin. Di Lella also identified Deuteronomy as 'nomic literature' in paraenetic form (1979: 388).

Another important study on the Farewell discourse is that of Kurz, 'Luke 22.14-38 and Greco-Roman and Biblical Farewell Addresses' (1985).[30] In Kurz's analysis the elements of the Farewell addresses

29. Lacomara also has noted the correspondence between Deuteronomy and the Farewell discourses of John. He concludes that the similarities are more than coincidental and, therefore, that 'the deuteronomic discourses of Moses were the model for the FD' (1974: 82).

30. In the Farewell address in the tradition of Plato's *Phaedo* the speaker (1) gives commands or names successors; (2) exhorts, and urges his disciples to remember his teachings; (3) sometimes curses enemies; (4) proclaims innocence or fulfilment of office; (5) defends what he did or why he is about to commit suicide; (6) reflects on his life; (7) sometimes seeks clemency; (8) shows courage facing death; (9) sometimes expresses sorrow; and (10) turns over his soul to the gods (Kurz 1985: 255). These are similar to the elements Stauffer listed: (1) revelations of the speaker's coming death; (2) final orders; (3) installation of his successor; (4) a speech to the people about the speaker's life; (5) warnings for the future; and (6) woes or consolations (Stauffer 1950: 31). According to Kurz the structure of the Farewell address in Luke is as follows: (1) Jesus refers to his imminent death; (2) instructs about the

consists of the following: (1) summoning of successors; (2) recollection of the mission and example of the departing person; (3) recollection of the innocence and faithfulness of the departing person; (4) impending death; (5) exhortation; (6) warnings and final injunctions; (7) blessings; (8) farewell gestures; (9) tasks for successors; (10) a theological review of history; (11) the revealing of the future; (12) promises; (13) appointment of successors; (14) mourning over the departure; (15) prophecy concerning future degeneration; (16) renewal of the covenant; (17) care of those left; (18) consolation to inner circle; (19) didactic speech; and (20) *ars moriendi*. Kurz, like Michel, sees the Farewell discourse functioning as a paraenesis.

I conclude that John 13–17 does reflect the style and character of the Jewish Farewell discourse. This has been shown by the studies mentioned above. The question for me is how John 17 relates to its preceding Farewell speeches. Is John 17 another new version of Jesus' farewell to his disciples, or should it be regarded as a summary of the speeches? I think that the answer lies somewhere in between these two alternatives. John 17 is not simply a summary or a synthesis of the Farewell discourses but rather its climax; it is the end result of the community's reflection on its purpose after the departure of the Redeemer. We notice several common themes between the Farewell speeches and the prayer, for example, the themes of glory (δόξα, δοξάζω; cf. 13.31-32; 14.13; 15.8; 16.14; 17.1, 4, 5, 10, 22, 24), life (ζωή; cf. 14.6; 17.2, 3), revelation (cf. 14.9-10, 21, 24-25; 16.12-15; 17.6, 8), election (cf. 15.16; 17.2, 6-9, 12, 14-16), struggle with the world (κόσμος; cf. 14.17, 19, 22, 27, 30-31; 15.18-19; 16.11, 20-21, 33; 17.6, 9, 12-16, 25), belief (πιστεύω; cf. 14.1, 11-12, 29; 16.9, 27, 30-31; 17.8, 20-21), joy (χαρά; cf. 15.11; 16.20-22, 24; 17.13), and love (ἀγάπη, ἀγαπάω; cf. 13.34; 14.15, 21, 23-24, 31; 15.9-10, 13, 17; 17.23-24, 26). These key words and themes tie the whole section of the Redeemer's farewell together. Therefore, John 17 must be regarded as part of the Farewell discourses in John. We notice, however, that though many themes of the Farewell discourses are present in the prayer there are significant omissions, for example, the role of the Spirit is completely absent from the prayer. There is also new material in the prayer, such as the emphasis on unity, and the theme of

eucharist; (3) institutes the new covenant; (4) predicts betrayal; (5) discusses rank; (6) transfers his authority; (7) singles out Simon; and (8) foreshadows the impending crises.

sending. Therefore, the prayer cannot be regarded as a simple summary of the Farewell discourses. It contains further reflection that
goes beyond the thought of the previous Farewell discourses.

A hypothesis concerning the *Sitz im Leben* of the prayer when it
was composed in its final form and inserted into the Gospel may help
us to account for the absence and presence of certain themes. The
most reasonable explanation to account for the absence of the Spirit as
the giver of revelation appears to be that the evangelist is trying to
curb the activity of Spirit-enthusiasts. This may reflect the earlier
struggle that Woll suggested lay behind the first Farewell discourse.[31]
The insistence in the prayer on Jesus' work on earth and the word he
gave to the disciples would counteract sole dependence on new revelation that is independent from the tradition of Jesus. Therefore, it is
probable that John 17 was the last addition made to the Farewell discourses, or, at least, contains the reflection of the evangelist that took
place after the situations that produced the Farewell discourses. Moreover, the absence of the danger of apostasy (sin) and of any strong
language against any who would leave the community,[32] indicates that
the prayer was composed before 1 John was written. I conclude that
the final form of John 17 was composed after the decisive break with
the synagogue, but before the schism that occurred within the community. Therefore, the *Sitz im Leben* of the prayer reflects the situation of the Johannine community after the split with the synagogue as
the community defines its place in the 'world', but before 1 John
(where the prominence of sin [ἁμαρτία], that is, apostasy, is central).
We may, then, regard the Farewell discourses as presenting the
struggle in the community's reflection to come to terms with its position in the world. The Farewell discourses contain glimpses of how
the community responded to different threats to its existence. John 17
is the community's definitive statement concerning itself and its mission before the schism. Indeed, many scholars regard the prayer as a
later addition to the Gospel, and as such reflect the developed theology
of the Johannine community.[33] Therefore, in our analysis John 17

31. Käsemann also recognized the prominent role played by the Spirit in the
Johannine community (1978: 31-32).

32. Though the prayer emphasizes unity, I do not think that it reflects the schism
that occurred later on within the community.

33. For example, R.E. Brown sees the prayer as an independent composition
added later corresponding to the style of the Prologue (1966: II, 745). Likewise,

reflects the final ecclesiological statement of the Gospel.

What, then, is the function of the prayer in its present context? Since John 17 is to be regarded as part of the Farewell discourses, it is not a true historical prayer,[34] but functions chiefly as a paraenesis. We have seen in the analysis of Michel the importance of paraenesis in the Jewish Farewell genre. The prayer also recalls the foundation of the community's teachings in the earthly life of Jesus, and as such serves as an apologia for the community against threats on its existence. From this basis the prayer seeks to encourage the community to fulfil its place in the world. Therefore, though the prayers underlying John 17 had an apologetic purpose, the present prayer has a paraenetic function.

In addition we may note that the prayer is remarkable for its comprehensiveness; it addresses the community's stance vis-à-vis the synagogue, the world and fellow believers. Moreover, the prayer encompasses the past, the present and the future. John 17 is therefore a theological overview of the community's place in the world. It is not just a polemic against other Christians (as is 1 John), but an apologia and paraenesis for the community's existence and its sending into the world. John 17 describes ecclesiology: the community must continue its mission into the world (cf. 17.18, 21). The broader concern of mission of John 17 is in stark contrast with the Farewell discourses which contain no mission sentiment, except for the concept of fruit in the parable of the vine[35] (Jn 15.1-8). Most of the Farewell discourses were composed during the height of the community's struggle against the synagogue. After the dust of the conflict has settled the prayer of John 17 serves to remind the community again of its mission in the world. John 17 is a summary and reflection on the history of the community and defines its future character.[36]

---

both Painter (1981: 256) and Schmithals (1992: 401) regard Jn 17 as a later addition by the evangelist.

34. Prayers in the mouths of the protagonists are also found in *4 Ezra* and *2 Bar.* (Flusser 1984: 575), which were written around the same time as John.

35. In the New Testament the figure of fruit generally denotes the presence of spiritual virtues, as in Gal. 5.22. However, in John καρπός is defined in terms of harvest, i.e. salvation of people for eternal life (cf. Jn 4.36; and 12.24; also Jn 15.2, 6, 8, 16).

36. In the words of Becker, 'Das Gebet ist so nie von Jesus gesprochen worden, noch im Gottesdienst der Gemeinde verwendet worden' (1991: II, 611).

4. *The Structure of the Prayer*

We are now in a position to turn to the discussion concerning the structure of the text.[37] First of all, John 17 does present us with a clearly defined literary unit. John 17.1, ταῦτα ἐλάλησεν Ἰησοῦς (After Jesus spoke these words), signals the beginning of a new section. Jesus then prays continuously until the end of the chapter. There are no breaks in the prayer except for some explanatory notes. The beginning of John 18 again signals the start of a new section with the expression, ταῦτα εἰπὼν (after speaking these words). Furthermore, the key concept of δόξα in the prayer forms an inclusion—it is mentioned in the first request of Jesus (v. 1), and again near the end of the prayer (v. 24).

Becker has provided a thorough analysis of how John 17 has been divided by the commentators (1969: 56-61). I do not need to repeat his work here and have opted for the common threefold division of the text: (1) Jesus prays concerning himself (vv. 1-8); (2) Jesus prays concerning his disciples (vv. 9-19); (3) Jesus prays concerning future believers (vv. 20-26). I have based this division on the following reasons: First, the division follows closely the time perspective of John as outlined by Onuki. John is concerned not only with the past and present but also with the future. Jesus' prayer concerning himself reflects on the past. His prayer concerning his disciples describes the present, whereas Jesus' prayer for those who will believe through the disciples' word prophesies about the future. Secondly, key structural markers suggest this threefold division of the prayer. The address to the Father, πάτερ, in v. 1 opens Jesus' prayer, then at v. 9 the expression, ἐγὼ περὶ αὐτῶν ἐρωτῶ, occurs indicating that Jesus is progressing to a new subject. Then again a similar expression occurs at v. 20, οὐ περὶ τούτων δὲ ἐρωτῶ μόνον, ἀλλὰ καὶ περὶ τῶν πιστευόντων διὰ τοῦ λόγου αὐτῶν εἰς ἐμέ, indicating that another transition is made. Thirdly, the content also lends itself to a threefold division. In the first section Jesus prays for his own glorification and recounts his work on earth, especially revealing the Father to the disciples. In the second section the attention is on the disciples who are in need of protection and sanctification. In the third section the focus shifts to future

37. Important articles on the structure of Jn 17 are those of J. Becker (1969), Malatesta (1971), Schnackenburg (1973), and D.A. Black (1988).

believers, and the need for oneness and love. And fourthly, vv. 6 to 8
have been grouped with the first part of the prayer because no new
request is made and the focus is still on what Jesus has done. Taking
these verses with the first part of the prayer also allows for a more
symmetrical division of the prayer.[38]

This prayer shares all the Johannine characteristics of style.[39] The
most important of these are: parallelism; repetition of words and
ideas, repetition of syntactical structures, the literary device of inclusion, chiastic structures, explanatory notes, and the frequent use of
ἵνα and ὅτι clauses. I propose the following structure (and translation) of the prayer:[40]

Part I: Jesus prays concerning himself (verses 1-8)

1a ταῦτα ἐλάλησεν Ἰησοῦς
1b καὶ ἐπάρας τοὺς ὀφθαλμοὺς αὐτοῦ εἰς τὸν οὐρανὸν
1c εἶπεν·

1d πάτερ, ἐλήλυθεν ἡ ὥρα·
1e δόξασόν σου τὸν υἱόν,
1f   ἵνα ὁ υἱὸς δοξάσῃ σέ,
2a   καθὼς ἔδωκας αὐτῷ ἐξουσίαν πάσης σαρκός,
2b   ἵνα πᾶν ὃ δέδωκας αὐτῷ δώσῃ[41] αὐτοῖς ζωὴν αἰώνιον.
3a   αὕτη δέ ἐστιν ἡ αἰώνιος ζωὴ
3b   ἵνα γινώσκωσιν σὲ τὸν μόνον ἀληθινὸν θεὸν
3c   καὶ ὃν ἀπέστειλας Ἰησοῦν Χριστόν.
4a   ἐγώ σε ἐδόξασα ἐπὶ τῆς γῆς
4b   τὸ ἔργον τελειώσας ὃ δέδωκάς μοι
4c   ἵνα ποιήσω·
5a   καὶ νῦν δόξασόν με σύ, πάτερ, παρὰ σεαυτῷ
5b   τῇ δόξῃ ᾗ εἶχον πρὸ τοῦ τὸν κόσμον εἶναι παρὰ σοί.

1a Jesus said these (things).
1b And lifting his eyes into heaven,
1c he said:

38. The structural division here is also followed by Moloney (1982).
39. For a discussion of Johannine style see N. Turner (1976: 64-79), R.E.
Brown (1966: I, cxxix-cxxxviii), Freed (1964), and D.A. Black (1988).
40. I have adopted the 26th edition of the Nestle-Aland text here and shall deal
with the important textual variants in the exegesis.
41. I shall discuss the textual variant at this point in the next chapter.

1d 'Father, the hour has come.
1e Glorify your Son,
1f   in order that the Son may glorify you.
2a   Because you gave him authority of all flesh,
2b   in order that to all which you have given him he may give them
            life eternal.
3a   And this is the eternal life
3b   that they may continue to know you, the only true God,
3c   and Jesus Christ whom you sent.
4a   I glorified you on the earth,
4b   by completing the work which you have given me
4c   to do.
5a And now you, Father, glorify me with yourself,
5b with the glory which I had with you before the world was.

6a ἐφανέρωσά σου τὸ ὄνομα τοῖς ἀνθρώποις
6b   οὓς ἔδωκάς[42] μοι ἐκ τοῦ κόσμου.
6c   σοὶ ἦσαν
6d   κἀμοὶ αὐτοὺς ἔδωκας
6e καὶ τὸν λόγον σου τετήρηκαν.

7a νῦν ἔγνωκαν
7b   ὅτι πάντα ὅσα δέδωκάς μοι παρὰ σοῦ εἰσιν·
8a   ὅτι τὰ ῥήματα ἃ ἔδωκάς μοι δέδωκα αὐτοῖς,
8b   καὶ αὐτοὶ ἔλαβον
8c   καὶ ἔγνωσαν ἀληθῶς
8d   ὅτι παρὰ σοῦ ἐξῆλθον,
8e   καὶ ἐπίστευσαν
8f   οτι σὺ με ἀπέστειλας.

6a I manifested your name to the people
6b   whom you have given me among the world.
6c   They were yours
6d   and you gave them to me
6e and they have kept your word.

7a Now they have come to know
7b   that all you have given me are from you.
8a   Because the words which you gave me I have given them,
8b   and they received [them],
8c   and they came to know truly
8d   that I came from you,

42. I shall discuss the textual variant at this point in the next chapter.

8e   and they believed
8f   that you sent me.

Part II: Jesus prays concerning his disciples (verses 9-19)

9a ἐγὼ περὶ αὐτῶν ἐρωτῶ,
9b   οὐ περὶ τοῦ κόσμου ἐρωτῶ
9c   ἀλλὰ περὶ ὧν δέδωκάς μοι,
9d   ὅτι σοί εἰσιν,
10a   καὶ τὰ ἐμὰ πάντα σά ἐστιν
10b   καὶ τὰ σὰ ἐμά,
10c   καὶ δεδόξασμαι ἐν αὐτοῖς.
11a | καὶ οὐκέτι εἰμὶ ἐν τῷ κόσμῳ,
11b   καὶ αὐτοὶ ἐν τῷ κόσμῳ εἰσίν,
11c   κἀγὼ πρὸς σὲ ἔρχομαι.

9a I am asking concerning them,
9b   I am not asking concerning the world,
9c   but concerning those you have given me,
9d   because they are yours.
10a   And all mine are yours,
10b   and yours mine,
10c   and I have been glorified by them.
11a   And I am no longer to stay in the world,
11b   but they are to stay in the world,
11c   and I am coming to you.

11d πάτερ ἅγιε, τήρησον αὐτοὺς ἐν τῷ ὀνόματί σου ᾧ δέδωκάς μοι,
11e   ἵνα ὦσιν ἓν
11f   καθὼς ἡμεῖς.
12a   ὅτε ἤμην μετ᾽ αὐτῶν
12b   ἐγὼ ἐτήρουν αὐτοὺς
12c   ἐν τῷ ὀνόματί σου ᾧ δέδωκάς μοι,
12d   καὶ ἐφύλαξα,
12e   καὶ οὐδεὶς ἐξ αὐτῶν ἀπώλετο εἰ μὴ ὁ υἱὸς τῆς ἀπωλείας,
12f   ἵνα ἡ γραφὴ πληρωθῇ.
13a   νῦν δὲ πρὸς σὲ ἔρχομαι
13b   καὶ ταῦτα λαλῶ ἐν τῷ κόσμῳ
13c   ἵνα ἔχωσιν τὴν χαρὰν τὴν ἐμὴν
                        πεπληρωμένην ἐν αὐτοῖς.
14a   ἐγὼ δέδωκα αὐτοῖς τὸν λόγον σου
14b   καὶ ὁ κόσμος ἐμίσησεν αὐτούς,
14c   ὅτι οὐκ εἰσὶν ἐκ τοῦ κόσμου
14d   καθὼς ἐγὼ οὐκ εἰμὶ ἐκ τοῦ κόσμου.

15a οὐκ ἐρωτῶ
15b   ἵνα ἄρῃς αὐτοὺς ἐκ τοῦ κόσμου,
15c   ἀλλ᾽ ἵνα τηρήσῃς αὐτοὺς ἐκ τοῦ πονηροῦ.
16a   ἐκ τοῦ κόσμου οὐκ εἰσὶν
16b   καθὼς ἐγὼ οὐκ εἰμὶ ἐκ τοῦ κόσμου.

11d Holy Father, keep them in your name which you gave me,
11e   in order that they may be one
11f   as we (are).
12a   When I was with them,
12b   I was keeping them
12c   in your name which you have given me,
12d   and I guarded (them),
12e   and no one out of them perished except the son of
                perdition,
12f   in order that the Scripture might be fulfilled.
13a   But now I am coming to you
13b   and I am speaking these things in the world
13c   in order that they may have my joy made
                complete in themselves.
14a   I have given them your word
14b   and the world hated them,
14c   because they are not from the world,
14d   just as I am not from the world.
15a I am not asking
15b   that you take them out of the world,
15c   but that you keep them away from the Evil One.
16a   They are not from the world,
16b   just as I am not from the world.
17a ἁγίασον αὐτοὺς ἐν τῇ ἀληθείᾳ·
17b ὁ λόγος ὁ σὸς ἀλήθειά ἐστιν.
18a   καθὼς ἐμὲ ἀπέστειλας εἰς τὸν κόσμον,
18b   κἀγὼ ἀπέστειλα αὐτοὺς εἰς τὸν κόσμον·
19a καὶ ὑπὲρ αὐτῶν ἐγὼ ἁγιάζω ἐμαυτόν,
19b   ἵνα ὦσιν καὶ αὐτοὶ ἡγιασμένοι ἐν ἀληθείᾳ.

17a Consecrate them in the truth:
17b   your word is truth.
18a   Just as you sent me into the world,
18b   I also sent them into the world.
19a And I am consecrating myself on behalf of them,
19b   in order that they also may be consecrated in truth.

Part III: Jesus prays concerning future believers (verses 20-26)

20a οὐ περὶ τούτων δὲ ἐρωτῶ μόνον,
20b ἀλλὰ καὶ περὶ τῶν πιστευόντων διὰ τοῦ λόγου αὐτῶν εἰς ἐμέ,
21a   ἵνα πάντες ἓν ὦσιν,
21b   καθὼς σύ, πάτερ, ἐν ἐμοὶ
21c   κἀγὼ ἐν σοί,
21d   ἵνα καὶ αὐτοὶ ἐν ἡμῖν ὦσιν,
21e   ἵνα ὁ κόσμος πιστεύῃ ὅτι σύ με ἀπέστειλας.
22a κἀγὼ τὴν δόξαν ἣν δέδωκάς μοι δέδωκα αὐτοῖς,
22b   ἵνα ὦσιν ἓν
22c   καθὼς ἡμεῖς ἕν·
23a   ἐγὼ ἐν αὐτοῖς
23b   καὶ σὺ ἐν ἐμοί,
23c   ἵνα ὦσιν τετελειωμένοι εἰς ἕν,
23d   ἵνα γινώσκῃ ὁ κόσμος ὅτι σύ με ἀπέστειλας

23e καὶ ἠγάπησας αὐτοὺς
23f καθὼς ἐμὲ ἠγάπησας.

20a But I am not only asking concerning these,
20b but also concerning those who will believe through their word in me,
21a   in order that all may be one,
21b   just as you, Father, in me,
21c   and I in you,
21d   in order that they also may be in us,
21e   in order that the world may believe that you sent me.
22a And the glory which you have given me I have given them,
22b   in order that they may be one
22c   just as we (are) one,
23a   I in them
23b   and you in me,
23c   in order that they may be perfected into one,
23d   in order that the world may come to know that you sent me

23e and loved them
23f just as you loved me.

24a πάτερ, ὃ δέδωκάς μοι, θέλω
24b   ἵνα ὅπου εἰμὶ ἐγὼ κἀκεῖνοι ὦσιν μετ' ἐμοῦ,
24c   ἵνα θεωρῶσιν τὴν δόξαν τὴν ἐμήν, ἣν δέδωκάς μοι
24d   ὅτι ἠγάπησάς με πρὸ καταβολῆς κόσμου.

25a πάτερ δίκαιε, καὶ ὁ κόσμος σε οὐκ ἔγνω,

25b ἐγὼ δέ σε ἔγνων,

25c καὶ οὗτοι ἔγνωσαν ὅτι σύ με ἀπέστειλας·

26a καὶ ἐγνώρισα αὐτοῖς τὸ ὄνομά σου

26b καὶ γνωρίσω,

26c   ἵνα ἡ ἀγάπη ἣν ἠγάπησάς με ἐν αὐτοῖς ᾖ

26d   κἀγὼ ἐν αὐτοῖς.

24a Father, I want that those you have given me

24b   may be where I am that they may be with me,

24c   in order that they may see my glory which you have given me,

'24d   because you loved me before the foundation of the world.

25a Righteous Father, even the world did not know you,

25b but I have known you,

25c and these have known that you sent me.

26a And I made your name known to them

26b and I will make (it) known,

26c   in order that the love with which you loved me may be in them,

26d   and I (may be) in them.'

The first five verses of the prayer form a chiastic structure around the concept of glory (δόξα and δοξάζω). In v. 1 the Johannine Jesus prays that the Father may glorify him, and at v. 5 he prays again that the Father may glorify him, but now the idea is expanded with the addition of v. 5b. Verses 1e, 1f and 2 give the reason or justification of the Son's request, which is again reflected in v. 4. Verse 3 is a note (probably a later insertion) on the last concept mentioned in v. 2, namely, life eternal.

Verses 6 to 8 continue to describe the work of the Son, and as such serve as further justification of the requests in vv. 1 and 5. The Son's work is primarily seen as that of a revealer of the Father's name or word to his community. As such, the nature of the community features prominently as well. Verse 6 also contains a chiastic structure: 6a and 6e deal with the revelation the Son has brought; 6b, 6c and 6d describe the people (τοῖς ἀνθρώποις) to whom the Son has revealed the Father's name. Verses 7 and 8 focus particularly on the response of the disciples to the Son's revelation. But since v. 8a connects these verses to the Son's revelation of the Father, these verses are still part of the section begun in v. 6. The disciples have known that everything the Son revealed is from the Father and that they have received that revelation. Their reception of the Son's revelation is described in three clauses that are in parallel construction, namely, vv. 8b, 8c, and 8e.

Verses 9 to 19 form the second major division of the prayer. Verses 9 to 11c serve as an interlude to the specific requests of the Johannine Jesus for the disciples. Jesus does not pray for the world but only for those the Father has given to him. Verses 9d to 11c, though v. 10 is somewhat of an interruption in the thought, give several reasons why Jesus only prays for his disciples: they belong to the Father; Jesus has been glorified in them; Jesus will no longer be in the world, but the disciples will remain in the world. Verse 11c reflects v. 11a.

The two requests for the protection and consecration of the disciples form two sections respectively. A chiastic structure may again be detected in these two sections. In v. 11d Jesus prays that the Father may keep (τήρησον) the disciples in his name, and at v. 15c Jesus prays that the Father may keep (τηρήσῃς) the disciples from the evil one. Verse 14 reflects v. 12: the Son has kept the disciples by the revelation he has given to them. Verse 13 is another note giving the reason for Jesus' prayer. Similarly, Jesus' request for the disciples' consecration (ἁγίασον) in v. 17a is reflected in the Son's consecration (ἁγιάζω) on behalf of his disciples in v. 19. Verse 18 serves to explain the nature of the consecration that is in view.

Verse 20 begins the final section of the prayer. Jesus not only prays for his current disciples but also for those who will believe through their word. The thought contained in vv. 20 to 23 is complex, but nevertheless a parallel structure can be detected. The reason for the Son's prayer for future believers is given in vv. 21 to 23, with vv. 22 to 23 generally reflecting the thought contained in v. 21.

In v. 24 the Johannine Jesus prays that the disciples may be with him to see his glory (δόξα). Verse 24, therefore, incorporates the whole prayer in an inclusio around the theme of glory (δόξα). Lastly, vv. 25 and 26 returns to the difference between Jesus, the disciples of Jesus, and the world. The world did not know the Father, but Jesus and his disciples have known him. Jesus will continue to reveal the Father's name to the community so that the love with which the Father has loved the Son may be in them.

5. *Thematic Overview of John 17*

The central idea of the prayer, which is also its unifying factor, is the concept of glory. The opening request is to glorify the Son that the

Son in turn may glorify the Father. This request provides the tone of the whole prayer. Jesus goes on to say that he has already glorified the Father by completing the work (ἔργον) the Father gave him to do. In fact, the Son had glory even before the world (κόσμος) began. Jesus returns to the theme of glory at v. 10 by saying that he received glory through the disciples. At the end of the prayer glory again becomes prominent when the Son says that he has given his glory to the disciples. The Johannine Jesus' last request is that his disciples may be where he is and that they may see his glory. The concept of glory, then, is one of the major theological themes of the prayer. Chapter 5 will deal with the Johannine concept of glory in greater detail.

Other prominent ideas of the prayer are those of revelation, election and unity. Jesus characterizes his work as having revealed the Father's name (ἐφανέρωσά σου τὸ ὄνομα) to his disciples, and as having given the Father's words (τὰ ῥήματα in v. 8 and τὸν λόγον σου in v. 14) to his disciples. This is obviously a reflection on the earlier narratives and discourses of the Gospel.

Another very important concept in the prayer, and one which has not yet received adequate attention in Johannine scholarship, is that of election. This concept is taken up in the verb δίδωμι, which occurs not less than 17 times in the prayer. On eight occasions the verb occurs in the context of election—the Father *has given* the disciples to Jesus (vv. 2, 6, 7, 9, 11, 12, 24). On four other occasions the disciples are also described by this term (Jn 5.36; 6.37, 39; 10.29). The concept of unity or oneness becomes central in the third section of the prayer. The Son prays specifically that both the disciples (v. 11) and future believers may be one (vv. 20-23). The word ἕν occurs six times in the prayer. Chapter 4, the exegesis of Jesus' prayer, will return to these issues.

Ecclesiological concerns occupy a prominent place throughout the prayer. The prayer opens with the request to glorify the Son. The justification of this request is that the Father has given the Son authority to bestow eternal life on those the Father has given him, that is, on the elect. Therefore, from the beginning the prayer is concerned with the Johannine community, that is, those who belong to the Son. In vv. 6 to 8 the praying Jesus describes his work on earth which is exclusively concerned with the disciples. He has revealed the Father to them. They stand in sharp contrast to the world (κόσμος). The distinction between the world and the elect is that the elect are those who receive the word and believe that the Father sent Jesus. Therefore, we see that though in the first section of the prayer Jesus prays for himself, his concern is nearly always directed towards the disciples.

From v. 9 onwards the community of disciples, whether present or future believers, become the main subject of the prayer. Concerning present believers Jesus prays that they may be protected from the world. He protected them while he was with them by the name of the Father. Jesus also prays that the community may be sanctified through the word. Therefore we see that the community is protected through recourse to the word. There is also the reminder that as the Father has sent Jesus, so Jesus is sending his disciples into the world.

In the final section the emphasis falls on unity and love in the community (the concept of unity has already been mentioned in v. 11). Jesus prays that they may be one so that the world may believe that the Father sent him. Again reference is made to the mission of the community with respect to the world. Unity is indispensable for the community in order to continue their mission. Jesus further says that he has given his glory to the community and he asks that they may be with him to see his glory. Glory thus becomes not only the goal of Jesus' mission but also of the community's mission. Lastly, the prayer concludes with the reminder that they must love one another.

6. *Conclusion*

On the basis of these observations, it is proposed that John 17 particularly reflects the Johannine community's understanding of itself, and that the prayer is therefore crucial for understanding Johannine ecclesiology. The *Sitz im Leben* of the prayer has its original context in the community's petitionary prayers in its conflict with the synagogue. John 17, in other words, reflects the early prayers of the Johannine community as it sought vindication from God for its christological beliefs. As such, strong apologetic motifs for the legitimacy of the Johannine community within a Jewish context surface in the prayer. Moreover, the *Sitz im Text* of the prayer also shows that ecclesiology is the primary concern of John 17. The Farewell discourses, of which John 17 is a part, are an attempt of the Johannine community to come to grips with its place in a hostile world. The Farewell discourses serve to consolidate the existence of the Johannine community, and as such have didactic and paraenetic functions.

We have also seen that the prayer itself focuses particularly on the origin, the nature, and the purpose of the Johannine community. Though the christological concern plays a major role it serves primarily to provide the necessary foundation for an ecclesiology. The origin of the community can be traced back to the revelation that Jesus had given it. The prayer emphasizes the past and definitive character of this revelation. Moreover, the community consists of those whom the Father had given to Jesus and its origin is totally dependent on Jesus. The nature of the community is seen in terms of concepts such as unity, joy, and love. And lastly, the community exists in order to continue the sending of Jesus in the world, that is, that the world may also believe that the Father sent Jesus. In the following chapter I shall explore these ideas more fully.

Chapter 4

THE EXEGESIS OF JESUS' PRAYER

1. *Introduction*

We are now able to turn to the exegesis of John 17. It should be pointed out at the beginning that this chapter does not intend to provide a detailed discussion of all the questions presented by the text.[1] Instead, on the justification provided in Chapter 2, and according to the purpose of the study, I shall consider the Johannine prayer in terms of its ecclesiological perspective. The aim is to discover the ecclesiological concerns of the Johannine community and the answers given to those concerns. Therefore, I shall especially focus on terms and concepts that relate to Johannine ecclesiology. The underlying method of my exegesis will be to ask what is specific to the text with respect to Johannine ecclesiology. Indeed, the temptation of exegesis is to read too much into the text (eisegesis). Though many interpretations of the text may be possible one must always ask what is specific to the text in the overall context and purpose of the literary narrative. I have already pointed out that ecclesiology is indeed a major concern of John 17, and may therefore legitimately ask ecclesiological questions in my exegesis.

On the basis of the analysis of the structure of the prayer in Chapter 2 I shall divide the exegesis into three parts: Part I, Jesus prays concerning himself (vv. 1-8); Part II, Jesus prays concerning his disciples (vv. 9-19); and Part III, Jesus prays concerning future believers (vv. 20-26). Since I shall deal with the major concepts of the prayer as

---

1.   For detailed exegetical studies on Jn 17 see Thüsing (1975) and Ritt (1979), and the commentaries of Hoskyns (1940), Barrett (1955), R.E. Brown (1966), Schnackenburg (1990), Bultmann (1971), Lindars (1971), Haenchen (1984), Beasley-Murray (1987), J. Becker (1991), and Carson (1991).

they are introduced, Part I will be the longest section of the three. Furthermore, I shall deal with the textual variants at the beginning of each section, and a translation of the passage into English will be provided at the end.

2. Part I: Jesus Prays concerning himself (verses 1-8)[2]

a. *Exegesis*

In the first section of the prayer Jesus is praying concerning himself (vv. 1-8). The first sentence of ch. 17 serves to make a transition from the previous Farewell speeches and to introduce the prayer, ταῦτα ἐλάλησεν Ἰησοῦς καὶ ἐπάρας τοὺς ὀφθαλμοὺς αὐτοῦ εἰς τὸν οὐρανὸν εἶπεν. The evangelist uses the expression ταῦτα ἐλάλησεν Ἰησοῦς, as in Jn 12.36 and 18.1, to provide the transition from Jesus' Farewell speeches to the prayer.[3] A similar expression occurs in Jn 16.33, ταῦτα λελάληκα, which makes its repetition here verbose. These observations support the suggestion that the material of John 17 was added later and that it stands somewhat apart from the Farewell speeches. John 17 was composed as the evangelist's final statement for his community's place and purpose in the world.

Nevertheless, the prayer flows out of the preceding speeches as can be seen in the fact that the last verse of John 16 provides a good description of the tone behind the composition of the prayer, 'I have said this to you, so that in me you may have peace. In the world you face persecution. But take courage; I have conquered the world!' Though the history of the community has been characterized by conflict, the Johannine Jesus wants the community to have peace and courage.

It is important to note that the historical aorist of the verb λαλέω is used, since the verb often describes the revelation brought by the Johannine Jesus (cf. Jn 6.63; 7.17-18, 46; 8.38; 12.49-50; 14.10, 25;

---

2. I shall generally follow the text of the 26th edition of the Nestle-Aland Greek New Testament. I shall only deal with text critical matters at vv. 2 and 6 where I might disagree with the Nestle-Aland text. The criteria that I have adopted for the determination of the 'better' reading are those proposed by Metzger (1971: xxiv-xxxi).

3. Cf. Barrett, 'ταῦτα refers to the discourse of chs. 13-16. John emphasizes that the address of Jesus to the disciples is over, and clearly distinguishes it from his address to the Father' (1955: 418).

15.3; 16.25). The aorist is used to refer to the revelation given by
Jesus during his earthly life and underscores its definitive quality. The
absence of any reference in the prayer concerning the παράκλητος,
who will tell of things to come (Jn 16.13), makes the emphasis on
Jesus' revelation in the prayer significant. The community must be
defined in terms of the Johannine tradition about Jesus' teachings and
not on new revelations through the παράκλητος.[4]

The expression ἐπάρας τοὺς ὀφθαλμοὺς αὐτοῦ εἰς τὸν οὐρανὸν is
a semitic idiom and is often found in the Old Testament for 'looking
up' (cf. Gen. 13.10; 18.2; 22.4, etc.).[5] The action of the participle,
ἐπάρας, introducing the adverbial clause of manner, is antecedent to
the action of the main verb, εἶπεν. Jesus first looked up and then he
said (εἶπεν) the prayer. A simple verb of speaking is used, instead of
the more definite term προσεύχομαι.[6]

The prayer itself begins with the address to the Father, πάτερ,
which is in the vocative case.[7] πατήρ was a common address early
Christians used for God in prayer,[8] and this usage probably went back
to Jesus himself (Vermes 1993: 152-83). The term, contrary to Jeremias (1967: 15), was also popularly used in Judaism for God.[9] The
opening of this Johannine prayer by the term πατήρ has led some
scholars to postulate that John 17 is another version of the Lord's
Prayer found in Q. This is however improbable. Though the evangelist may have been familiar with the Lord's Prayer there is no indication that John 17 is a deliberate reinterpretation of it. Of course, there
are similarities between the Lord's Prayer and John 17, but it appears

4. In view of this observation one may wonder if there is a polemic here against
other Christian groups that emphasized pneumatic experiences.

5. This expression is also common in the Synoptic Gospels, though it is not
used to introduce a prayer, cf. Mt. 17.8; Lk. 6.20; 16.23; 18.13; also cf. Jn 6.5.

6. This term does not occur in John but is common in the Synoptic Gospels.

7. Jeremias's popular argument that the Aramaic אבא in the New Testament represents the vocative case and is the familiar address of a little child to his or her father
has been correctly criticized by Barr (1988: 28-47) and Vermes (1993: 180-83).

8. See, for example, Matthew's version of the Lord's Prayer, Mt. 6.9; also cf.
Did. 10.2.

9. Examples of its usage in Judaism can be gleaned from Vermes's discussion
of the sources (1993: 173-79).

that the dissimilarities, which I have already pointed out in Chapter 2, are more obvious.[10]

The term πατήρ is frequently used in all the gospels for God but its usage is especially pronounced in John, where it occurs more than 100 times.[11] Moreover, the term πατήρ has a much more specialized meaning in the Gospel of John than in the Synoptics. In reference to God, the term is exclusively on the lips of Jesus, with the exception of Jn 20.17, and designates his special relationship with the one who sent him. This usage is in sharp contrast with the Synoptic Gospels where the pronoun 'our' or 'your' is added before the term to indicate the status of sonship of believers.[12] In John the Father is primarily 'my Father', that is, Jesus' Father. In other words, the expression 'our Father' of the Lord's Prayer in Matthew does not fit well into Johannine theology. As I have pointed out, the expression 'your Father' occurs only once in Jn 20.17, and there it is obvious that Jesus' solidarity with the disciples is in view.[13] The Johannine Jesus is the one who is sent by the Father, that is, he acts on the authority and commission of the Father (cf. Jn 5.36; 8.16, 18; 12.49; 14.24; 20.21). In John only the Son can truly speak in terms of 'my Father', because he alone is the 'only begotten' of the Father (μονογενοῦς παρὰ πατρός) (Jn 1.14; also cf. Jn 1.18). In fact, the Johannine Jesus denies that the Jews can regard God as their Father (cf. Jn 8.41-44). The Johannine Jesus comes from the Father and goes back to the Father (cf. Jn 5.43; 6.46; 13.1; 14.12, 28; 16.10, 16, 17, 28; 20.17). And there is a perfect

10. Jn 17 and the Lord's Prayer are similar in that the address 'Father' occurs in both, the request to glorify the Father's name in Jn 17 reflecting the request 'hallowed (ἀγιάζω) be your name' (Mt. 6.9) in the Lord's Prayer, and the request in Jn 17 that the disciples may be protected from the evil one (v. 15) reflects the request in the Lord's Prayer 'bring us not into temptation but deliver us from the evil one' (Mt. 6.13).

11. The term occurs 5 times in Mark; 44 times in Matthew; 16 times in Luke; and 122 times in John.

12. Vermes has analysed the usage of Father in the Synoptics under the following categories: (1) the forgiving Father; (2) the caring Father; (3) the Father who sees in secret; (4) *imitatio Patris*; and (5) Father in apocalyptic sayings (1993: 154-60).

13. The expression is ἀναβαίνω πρὸς τὸν πατέρα μου καὶ πατέρα ὑμῶν καὶ θεόν μου καὶ θεὸν ὑμῶν. The use of Father with God here detracts from the peculiarity of the term Father, since on other occasions the Gospel seems to equate Jesus with God. Instead, Jesus' solidarity with the disciples is in view here.

harmony in word and deed between the Father and the Son (cf. Jn 5.19, 26; 8.19, 28, 38; 10.15, 25, 32, 37, 38; 14.8-11). This close relationship between the Father and Jesus is summed up in Jesus' words that 'I and my Father are one' (Jn 10.30). This exclusive christological reference of the term in John is also seen in the reaction of the Jews who accuse Jesus with the charge that he said that God was his Father (Jn 5.18).[14]

Furthermore, the close relationship between Jesus and the Father identifies Jesus as not belonging to this world and must be understood in the light of the Johannine dualism.[15] The Johannine Jesus is only in the world because he has been sent from the Father. And since the world (the synagogue) is in darkness it cannot recognize him. In the prayer the term πατήρ is also used in connection with the sending of the Son and recalls the purpose for which he was sent, that is, to save the world (Jn 3.17). Therefore, πατήρ is a term that identifies the Johannine Jesus, instead of the Jewish leaders or the synagogue, as the legitimate Revealer of God.

The expression ἐλήλυθεν ἡ ὥρα, provides the basis for the request of glorification that is to follow. The concept ἡ ὥρα is very prominent in John and it plays an important eschatological role (cf. Jn 1.39; 2.4; 4.6, 21, 23, 52, 53; 5.25, 28, 35; 7.30; 8.20; 11.9; 12.23, 27; 13.1; 16.2, 4, 21, 25, 32; 17.1; 19.14, 27). Used in close connection with ὥρα is the adverb νῦν (cf. Jn 4.23; 5.25; 12.31; 13.31; 16.32). These time words stress that the age of salvation, or everlasting life in Johannine terms, has already arrived. The importance of ἡ ὥρα in John has been highlighted by Feuillet, who says the 'hour of someone' in John refers to the accomplishment of the work for which one is particularly destined (1962: 13),[16] and for Jesus, 'It is clear that all the events of his public life without exception were orientated to the hour as to a climax' (1962: 14). Though the hour of the Son's glorification includes the suffering, death, resurrection, and the departure of the Son, it refers particularly to the lifting up of the Son on the cross with

14. The historical *Sitz im Leben* for the community behind this charge in the Gospel must be seen in the synagogue's challenge concerning the legitimacy of Jesus and hence that of the community. The history of Jesus repeats itself in the history of the community (Martyn 1979: 30).

15. In the Old Testament God as the Father of Israel included the idea of Israel's election (Jeremias 1967: 13). This notion is not apparent in John's usage of the term.

16. Cf. Jn 16.3-4, 21.

everything that it entails (cf. Jn 12.27-33). Moreover, the perfect ἐλήλυθεν not only indicates that the time of the glorification of the Son has arrived, but also that the time of glorification is continuing into the present existence of the community. In other words, the time of the glorification of the Son has taken place in the earthly history of the Son, and is also continuing in the present time of the community. In this connection Thüsing's insight concerning ἡ ὥρα in v. 1 is significant, 'Thereby we have at the same time the beginning of a keyword (*Stichwort*), which is crucially important for the understanding of the *whole* prayer' (1975: 11).[17] The entire prayer has thus to do with the eschatological hour. As the community exists in the special time of the glorification of the Son, it is therefore still praying for the continuing glorification of the Son. The glorification of the Son was not an event that happened once for all but is continuing to happen in the history of the Johannine community. In this way the author links the time of Jesus with the time of the community. In other words, the history of Jesus is also the history of the community; there is no theological distinction in time between Jesus and the community.[18] The νῦν and ἡ ὥρα of Jesus' time is the same as the νῦν and ἡ ὥρα of the community's time. Therefore, the significance of the community's time is not that the *parousia* is near, but that it is the time of Jesus' glorification. As such the community's focus shifts from the future to the present.

Many commentators have already pointed out that vv. 1 to 5 form a chiastic structure around the concept of glory:[19]

---

17. 'Damit ist gleich zu Beginn ein Stichwort gefallen, das wiederum außerordentlich wichtig ist für das Verständnis des *ganzen* Gebets'. The emphasis is mine.

18. This is in contrast to Conzelmann's portrayal of Lukan theology as dividing history into three periods: (1) the period of Israel; (2) the period of Jesus; and (3) the period of the church (1982: 150).

19. See Waldstein (1990: 320) and Malatesta (1971: 195-98). Chiastic structures are a common characteristic of Johannine style (Turner 1976: 65). The identification of a chiastic structure here does not negate our previous suggestion that the prayer of Jn 17 has its original *Sitz im Leben* in the 'Law-court' prayers of a community in conflict with a synagogue. It is probable that the early prayers of the community were developed or adapted according to the context of the Gospel and the didactic purposes of the author(s).

(A)   πάτερ, ἐλήλυθεν ἡ ὥρα·
(B)   δόξασόν σου τὸν υἱόν,
              ἵνα ὁ υἱὸς δοξάσῃ σέ,
              2 καθὼς ἔδωκας αὐτῷ ἐξουσίαν πάσης σαρκός,
              ἵνα πᾶν ὃ δέδωκας αὐτῷ δώσῃ αὐτοῖς ζωὴν αἰώνιον.
(C)   3 αὕτη δέ ἐστιν ἡ αἰώνιος ζωή
              ἵνα γινώσκωσιν σὲ τὸν μόνον ἀληθινὸν θεὸν
              καὶ ὃν ἀπέστειλας Ἰησοῦν Χριστόν.
(B')   4 ἐγώ σε ἐδόξασα ἐπὶ τῆς γῆς
              τὸ ἔργον τελειώσας ὃ δέδωκάς μοι
              ἵνα ποιήσω·
(A')   5 καὶ νῦν δόξασόν με σύ, πάτερ, παρὰ σεαυτῷ
              τῇ δόξῃ ᾗ εἶχον πρὸ τοῦ τὸν κόσμον εἶναι παρὰ σοί.

The first request of the prayer is for the Father to glorify the Son in order that the Son may glorify the Father. In v. 2 this glorification is explained in terms of the bestowal of everlasting life. Verse 3 forms an explanatory note on eternal life, and serves as the climax of the chiasm. Then v. 4 returns to the concept of glory by identifying Jesus' work in terms of glory. Verse 5 again requests that the Son may be glorified, but at this time the glory is equated with the Son's protological glory. This chiastic structure underscores the importance of the concept of glory in the prayer of Jesus. I have already noted that at the end of the prayer Jesus returns again to the concept of glory. The concept is therefore central to the whole prayer and has important implications for ecclesiology, since Jesus has given his glory to the disciples (Jn 17.22). As I shall turn later to a detailed discussion of the concept of glory in John, I only want to mention here that it does not refer to some sort of 'visible splendour' (contra Turner 1976: 69; and Brückner 1988: 42-43), but refers especially to the death of Jesus on the cross.[20] And since glory is the central and unifying concept of the prayer, it follows that the concept of glory should feature prominently in a description of Johannine ecclesiology.

The first request of the prayer is δόξασόν σου τὸν υἱόν. The aorist imperative δόξασόν indicates that the glorification of the Son is accomplished by the Father in the event of the cross. As the Father sent the Son into the world, the Father is now called upon to finalize

20. The concept also incorporates the ascension, although not explicitly described in John, of the Son to the Father.

the Son's sending in his glorification. The use of the term 'Son' (υἱός) with its related expressions, is very problematic in New Testament scholarship.[21] I do not need to go into a detailed discussion of these matters at this point, but merely to point out that in Johannine usage it is clear that the term has to be understood in correlation with the concept of 'Father'. Since John understands Jesus primarily in respect to his relationship with the Father, it is natural that the preferred title for Jesus in John is the absolute use of the term 'Son'.[22] John wants to imply the closest possible relationship between Jesus and God in the use of the terms 'Father' and 'Son'.

In what way, then, should we understand the relationship between the Father and the Son? They are certainly not identified in an ontological sense as one entity. The Son is always distinct from the Father. Rather, the unity between the Father and the Son must be seen in terms of function, that is, the Son is the perfect revelation of the Father's word and works (cf. Jn 5.19). If anyone has seen Jesus, he or she has also seen the Father (Jn 14.9). Therefore, the terms 'Father' and 'Son' (υἱός) in John underscore the unity between Jesus and God, and identify Jesus as the true Revealer of the Father. Though many scholars have interpreted the expression 'Son of Man' (υἱὸς τοῦ ἀνθρώπου)—which is closely related to 'Son' (υἱός) in John—in an apocalyptic and eschatological judgment sense, especially in Mark, and thus as relating to the suffering of Jesus, this does not appear to be the emphasis in John. The Johannine emphasis is that the Son is the true revelation of the Father in every respect. Therefore, Schnackenburg has correctly pointed out that the 'Johannine Son-Christology is essentially the doctrine of salvation for believers,' and that it has a 'functional' character (1990: II, 184). Soteriology always plays a part in Johannine Christology. In addition, Scroggs made the observation that John especially uses the term 'Son' in conflict settings which reflect the arguments between John's community and the synagogue (1988: 68). This suggests, therefore, that the term 'Son' is a term of identification

21. See Cullmann (1959), Marshall (1966; 1970), Hahn (1969), Hengel (1976), Gnilka (1977), Smith and Spivey (1989: 218-22) and Moule (1995) *et al.*

22. χριστός occurs 17 times, κύριος 14 times, and υἱός 39 times. The expression 'Son of God' occurs nine times, 'Son of man' 12 times, and 'Son' (ὁ υἱός) 18 times (Scroggs 1988: 68). The absolute use of 'Son' occurs only three times in the Synoptics and five times in Hebrews (Schnackenburg 1990: II, 172).

in John, and establishes the legitimacy of Jesus as above that of the synagogue.

The particle ἵνα with the subjunctive δοξάσῃ introduces the final clause. The Father must glorify the Son, in order that the Son may glorify the Father. Therefore, the ultimate purpose of Jesus' sending is the glorification of the Father.

The nature of the glorification of the Father is further explained in v. 2. The Son's glorification consists in that he has the authority or power (ἐξουσία) to bestow life everlasting (ζωὴν αἰώνιον).[23] The aorist ἔδωκας is a historical aorist indicating that the action was a simple event of the past. The prayer does not specify when the Father gave the Son this authority, neither is there any event in the Gospel that signifies such a transaction.[24] Therefore, this event could be traced back to the time of the pre-existence of the *Logos* with God. At the incarnation the Johannine Jesus already possessed this glory and authority (Jn 1.14). In other words, the Son did not receive his glory at the incarnation but already possessed it before his earthly appearance (cf. Jn 17.5). The Son received from the Father the ἐξουσία to bestow life eternal, since all ἐξουσία is in the hands of God (cf. Jn 19.10-11). In John ἐξουσία is the prerogative which includes the ability to do something (cf. Jn 1.12; 5.27; 10.18). Here it is the ability to grant life everlasting. And this prerogative to give life is over all flesh (πάσης σαρκός),[25] that is, the Son is able to bestow life on all human beings. In other words, this expression has to be understood positively. This is in contrast to R.E. Brown who suggests that judgment is in view here (1966: II, 740). Instead, J. Becker has seen the positive aspect of the text when he says, 'Also here Christology comes

---

23. Cf. Mt 28.18, where the disciples are commissioned or sent as a result of the authority of Jesus. The Johannine usage of the term here is not that foreign to the Matthean usage, since, as I shall point out later, the sending of the disciples and life in John are closely related.

24. The baptism of Jesus by John the Baptist is not mentioned in John but is only alluded to at Jn 1.32-34. Even so, in this passage the baptism of Jesus only serves as a testimony to the superiority of Jesus, and not as an anointing of Jesus with special power or to a privileged office. The Johannine Jesus has always been the pre-existent *Logos* who was with God.

25. This expression is a semitism (כל בשר) and occurs only here in John (Barrett 1955: 419). For R.E. Brown the usual Johannine dualism is probably not in mind here (1966: II, 740).

to the fore only in terms of its meaning for soteriology' (1991: II, 619).

This thought of the Son's authority is further explained with the final (epexegetic) clause introduced by ἵνα.[26] The Son's authority consists in his prerogative to give life to all the Father has given him. The transition between πάσης σαρκός to πᾶν ὃ δέδωκας αὐτῷ is important.[27] Though the Son has the power to grant life to everyone, it is only granted to a select few, that is, to those whom the Father has given to the Son (ὃ δέδωκας αὐτῷ). It is the Son therefore that has the power to call a special community, distinguished by the possession of life, into existence. The full force of the perfect indicative δέδωκας should be insisted upon here. It is a perfect of existing state and it identifies those belonging to Jesus as the ones given to him by the Father and who continue to belong to him. The neuter πᾶν with the following relative pronoun ὅ should be translated as 'the whole which' and underscores the collective nature of believers. Therefore, believers are viewed in terms of a collective or a community, rather than individually. Similarly, Barrett comments:

> The αὐτοῖς which follows shows that πᾶν, although neuter singular, refer to the disciples. Their unity is thus represented in the strongest possible way (not πάντες, 'all', but 'the whole') (1955: 419).

Therefore, the Son glorifies the Father by giving his *community* life, and not just individual believers.

At this point we may note that v. 2 has four textual variants for the expression δώῃ αὐτοῖς. (1) Some documents have δώσει αὐτοῖς [B Ψ 054 f^{13} (1) 𝔐]; (2) some have δώσω αὐτῷ (ℵ* 0109 *pc*); (3) others have the reading δῷς αὐτῷ [W (L.-τοις)]; and (4) D contains the reading ἔχῃ. The reading of the Nestle-Aland text is supported by ℵ² A C K 0250. 33 *al.* The readings supported by W and D can be discarded as these manuscripts are relatively late (fifth century). However, the readings supported by B and ℵ* are worthy of consideration especially since the support for the current reading is

26. See Burton's discussion on epexegetic clauses introduced by ἵνα (1976: 91-92). These clauses may serve as an epexegetic limitation of nouns, adjectives, and verbs. In this case the epexegetic clause serves as an epexegetical limitation of the noun ἐξουσία. Another example of this Johannine usage is found at Jn 15.8, ἐν τούτῳ ἐδοξάσθη ὁ πατήρ μου, ἵνα καρπὸν πολὺν φέρητε.

27. σάρξ in John does not have ethical connotations as in Paul but is a generic term that denotes human life in the realm below.

not that substantial. On internal considerations the reading of B seems better than א*. The context requires that the language of v. 2b be in the third person, that is, 'he will give' rather than 'I will give'. It is also possible to argue that δώσει αὐτοῖς is a better reading than the present one. The documents that support the present reading, א² A C.K 0250. 33 *al*, are relatively late and apart from C belong to the inferior Syrian manuscript family. It is easy to imagine that a scribe copying from dictation confused δώσει αὐτοῖς for δώσῃ αὐτοῖς (an instance of itacism). The reading δώσει αὐτοῖς is not only supported by the earlier and more reliable Codex Vaticanus but also has wide geographical distribution and should therefore be regarded as superior. Lastly, I may mention that the future of δίδωμι occurs regularly in John: cf. Jn 4.14; 6.27, 51; 13.26; 14.16; 16.23; also cf. 1 Jn 5.16 (Burton 1976: 86). The statements in Jn 4.14 and especially in Jn 6.27 show that the blessing the Son gives may have a future reference. Everything is not absorbed into John's realizing eschatology. Therefore, the reading adopted in the earlier edition of the Nestle-Aland text may have been the better one, or at least we must be open as to the reading of the *Urtext* here.

Several scholars have postulated that v. 3 is a later addition or parenthesis to the prayer.[28] The use in the text of Ἰησοῦς Χριστός as a proper name only occurs here in the Gospel, and the expression αἰώνιος ζωή occurs only here in this order. When αἰώνιος is used to qualify ζωή the order is always ζωὴ αἰώνιος (cf. Jn 3.15, 16, 36; 4.14, 36; 5.24, 39; 6.27, 40, 47, 54, 68; 10.28; 12.25, 50). We may also ask whether τὸν μόνον ἀληθινὸν θεόν is a Johannine expression. It seems to reflect the theological language of Paul in 1 Thess 1.9, though it also occurs in 1 Jn 5.20. Therefore, it is possible that the expressions αὕτη δέ ἐστιν ἡ αἰώνιος ζωή, τὸν μόνον ἀληθινὸν θεόν, and Ἰησοῦν Χριστόν, in apposition to ὃν ἀπέστειλας, are later insertions into the text. If that is the case, the original wording contained only the following: ἵνα γινώσκωσιν σὲ καὶ ὃν ἀπέστειλας. That most of v. 3 is a latter addition may well be the case, though its theology is still very Johannine.

Verse 3 serves to explain the concept of everlasting life. The subordinating conjunction ἵνα introduces an epexegetical clause explaining the nature of eternal life, that is, to know the only true God and

28. For example, see Barrett (1955: 503), R.E. Brown (1966: II, 752), Beasley-Murray (1987: 296) and Lindars (1972: 519).

the one he sent, Jesus Christ. Therefore, eternal life consists in know-ing God and the Johannine Jesus who was sent. The present subjunc-tive γινώσκωσιν indicates a continual experience of knowing on the part of the believer and denotes personal fellowship with God and Christ. J. Becker has correctly observed that in John eternal life con-stitutes the salvation concept (1991: II, 621). Later in the section on life we will pay more attention to this concept.

An important exegetical question at this point and for the whole of the prayer is what John means by γινώσκειν. Since this term is closely related to πιστεύειν, it is helpful to consider the two terms together. Barth has pointed out that πιστεύειν is 'orientated less toward the soteriological significance of Jesus' death and resurrection than to the fact that God has revealed himself in Jesus' (1993: 95). The content of Johannine faith is therefore defined in terms of the 'I am' sayings of the Gospel (Barth 1993: 96). This may be seen as the cognitive aspect of belief in John. However, the experiential aspect of faith is more prominent.[29] The term is often used in relation to the miracles per-formed by Jesus, and as such denotes belief that comes through a his-torical process. It can stand for coming to Jesus (Jn 5.20; 6.35, 37, 44, 65, 7.37), receiving Jesus (Jn 1.12; 5.43), drinking the water Jesus gives (Jn 4.13-14; 6.35; 7.37), following Jesus (Jn 8.12), and loving Jesus (Jn 14.15, 21, 23; 16.27). Historical experience, or the activity of the disciple, is therefore an integral part of belief. It is my con-tention that the Johannine concept of knowledge has to be understood in a similar sense.[30] As such this Johannine concept reflects the Hebrew concept of the knowledge of God which means obedience to God's will. 'It connotes experience rather than contemplation or ecstasy' (Ladd 1974: 261).[31] And since the content of the knowledge concerns the sending of the Son by the Father, an appropriate response to that sending is implied. In Ladd's words, 'Knowledge of Jesus includes knowledge of the meaning of his mission' (1974: 262). Therefore,

29. In this connection it is interesting to note that faith is an exclusively verbal concept in the Gospel—the noun πίστις never occurs.

30. For a discussion on the relationship between οἶδα and γινώσκειν in John, see Horstmann (1991: 1206-1209), Tietze (1954), de la Potterie (1959), and Carl (1984: 78-79).

31. Brown also rejects the idea that John reflects Gnosticism at this point and argues for an Old Testament background to the concept of knowledge here (1966: II, 752-53).

Bultmann is right when he says that γινώσκειν in John 'does not mean the knowledge of investigation, observation or speculation, nor of mystical vision remote from historical contacts or action; it achieves concrete expression in historical acts' (1964a: 711).[32] In this respect knowledge in John must be distinguished from that of later Gnosticism. Though John shares with Gnosticism the idea that knowledge is not an activity of the mind (νοῦς) but is a gift (χάρισμα), John is different in that it is not an ecstatic or mystical vision but is the experience of a concrete action, that is, the experience of salvation and life. John should further be distinguished from later Gnosticism in that the noun γνῶσις, which is a central term in the second-century Gnostic system, never occurs in John.[33]

Verse 4 continues the chiastic structure by returning to the theme of δόξα. The Johannine Jesus proleptically states that he has glorified (ἐδόξασα) the Father on the earth. The aorist ἐδόξασα may be designated as a historical comprehensive aorist, which would mean that Jesus has already glorified the Father in all his teachings and acts (including his death) performed on the earth. As such, the earthly life of the Johannine Jesus is described in terms of glorifying the Father.[34] Thus Thüsing points out that this glorification consists in the accomplishment of the work commanded by the Father (1975: 16). The glory here should be understood in the same terms as the glory of v. 1 (contra Barrett 1955: 420), and the aorist participle τελειώσας should be understood in a causal sense. In other words, the sentence can be translated as, 'I glorified you on the earth by completing the work which you have given me to do.'[35] τὸ ἔργον stands in an emphatic position, and refers to the commission that the Father gave Jesus to accomplish (cf. Jn 4.34). This Redeemer was to complete the ἔργον the Father gave him to do, which was to reveal the Father's name and thereby to establish the community. On this point Hoskyns has said:

> The incarnate Son of God has, therefore, completed his work by bringing into concrete existence in the world the messianic congregation of the faithful disciples. Thus the work of Jesus is not defined as a general

32. Though I do not share Bultmann's opinion that γινώσκειν is understood to be ἀγάπη.

33. This does not mean however that John is anti-Gnostic or stands outside a Gnostic trajectory.

34. The pronoun σέ is here in an emphatic position.

35. The clause ἵνα ποιήσω is a semitism (Turner 1976: 73).

proclamation of the Fatherhood of God and the Brotherhood of men, but rather as the creation of the Church, the *Ecclesia* of God, consisting of men of flesh and blood extracted from the world to which they had hitherto belonged—by the power of God (1940: 591).

The same opinion is expressed by Thüsing and Onuki. Thüsing observes that the expression concerning the accomplishment of his 'work' may indeed refer to the creation of the community of disciples (1975: 20).[36] For Onuki, similarly, the revelation event of Jesus serves as the cause and basis of the Johannine community.[37] We see, therefore, that the community sees its origin in the historical and earthly work of Jesus. This will be stressed throughout the prayer and is therefore an important aspect of Johannine ecclesiology.

It is interesting to note that the perfect tense is used in the expression ὃ δέδωκάς μοι. This seems to indicate that the work (ἔργον) the Father has given to the Son still remains the Son's commission though, as we will see, it is now carried on by the community. The existence of the community therefore should be understood as having the function of an agent. It continues the sending of the Son as the Son's functionary on the earth.

Verse 5 concludes the chiastic structure begun in v. 1. The Johannine Jesus again asks the Father to glorify him. But here the glory is described as παρὰ σεαυτῷ τῇ δόξῃ ᾗ εἶχον πρὸ τοῦ τὸν κόσμον εἶναι παρὰ σοί. While not adopting Bultmann's existential interpretation, one must recognize the validity of his statement that Jesus' return to the Father to his pre-existent glory 'accords fully with the thought-form of the Gnostic myth' (1971: 496).[38] R.E. Brown criticizes Bultmann at this point and proposes that 'Jewish speculation about personified Wisdom' provides the context of the verse (cf. Wis. 7.25). Brown's proposal is possible, but on the evidence a Gnostic 'influence' seems more probable. The Johannine dualism stands much closer to what we find in the Gnostic world-view than to Jewish Wisdom traditions. But the question is further complicated by the possibility that Jewish Wisdom traditions may have influenced Gnostic

36. 'Jesus hat seine Jüngergemeinschaft geschaffen: wenn man das umfassend genug versteht, kann es ebenfalls ein vollgültiger Ausdruck für sein "Werk" sein'.

37. 'Nach ihrem Selbstverständnis ist sie erst und allein durch das Offenbarungsgeschehen gesammelt und begründet' (1984: 58).

38. See Haenchen for a criticism of Bultmann's existential interpretation at this point (1984: II, 151-52).

thought as well. Nevertheless, the Johannine descent–ascent motif of the Revealer is nowhere more pronounced than in the Gnostic myth, which is at least a contemporaneous development with John. In addition, many terms and concepts in John, though some may have a slightly different meaning than that in the second-century Gnostic systems, are shared with Gnosticism, for example, world, light–darkness dualism, knowing, and so on. It would appear, therefore, that the Gnostic myth is reflected here.

At this point I have to disagree with Haenchen who assumes that the incarnation entailed a forfeiture of the Son's glory (1984: 152; also cf. Beasly-Murray 1987: 296). Käsemann is right when he highlights the emphasis on glory in the earthly life of Jesus, though he misinterprets the nature of Jesus' glory. It is best to understand the pre-existent glory of the Son mentioned here as the same as that for which the Son prays in the rest of the prayer. In the same way Stimpfle sees a connection between Jesus' earthly and heavenly glory (1990: 225). Stimpfle writes, 'The Johannine Christ already had δόξα in his pre-existence with the Father (17,5; cf. 1,1f.). He revealed his δόξα during his earthly existence (2,11)' (1990: 225). To understand the meaning of this verse it may be helpful to look at Jn 1.14. The glory that is expressed in the incarnation is not a new glory that the Son received for his ministry on the earth, but is in fact an expression of the glory he always had with God, or, in other words, his pre-existent glory. This suggestion will be further supported in the next chapter when I shall consider what is meant by the concept of glory in John. The Son prays here not for a restoration of a forfeited glory, but that, after the accomplishment of his work and his return to the Father, his glory may be completed. Laurentin's study on the phrase καὶ νῦν also supports my suggestion here. He points out that the phrase is often used to repeat a previous command (1964: 425). Similarly, Brown made the observation that 'In Johannine thought the 'now' is the 'now' of 'the hour'' (1966: II, 742). All these observations strongly suggest that the glory of v. 5 and the glory of v. 1 refer to the same entity.

Verse 6 continues to describe the work of the Johannine Jesus. As such it can be viewed as a commentary on v. 4. Jesus manifested (ἐφανέρωσά) the name of the Father to the believers.[39] The aorist is a

---

39. This verb is synonymous with γνωρίζω and ἀποκαλύπτω (Jn 12.38). The soteriological aspect is to the fore in 1 Jn 3.5.

historical aorist encompassing the totality of the Revealer's work.[40] It is interesting to note that here, in contrast to the Synoptic Gospels and Paul, Jesus' main work is understood in terms of revealing the name of the Father and not in terms of the atonement motif.[41] The general meaning of the verb φανερόω is to reveal something that is hidden. In Paul the term is often applied to the disclosure of the gospel (cf. Rom. 1.17; 3.21). The word is especially common in the Johannine writings occurring nine times in the Gospel,[42] nine times in 1 John,[43] and twice in Revelation.[44] The expression σου τὸ ὄνομα is a semitic idiom and refers to the character of a person (cf. Isa. 21.23; 57.6; Ezek. 39.7).[45] We see here that the Johannine Jesus revealed the Father's name only to a select few. The word ἀνθρώποις in the text is classified by an adjectival clause as those whom the Father has given to Jesus from among the world. The verb ἔδωκάς has an alternative as δέδωκας in $\mathfrak{P}^{60vid}$ C L Ψ 054. 0109 $f^{1.13}$ $\mathfrak{M}$. The text is supported by ℵ A B D K N W Θ *l* 844. We may prefer the reading δέδωκας for ἔδωκάς. The documents that support this reading have both an early date and a wide geographical distribution. Internal evidence also supports this reading since the perfect always seems to be used in the expression ὃ δέδωκάς μοι referring to the Johannine community in John 17.[46] I have already noted that the phrase οὓς ἔδωκάς (or δέδωκας) μοι is a Johannine expression referring to the community.

The prepositional phrase ἐκ τοῦ κόσμου further describes the community. The preposition ἐκ is best understood in a partitive sense denoting separation and, as such, should be translated as 'among'. Translating the preposition with 'from', denoting origin, would violate Johannine thought. Though the community exists in the world they are not of it, but are a separate entity. According to Johannine theology the origin of the community is not from, or out of, the

---

40. So Carson, 'The aorist *ephanerōsa* doubtless sums up all of Jesus' ministry, including the cross that lies just ahead' (1991: 558).

41. Of course, it may be argued that the atonement motif is included in the manifestation of the Father's name. But the task of the exegete is to ask what is distinctive about the text, or what makes the text unique.

42. Cf. Jn 1.31; 2.11; 3.21; 7.4; 9.3; 17.6; 21.1 (twice), 14.

43. Cf. 1 Jn 1.2 (twice); 2.19, 28; 3.2 (twice), 5, 8; 4.9.

44. Cf. Rev. 3.18; 15.4.

45. See F. Brown (1952: 1028).

46. Though we may note that the aorist form of the verb in the expression in v. 11 has good support ($\mathfrak{P}^{66vid}$ ℵ L W *pc*).

world but is from above or from the Father. This is clearly seen in
v. 7 where the community is described as those παρὰ σοῦ εἰσιν.[47]
Here παρά with the genitive denotes the origin of the community and
should be translated as 'from'.

The following compound sentence describes the true identity of the
community, σοὶ ἦσαν κἀμοὶ αὐτοὺς ἔδωκας καὶ τὸν λόγον σου
τετήρηκαν. We have here a good example of parataxis, that is, the
linking of clauses with the conjunction καί. It is interesting to note the
chronological progression in the thought expressed here. Initially the
community was the Father's, then it was given to the Son, and then it
kept the Father's word. Note that even before the community kept the
Word and was given to the Son, it was already belonging (ἦσαν) to
the Father. Moreover, the imperfect ἦσαν underscores the thought
that the community always belonged to the Father.[48] Therefore, any
attempt to play down the determinism of the Gospel is bound to fail.
In Bultmann's words, the community 'by their faith testify that their
origin does not lie in the world, but that from the very beginning they
were God's possession' (1971: 498).[49]

Verses 7 and 8 describe the community and further confirm the
Johannine concept of election. These two verses should be viewed
together as they express one thought. The adverb νῦν follows on from
the last clause καὶ τὸν λόγον σου τετήρηκαν. The perfect tense
(τετήρηκαν) indicates that the community is continuing to keep the
word. Therefore, the prayer does not reveal that any schism in the
community has taken place yet. Since the community is keeping the
word the Johannine Jesus knows that it belongs to the Father, παρὰ
σοῦ εἰσιν. Again we note the use of the linear tense: the community
always belongs to the Father. The origin of the community is from
above, they are not of this world. And this fact is not dependent on the
community's faith, rather their faith is an expression of the fact. In
other words, it is because they belong to the Father that they respond
positively to the Son's revelation.

Verse 8 gives the basis for the Son's assurance:

47. Pollard overlooked this occurrence when he said that 'παρά with the genitive
is never used of the relation of anyone other than the Son to the Father' (1977: 365).

48. Barrett is correct in recognizing the Johannine determinism here, 'The disciples belonged to God from the beginning, because from the beginning he had pre-
destinated them as his children' (1955: 421).

49. A similar thought occurs in *Odes* 17.12-16.

ὅτι τὰ ῥήματα ἃ ἔδωκάς μοι δέδωκα αὐτοῖς,
 καὶ αὐτοὶ ἔλαβον
 καὶ ἔγνωσαν ἀληθῶς ὅτι παρὰ σοῦ ἐξῆλθον,
 καὶ ἐπίστευσαν ὅτι σύ με ἀπέστειλας.

Here again we have parataxis. The ὅτι introduces the causal clause that gives the reasons for the previous fact stated. The uniqueness of the community lies in the fact that they were given the words (ῥήματα) of the Father by Jesus. Moreover, the community received the words the Son has given to it; it truly knew that the Son came out from the Father;[50] and they believed that the Father sent the Son. These three statements are important as they describe the characteristics of the community. Above all it is a community that treasures the Johannine tradition about Jesus. In Käsemann's words, it is a community that is under the Word. 'For John, the Church is basically and exclusively the fellowship of people who hear Jesus' word and believe in him; in short, it is a community under the Word' (1978: 40). The content of that Word is the Johannine tradition about Jesus as the last two statements clarify. Jesus is the one who came from God (παρὰ σοῦ ἐξῆλθον). Here the pre-existence, and consequently the pre-eminence, of the Son is emphasized. Jesus was the one sent by the Father. Therefore, receiving the Word, in Johannine terms, requires the acceptance of the Son's pre-eminence and sending.

It is necessary here to consider the Johannine usage of the terms ῥήματα and λογός. Barrett says:

> It is shown at 14.23f. that a distinction should be drawn between *word* (singular) and *words* (plural). The former means the divine message brought by Jesus as a whole, the latter is nearer in meaning to ἐντολαί, precepts (1955: 421).[51]

R.E. Brown, however, feels that it is difficult to maintain a distinction between these terms (1966: II, 743). It seems more probable that these two terms are used interchangeably in the Gospel because it accords with Johannine style. Both terms are used quite frequently in the Gospel though λογός is used more often.[52]

50. The object of the community's knowledge, i.e. Jesus' historical coming, among other things, distinguishes them from the Gnostics.
 51. Lindars (1972: 521-22) and Carson (1991: 559-60) expressed the same opinion.
 52. λογός occurs at Jn 1.1, 14; 2.22; 4.37, 39, 41, 50; 5.24, 38; 6.60; 7.36, 40; 8.31, 37, 43, 51, 52, 55; 10.19, 35; 12.38, 48; 14.23, 24; 15.3, 20, 25; 17.6, 14,

A crucial question for Johannine theology is how the concept of 'Word' within the Gospel relates to the Prologue. In the past most scholars have drawn a distinction between the origin of the Prologue and the rest of the Gospel, and therefore have interpreted the meaning of λόγος in the Prologue differently from the occurrence of the word-group elsewhere in the Gospel. Recently, however, this antithesis between the *Logos* concept in the Prologue and the rest of the Gospel has been questioned (Minear 1982; E.L. Miller 1993).

What meaning then does the concept have, and what role does it play? In an article 'Logos Ecclesiology in John's Gospel', Minear argues that the concept has primarily an ecclesiological function and conditions the Gospel's thinking about the Messiah (Minear's term). 'In his vocabulary the logos symbol disclosed rather the interdependence of ecclesiology and Christology' (1982: 95). Minear even goes so far as to say that

> Within the Johannine perspective, the doctrine concerning incarnation is a doctrine concerning the church; to understand the life of the church is required before an interpreter can grasp many nuances in John's thinking about Christ (1982: 110).

Minear makes a valid point: ecclesiology and Christology are closely related. And in general terms, what is said about the Johannine Christ can be said about the church, and vice versa.

In his article 'The Johannine Origins of the Johannine Logos' (1993), E.L. Miller criticizes the attempts to understand the term Logos in Jn 1.1 in isolation from the rest of the Gospel. Miller asserts that 'it is here [i.e. in the Gospel] *primarily, essentially*, and *exclusively* that we encounter the origin of the Logos concept...' (1993: 450). According the Miller, λόγος and ῥῆμα point beyond the meaning of simply 'word' to a 'Word' which is saving truth. As such, the term Logos has an implicit christological significance (1993: 452).

All these observations underscore the centrality of the Word in Johannine ecclesiology. The giving of the Word creates the community. And the community's possession of the Word identifies them as the legitimate community of the Father. Indeed, it is the Word that

---

17, 20; 18.9; 19.8, 13; and 21.23; while ῥῆμα occurs at Jn 3.34; 5.47; 6.63, 68; 8.20, 47; 10.21; 12.47, 48; 14.10; 15.7; and 17.8. The change from λόγος to ῥήματα also occurs at Jn 6.60, 63; 8.43, 47; 12.48; and 14.10, 23 (Schnackenburg 1990: III, 177-78).

separates the elected ones from the world. Where the Word is, there is the true community of the Father. Again, this concept should be understood against the background of the community's struggle with the synagogue.

The disciples believe that Jesus came from the Father (παρὰ σοῦ ἐξῆλθον). The term ἐξέρχομαι had important messianic connotations in the first century. Some groups in first-century Judaism often referred to the Messiah as the coming one (בא) (Arens 1976: 261-87). Likewise, the term possesses a significant theological meaning in John. Jesus did not come of his own accord, but was sent by the Father (cf. Jn 5.43; 7.28; 8.42; 10.10; 12.47; 16.30). In these verses there is certainly an apologetic motif. The term can also denote the resurrection of Jesus (cf. Jn 11.34, 41), going out on missionary work (cf. 3 Jn 7), and going to the crucifixion (cf. Jn 19.17).

In the last clause it is also stated that the disciples believed (ἐπίστευσαν) that the Father sent Jesus. In these verses 'knowing' and 'believing' are used in the closest parallelism (Barrett 1955: 422). The disciples have experienced that Jesus is indeed the true Revealer from God. Again the emphasis on Jesus as being the Revealer of God is unlike the rest of early Christian literature, and is to be explained in that John stands in some way in the trajectory of Gnosticism.

b. *The Function and Nature of Life in John*
The question concerning the purpose of the Fourth Gospel is one of the most crucial issues for Johannine research. The distinctive character of the Gospel in contrast to the Synoptics, and the explicit statement regarding its purpose (Jn 20.31) immediately invite the reflection of the scholar. Needless to say, the way this question is answered will determine a person's understanding of the Gospel. The most influential voices of the early church considered that the Fourth Gospel was only written to supplement the Synoptics, and that it does not add anything that is substantially different (Torm 1931: 130; Hendriksen 1961: 21-22). In more recent times, traditional scholarship has regarded the Gospel as a missionary document written to convert either Jews or Greeks (Carson 1987). During the last half of this century, however, the discussion has become much more sophisticated with the recognition that the Gospel was composed from a variety of sources which reflect different aims; missionary, pastoral and apologetic

concerns can be identified in the Gospel.[53] More and more scholars are shifting away from the opinion that John is a missionary document, emphasizing the pastoral and especially apologetic concerns.

Since Jn 20.31 explicitly contains a statement of purpose, and has long been a central verse in the discussion, it will serve as the starting point and basis for our inquiry. In Jn 20.31 the author (or redactor) expresses the purpose for recording the signs Jesus performed. Any discussion on the purpose of the Fourth Gospel needs to pay careful attention to this statement. I have therefore provided the text and a translation of the passage as follows:

> ταῦτα δὲ γέγραπται
>   ἵνα πιστεύ[σ]ητε
>   ὅτι Ἰησοῦς ἐστιν ὁ Χριστὸς
>   ὁ υἱὸς τοῦ θεοῦ,
> καὶ   ἵνα πιστεύοντες ζωὴν ἔχητε
>   ἐν τῷ ὀνόματι αὐτοῦ.

> But these things have been written
>   in order that you may come to believe
>   that Jesus is the Christ
>   the Son of God,
> and   in order that by believing[54] you may have life
>   in his name.

Two purposes are given for the writing of the Gospel, namely, (1) that the reader may believe; and (2) that the reader may have life. Discussion of this verse has focused on the important variant in the first ἵνα clause between the present πιστεύητε (that you may continue believing), and the aorist πιστεύσητε (that you may come to believe). The first reading would indicate that the Gospel was written to strengthen Christians in their faith; the second reading, on the other hand, would indicate that the Gospel was written to convert the reader, making the Gospel a missionary document.[55] Though the manuscript evidence is about equally divided between the two variants, the corrected text of Sinaiticus would slightly favor the aorist πιστεύσητε. When we look at usage in the Gospel itself, we find that ἵνα with the finite verb

53. See Schnackenburg (1990: I, 48-52) and R.E. Brown (1966: I, lxvii-lxxvii).

54. This translation is based on the adverbial participle used instrumentally (Burton 1976: 171).

55. See Metzger's comments at this point (1971: 256).

πιστεύω occurs on eight other occasions,[56] on five occasions the aorist is used, on two occasions the present is used, and in Jn 19.35 the textual evidence, as here, is ambiguous. Again this data would slightly favor the aorist reading. Therefore, it seems to me that the aorist reading is to be preferred above the present. This argument finds further support in the hypothesis that the Gospel was constructed on material from a signs source which had a missionary purpose (Fortna 1970). Therefore, on the basis of these arguments, the first purpose clause does express missionary intention. However, the unmistakable influence of a source behind this statement should make us wary of accepting it as adequately expressing the purpose of the Gospel or even the original Gospel.

In this section, I want to pay more attention to the second clause here expressing the purpose of the Gospel. Discussions concerning the purpose of the Fourth Gospel have neglected this statement, and thus have failed to appreciate its significance for understanding the purpose of the Gospel (Carson 1987), that is, the Gospel was also written in order that the reader may have life in the name of Jesus.

The first question that must be considered in discussing this second purpose clause is whether or not it originally stood together with the first purpose clause. Could it have been a later addition to the first clause by the proper author or redactor? Except for the resuscitation of Lazarus, life does not appear to be a prominent theme in the signs of Jesus. In 'the first of his miraculous signs' Jesus shows his power to change water into wine. There is no concern about life in the sign, instead the concern is for belief, 'He thus revealed his glory, and his disciples believed in him' (Jn 2.11). Likewise, the 'second miraculous sign', the healing of the official's son, Jesus performed that the people may believe, 'Unless you people see miraculous signs and wonders you will never believe' (Jn 4.48). This demonstrates that the concern for 'having life' does not come from the signs source, but is the concern of the proper author or redactor. This additional purpose clause may therefore be an addition that was made to the signs source that reflects the theological concern of the author or a later redactor.

The juxtaposition of two purpose clauses is a common feature of Johannine style (cf. Jn 1.7; 3.17; 12.47; 17.15, 21, 23, 24). Therefore, it is possible that this construction could have been written by the same author, and is not an addition by a later redactor. However, it is

56. Cf. Jn 1.7; 6.29; 9.36; 11.15, 42; 13.19; 17.21; 19.35.

also possible that it was indeed this stylistic feature of the Gospel that allowed such an addition to have been made. This question may be resolved with the results of source criticism. Since the concept of life is not prominent in those chapters that have been isolated as later additions to the Gospel, especially chs. 15, 16 and 21; and since the absence of the theme of life from the passion narrative is due to the fact that it attained a fixed form very early among Christians, a fact which is demonstrated in all the Gospels, it is possible that the second purpose clause comes from the hand of the author and not a later redactor. If this is correct, it follows that the second purpose clause is more significant than the first in ascertaining the purpose of the original Gospel.

Another question that needs to be considered is, 'What relationship exists between these two purpose clauses?' The proper author clearly had a reason for the first purpose clause, otherwise he would have omitted it. Was the original Gospel then written for two definite and separate purposes, that is, that the readers may believe that Jesus is the Christ, and that the readers may have life in his name? Or are these two clauses in parallel construction with each other, expressing the same idea in different words? A third possibility is that a logical progression is expressed, that is, the Gospel was written that the readers may believe in Jesus, and when they do so, they will have life. Careful analysis of the grammatical construction favors the last possibility. The second clause does not read ἵνα ζωὴν ἔχητε, but ἵνα πιστεύοντες ζωὴν ἔχητε, thereby building on the thought of the first clause. The purpose of the Gospel is not merely that the readers may believe, but that they may have life. Therefore, I conclude that the original Gospel had two purposes which are closely related and in logical progression, that is, that the readers may believe, and upon believing may have eternal life.

The conclusion, therefore, that the discussion has reached so far is that Jn 20.31 does contain a real statement of purpose by the proper author with respect to the original Gospel. The question that must now be asked is if the rest of the Gospel supports this conclusion.

A casual reading of the Gospel is enough to convince the reader that the concept of life is very important throughout the narrative.[57] The

---

57. The Johannine emphasis on life has been pointed out in the studies of Dodd (1953: 144-50), Filson (1962), Hill (1967), Coetzee (1972), Lindars and Rigaux (1974: 155-73), Moule (1975), Thompson (1989), and Luzarraga (1991) *et al.*

noun ζωή occurs 36 times, the verb ζάω occurs 17 times, and the verb ζωοποιέω occurs three times.[58] Often the noun is used with the adjective 'everlasting' (αἰώνιος) in the expression 'everlasting life' (cf. Jn 3.15, 16, 36; 4.14, 36; 5.24, 39; 6.27, 40, 47, 54, 68; 10.28; 12.25, 50; 17.2, 3). Studies have shown that these two expressions, 'life' and 'everlasting life', are used synonymously.[59] The centrality of the concept of life in the narrative is also striking. The reader is introduced to the concept already in the first few verses of the prologue: life was in the Word (Jn 1.4). Then in the conversation with Nicodemus, it is stressed that Jesus has come not to condemn the world but to give everlasting life to all who believe in him (Jn 3.17). In ch. 4, Jesus talks to a Samaritan women about living water springing up into everlasting life (Jn 4.13-14), and to his disciples about gathering fruit for everlasting life (Jn 4.36). In chs. 5 and 6, he argues with the Jews that as the Father has life in himself so he has given life to the Son and that Jesus is the bread that comes from heaven to give life to the world (Jn 5.26; 6.50-51). In ch. 6, the first 'I am' saying occurs when Jesus says, 'I am the bread of life' (Jn 6.48). In ch. 8, it is claimed that those who follow Jesus will not walk in darkness but have the light of life (Jn 8.12). Again in ch. 10, in the parable of the good shepherd, Jesus says that he has come that believers may have life in abundance (Jn 10.10). Before Jesus raises Lazarus from the dead another 'I am' saying occurs when he says to Martha, 'I am the resurrection and the life' (Jn 11.25). In ch. 14, Jesus says, 'I am the way the truth and the life' (Jn 14.6). Then in ch. 17, Jesus prays that the Father may glorify the Son in order that he may give life to those the Father has given him (Jn 17.1-2).

At this point it may be useful to note the similar importance that the concept of life has in 1 John. The subject of the apostolic proclamation is introduced as the 'Word of life' (cf. 1 Jn 1.1). And likewise the purpose of the epistle is identified as, 'I write these things to you who believe in the name of the Son of God so that you may know that you have eternal life' (1 Jn 5.13). This statement of purpose and concern is similar to that of the Gospel and may argue for a common author.

58. The noun ζωή occurs in Jn 1.4; 3.15, 16, 36; 4.14, 36; 5.24, 26, 29, 39, 40; 6.27, 33, 35, 40, 47, 48, 51, 53, 54, 63, 68; 8.12; 10.10, 11, 28; 11.25; 12.25, 50; 14.6; 17.2, 3; and 20.31. The verb ζάω occurs in Jn 4.10, 11, 50, 51, 53; 5.25; 6.51, 57, 58; 7.38; 11.25, 26; and 14.19.

59. See Coetzee (1972: 51) and Thompson (1989: 35).

This brief survey clearly indicates that the concept of life is a major theme in the Fourth Gospel.

I shall now proceed to provide an evaluation of the meaning of the concept of life in the Fourth Gospel, which is much more difficult than showing the importance and centrality of the concept in the Gospel. In the words of Marianne Thompson, 'it is easy to document the importance of the theme of life, it is more difficult to account for its prominence and to delineate the precise content of the Johannine concept of life' (1989: 5). As this comment suggests, there are two questions that must be considered: 'What reason might there be for the prominence of life in the Gospel?' And 'What is understood by this concept of life or everlasting life?' Of course, these questions are closely related, and the answer to one will help us to understand the other. Too often, the second question has been considered independently from the first by those who have attempted to deal with the purpose of the Fourth Gospel. In this study I shall also give prominence to the first question, and consider what light it might throw on the second. The answers that have been given to the second question range from 'that authentic existence, granted in the illumination which proceeds from man's ultimate understanding of himself,' (Bultmann 1971: 258) to the 'glorious and continued oneness with Christ and his Father' (Coetzee 1972: 51). No consensus has yet been reached on this question.

What, then, might have been the historical circumstances that occasioned the writing of the original Gospel? It is probable that the original Gospel was constructed on the basis of a signs source which had a definite missionary intent. This observation can already tell us much about the region in which the Gospel was written. If the proper author used a source it follows that the source must have had a high profile and influence among the Christians in the region. It seems to have been used by Christians as a tract for evangelism. These Christians were evidently a group with great evangelical fervor. However, the present Gospel demonstrates that the signs tract became inadequate to meet the needs of the Christians in the region, and needed supplementation. What was the need that lay behind this supplementation or addition to the signs source? Obviously, it was not a need for evangelistic material since the signs tract already served that purpose. Research has shown that the Gospel is saturated with a polemic against the 'Jews', who have to be identified with the Judean leaders in

Jerusalem. The 'Jews' are pictured, almost without exception, as being of the world and intent on persecuting Jesus. Their antagonism towards Jesus leads to the excommunication of his followers from the synagogue (cf. Jn 9.22, 12.42, 16.2). These findings lead to the conclusion that the Gospel reflects a major conflict between Christians and the synagogue. It was this crisis of being excluded from the synagogue that lies behind the writing of the original Gospel. Before, these Christians saw themselves as continuing the traditions of the Jews and coexisted with the synagogue, but now their validity is being challenged to the extent of being excommunicated from the Jewish establishment and worship. The enthusiasm of many Christians would have lessened as they feared excommunication from their religious tradition and faced the challenge of the synagogue regarding the validity of Jesus. Therefore, the Christians in the region of the proper author were not in need of evangelistic material, but in need of encouragement and a theological foundation for their existence and mission. The concept of life in the original Gospel can only be understood when this historical context is appreciated.

How, then, could the concept of life have served to meet these needs in the crisis the Christians faced? Why would the author have used this idea as an encouragement for the Christians in the Jewish community? Any attempt to understand how the author has used the concept of life needs to consider how the term was used at the time and see what connections there may be with the Johannine usage. Apart from the the Old Testament, the Pseudepigrapha, Dead Sea Scrolls and the Gnostic literature may also provide a context for understanding the term.

It does not appear that the Old Testament and the Pseudepigrapha provide any important leads since both collections have no definite concept of life similar to that of the Gospel (Hill 1967:163-75).[60] When we turn to the Dead Sea Scrolls and the Gnostic writings we find more similarity to the Gospel. The concept of life is not a very prominent concept in the Scrolls, only in a few instances is it used in the sense of 'eternal life' (Coetzee 1972: 60-61). Though it is important to note that it is used in a dualistic framework (cf. 1QS 2.3; 3.7; 4.7).

The concept of life is much more prominent in the Gnostic writings, especially in the Hermetic and Mandaean writings (Schnackenburg

---

60. The isolated references to eternal life in 1 En. 37.4 and 58.3 are probably of a late origin and may even be post-Christian (Hill 1967: 173).

1990: II, 357).[61] This context may help us to understand how the term life was used in the milieu of the proper author, and hence may help us to understand the use of the term in the Gospel. As in the Dead Sea Scrolls, life is seen in a dualistic framework. It comes from above, that is, from God. And it has the notion of energy or power associated with it. 'It is understood as a physical phenomenon, yet not as the vitality of cosmic being, but as indestructible duration and also as the underlying force which triumphs over all obstacles' (Bultmann 1964: 839). This notion of life as 'an absolutely otherworldly divine power' (Bultmann 1964: 841) may serve to encourage those who face opposition, and, as such, is a meaning that may lie behind the Johannine concept. Of course, much further research needs to be done on the way the concept is used in Gnosticism, but the appropriateness of what has been said of the Gnostic concept for the historical situation of the author of the Gospel is striking.

A feature that the Dead Sea Scrolls, the Gnostic literature, and the Fourth Gospel share is placing the concept of life in a dualistic paradigm. 'Eternal life' in the Gospel means life from above, that is, the divine life that comes from God. This life, however, does not consist in sharing in the essence of God, but rather consists in being empowered by God for the work of God. This life, in other words, does not denote a participation in the divine essence, but a participation in the divine mission.[62] To corroborate this assertion we need to look more closely at certain passages. A good place to start is with the definition of life that Jesus gives at the beginning of his prayer. He prays (Jn 17.2-3):

> ἔδωκας αὐτῷ ἐξουσίαν πάσης σαρκός,
> ἵνα πᾶν ὃ δέδωκας αὐτῷ δώσῃ αὐτοῖς ζωὴν αἰώνιον.
>
> αὕτη δέ ἐστιν ἡ αἰώνιος ζωή
>
> > ἵνα γινώσκωσιν σὲ τὸν μόνον ἀληθινὸν θεὸν
> > καὶ ὃν ἀπέστειλας Ἰησοῦν Χριστόν.

Here everlasting life is defined in terms of *knowing* the only true God and the one he sent. As most commentators think, it is probable that

---

61. Cf. Poimandres 1.9, 17; 12.21; 32, etc.

62. Coetzee's conclusion is correct, i.e. life in the Fourth Gospel means the 'glorious and continued oneness with Christ and his Father,' but it needs to be said that this 'oneness' is not in terms of essence but function (1972: 51).

v. 3 is an addition by a later redactor (Bultmann 1971: 494; Schnackenburg 1990: III, 172). If so, this statement provides important evidence of Johannine theology.[63] Without doubt, knowledge here is to be understood in terms of the Hebrew notion of knowledge and not, contra Bultmann, in terms of Greek thought or Gnosticism (Schnackenburg 1990: II, 360). The Hebrew concept of 'knowing God' has the meaning of 'having communion with God' (Schnackenburg 1990: II, 172). Therefore, life has to do with having communion with God. But the addition 'and the one you have sent' suggests that communion with God does not exhaust the concept of life, since the verb ἀποστέλλω has a definite theological function and plays an important role in the paradigmatic thought of the Gospel.[64] The term refers to the mission of Jesus as one coming from the Father to give life to the world. Therefore, the definition here suggests that life is more than having communion or fellowship with God, but that it also involves knowing, that is, sharing or participating in, the sending of Jesus. This understanding of life as communion with God and participating in the sending of Jesus is further supported by the close connection between ζωή and δόξα in this passage. Eternal life is a manifestation of the δόξα, which, according to Schnackenburg, replaces the phrase 'everlasting life' in the rest of the prayer (1990: III, 172). A careful study of δόξα in the Gospel reveals that it refers to the grace of God displayed in the sending of Jesus to save the world. Thus the idea of the mission or the sending of Jesus underlies the prayer of Jesus.

Therefore, on the basis of this passage I want to propose that the concept of life in the Fourth Gospel includes the participation of the believer in the sending of Jesus. In other words, life in the Gospel is more than an existential communion or fellowship with God, it also involves the experience of sharing in the sending of Jesus. This experience of the believer in the sending of Jesus has both an objective and a subjective side. First, the believer is the object of Jesus' sending, that is, the sending of Jesus saves the believer. Secondly, the believer in turn comes to participate in the sending of Jesus by continuing that sending or mission in the world. Everlasting life is to know God, the one who sent Jesus to give life to the world, in the sense of 'an inner

63. The expression 'Jesus Christ' is found only here in the Gospel.
64. God is the one who sends Jesus, Jesus is the one sent, and the disciples are those being sent by Jesus.

apprehension and participation' (Schnackenburg 1990: II, 360) in the sending or mission of God and Jesus. In this connection, I may point out that the Aramaic word for life חיה can mean both life and salvation.[65]

When we look at the rest of the Gospel it seems that the above proposal can be supported. In Jesus' conversation with the disciples at Jacob's well he says, 'even now he [the one reaping] is gathering fruit for (εἰς) eternal life' (Jn 4.36). Here the idea of eternal life is closely associated with 'gathering fruit', a metaphor for mission. Schnackenburg's comment is to the point:

> The reward is probably the gathering of the harvest itself; the καί, therefore, gives the precise explanation of the reward. Otherwise the sequence would be very strange: one does not expect payment before the work is done (1990: I, 450).

In other words, 'eternal life' consists indeed in 'gathering fruit,' that is, in participating in the mission of Jesus.

Another passage that may support the notion that life in John involves participation in the sending of Jesus is found in Jn 8.12. Following Jesus means that the person will have life. Note that life is not the end result of 'following', but that it is in the following that the person has life. This same idea underlies the Good Shepherd narrative in ch. 10 (cf. Jn 10.1-2, 10, 27-28).

In conclusion, this section shows that the concept of life is crucial for the purpose of the Fourth Gospel, and that this concept may have apologetic and missionary connotations. The Christians for whom the proper author wrote appear to have been active in persuading other Jews (and Gentiles) to believe that Jesus is the Christ. Because of the crisis that group of Christians faced in being challenged and excommunicated by the synagogue, their faith needed an apologetic against the synagogue and their mission encouragement. The Gospel was written that the reader may have life, that is, a life that consists in participating in the mission of Jesus and God. Therefore, though the Fourth Gospel may not have been a missionary document, it may have been a document for missionaries. The Gospel, among other things, could have served to encourage the community to continue in their witness that Jesus is the Christ, the Son of God (Jn 20.31). This suggestion

---

65. Similarly, the Syriac New Testament uses the same word ܚܝܐ for both ζωή and σωτηρία.

requires further reseach, which should include an investigation of how such a purpose may be substantiated in the narrative.

c. Kosmos *in John*

The term κόσμος occurs frequently in the Johannine writings. It occurs 78 times in the Gospel and 24 times in the letters. Whereas it occurs only twice in Mark,[66] nine times in Matthew, and three times in Luke. The word mostly used for earth or land in the Synoptic Gospels is γῆ. This word γῆ occurs 13 times in John and only once in the letters.

In Greek philosophy the word κόσμος denotes the basic world order or the world system (Sasse 1965: 868-80). The usage of the term in John covers a wide range of meanings.[67] However, generally in John, it does not denote a physical or metaphysical reality but it is an ethical term. 'In the statements regarding the κόσμος in Johannine theology the concern is with the nature of the world that has fallen away from God and is ruled by the evil one' (Balz 1991: 312). This is akin to Gnosticism, but it differs from the concept in Gnosticism in that the world is not rejected; instead the Father loves the world and sends the Son into the world to save the world (Jn 3.16-17). 'Thus the κόσμος itself is not rejected, but is overcome (16.33; 1 John 5.4-5)' (Balz 1991: 312). However, John does not go as far as Paul, for whom God is reconciling the κόσμος to himself (2 Cor. 5.18-19). In John the κόσμος is not redeemed or renewed (cf. 2 Peter 3.7, 10), instead the elect ones are drawn out from it. John is therefore halfway between Paul, who like the apocalyptic movement expected the renewal of the world, and Gnosticism, where the world is rejected. In John, Jesus does not reconcile the world, but overcomes the world. 'John is not interested in the liberation *of* the world but only in the deliverance *from* the world, i.e. the gathering and uniting of those predestined

66. I have disregarded the occurrence in Mk 16.15 as Mk 16.9-20 was not part of the original text.

67. Hendriksen has distinguished six different meanings of the term in John: (1) it is used for the universe and the earth, Jn 15.5; 21.25; (2) it refers to the human inhabitants of the earth, Jn 16.21; (3) it can refer to the general public, Jn 7.4; (4) it has an ethical sense, i.e. humanity is alienated from God and is in need of salvation, Jn 3.19; (5) as in usage (4) with the added idea that no distinction is made with respect to race or nationality, Jn 4.42; and (6) it can refer to the realm of evil as in (4) but with the added idea of hostility to God, Jn 7.7; 8.23, etc. (1961: 79).

who are to be protected *against* the world' (Lattke and Franzmann 1994: 152). This halfway stance between Paul and Gnosticism makes John's use of the term ambiguous.

Indeed, John's view of the κόσμος seems contradictory. On the one hand, there is the sharpest antithesis between Jesus and the world (cf. Jn 7.7; 8.23; 14.17); but, on the other hand, it is said that God loves the world (cf. Jn 3.16),[68] that Jesus takes away the sin of the world (Jn 1.29), that he was sent to save the world (Jn 3.17; 12.47), that he is the Saviour of the world (Jn 4.42), and that he gives life to the world (Jn 6.33, 51). This contradiction also appears in the prayer of Jesus. In Jn 17.9 he does not pray for the world, but in v. 21 he prays that the world may believe. How is this tension to be resolved then?

It is best to avoid any attempt to give a strict definition or description of the usage of κόσμος in John. The use of the term in the Gospel is a complex problem. First, it is necessary to note that the term has different meanings in different contexts.[69] Secondly, the Gospel presents the reader with different layers of tradition.[70] To make a generalization, the basic Johannine concept of κόσμος is best understood as that which opposes the sending of Jesus and the community. In John the κόσμος generally represents the Jerusalem Jewish leaders.[71] Onuki has correctly pointed out that the Jews in John are not merely a symbol of the world opposing Jesus, but are the actual opponents of the Johannine community (1984: 29-35). Therefore, a strict definition is impossible and misleading. The κόσμος for the community is both a place of danger and a place of potential. It is never stated that the world cannot believe. The elected ones are indistinguishable from the κόσμος when they do not believe. Therefore, there is not a total rejection of the κόσμος in John. The κόσμος can still believe, and is the

68. Lattke regards Jn 3.16 as uncharacteristic of John, although not as inauthentic (1975: 64-85). I agree with Lattke then that the Johannine κόσμος is not the object of Salvation History (*Erlösungsgeschichte*) (1975: 245).

69. For example, see Hendricksen (1961: 79).

70. For Baumbach Jn 1.10 reveals two understandings of the world: Old Testament and Gnostic. For Schmithals (1992: 309), the *Grundevangelium* talks of a neutral world (Jn 1.9-10; 6.14; 8.12; 11.27; 13.1; 14.19, 27, 30; 15.18; 16.20-21). The evangelist takes a negative meaning.

71. It should be noted that the enemies of Jesus in John are not simply the Jews as such, but particularly the Jewish leaders at Jerusalem. Therefore, John should not be viewed as an anti-Jewish document. After all, the Johannine Jesus and the disciples are still Jews.

object of both Jesus' and the community's sending. This difference in the concept of κόσμος between John and Gnosticism is because in John dualism serves a soteriological function, whereas in Gnosticism dualism is based on the cosmological order.[72] In Gnosticism the created world is intrinsically bad or evil, but not in John (cf. Jn 1.3, 10).

The *religionsgeschichtliche* context of the Johannine usage of κόσμος is an important issue for Johannine theology. The only real equivalent to the Johannine usage in Jewish literature is found in the apocalyptic document 2 Esdras, which is roughly contemporaneous with John. In 2 Esdras the world becomes a place of corruption and evil (cf. 2 Esd. 4.11; 9.20; 14.17, 20). Since 2 Esdras does not precede John in time one cannot deduce that John depends on this Jewish tradition. It is possible that 2 Esdras and John share the same strand of tradition here from another source.

Gnostic documents provide more abundant comparison. The *Gospel of Thomas* makes for a very interesting comparison with the usage of the terms γῆ and κόσμος in John. In the *Gospel of Thomas* there is a definite distinction between ⲕⲁϩ and ⲕⲟⲥⲙⲟⲥ. The term ⲕⲁϩ is theologically neutral and is used for 'earth', 'land', or 'soil' (cf. *Gos. Thom.* 34.8, 11, 30; 35.20, 35; 36.31; 40.30; 48.23; 51.6, 17). As such it corresponds to the usage of the term γῆ in the Synoptic Gospels and John. On the other hand, ⲕⲟⲥⲙⲟⲥ is used in an ethical sense for 'world' as the realm of evil, (*Gos. Thom.* 34.15; 35.33; 37.11; 38.9, 18, 21, 27, 28; 42.10, 30, 32; 47.13, 14; 51.5, 10). This is particularly clear in Jesus' statement, 'Whoever has come to understand the world (ⲕⲟⲥⲙⲟⲥ) has found a corpse, and whosoever has found a corpse is superior to the world (ⲕⲟⲥⲙⲟⲥ)' (*Gos. Thom.* 42.30-32, cf. 47.13-14). This is similar to the concept of κόσμος in John.

In the *Gospel of Philip*, which is later than the *Gospel of Thomas* and John, ⲕⲟⲥⲙⲟⲥ also plays a very important role and here it functions within a decidedly Gnostic dualism.[73] In *Eugnostos the Blessed*

72. For Ashton κόσμος implies a 'vertical opposition' (1991: 207), moral or ethical, not cosmological nor metaphysical. Barrett has pointed out that the expression ὁ κόσμος οὗτος, is not contrasted with the future world, but with an existing world that is above (1955: 135).

73. Cf. *Gos. Phil.* 52.20, 26, 27; 53.8, 13, 22, 36; 54.2, 6, 14; 55.7, 19; 58.27; 59.25; 61.24; 62.32, 34; 63.24; 64.32, 34; 65.27, 29; 66.7, 14, 16, 22; 67.10; 72.1, 17; 73.19; 75.3, 8, 9; 76.4, 6, 32-33; 77.12, 21; 78.21, 23; 79.18; 81.7; 82.3, 30; 83.6; 86.11, 12, 13.

and in *The Sophia of Jesus Christ*, which are probably first-century documents, kosmos occurs often but it lacks the theological meaning found in John and later Gnostic writings. Later, in the *Hermetica* κόσμος becomes a metaphysical being and even a second God.

In the *Odes of Solomon* we find ideas similar to and dissimilar from John.[74] In *Odes* 10.4 Christ is depicted as capturing the world for the glory of the Father; in *Odes* 20.3 the Lord's thought is contrasted to the thought of this world; in *Odes* 38.11 the Deceiver caused the world to err; and in *Odes* 41.15 it is said that the Messiah was known before the foundation of the world (cf. Jn 17.5, 24). These ideas are similar to what we find in John. However, *Odes* 22.11 and 33.12 talk about the renewal of the world (ܥܠܡܐ) and the new world (ܥܠܡܐ) respectively, which is akin to Jewish apocalyptic thought.[75]

From these observations, it would appear that John's usage of κόσμος is akin to that of Gnosticism. However, we have noted that there are important differences too. The Johannine tradition may have been influenced by the early Gnostic trajectory in its usage of κόσμος, but instead of making an absolute rejection of the κόσμος, the Johannine community, according to its Old Testament background and especially in embracing the Johannine Jesus tradition, affirms the potential of the κόσμος for mission.

d. *Election in John*

The concept of election is a major theme of the Gospel and especially in the prayer of Jesus. The verb ἐκλέγομαι occurs at Jn 6.70; 13.18; and 15.16 (twice), 19. Though believers are often described as 'the elect' (ὁ ἐκλεκτός) in the Synoptics,[76] the noun does not occur in John. Other verbs in the Gospel that describe the concept include: 'to draw' (Jn 6.44, ἕλκω), 'to call' (Jn 10.3, φωνέω), 'to know' (Jn 10.14, γινώσκω), 'to lead' (Jn 10.16, ἄγω), 'to appoint' (Jn 15.16, τίθημι), and 'to give' (Jn 17.2, δίδωμι).

The prominence of election in the Gospel again underscores its dependence on Jewish thought. Election is important in the Old Testament concept of the salvation history of Israel. The Hebrew word בחר

---

74. It is a debated question whether the *Odes* should be classified as Gnostic or not.

75. *Odes* 11 is very interesting and needs further research. The Syriac term ܥܠܡܐ does not occur in the Ode, instead ܐܬܪ is used.

76. Cf. Mt. 20.16; 22.14; 24.22, 24, 31; Mk 13.20, 22, 27; Lk. 18.7; 23.35.

(to choose) occurs 164 times in the Old Testament, and in most cases God is the subject. Israel's history begins with the choice and call of Abraham (Gen. 12.1-4), and the subsequent covenant God made with Abraham (Gen. 15.1-16). The concept takes on greatest prominence in the exodus of Israel out of Egypt (Exod. 2.23-25). It is especially in the exodus that the basis of the election of Israel is revealed, namely, the love of God (Deut. 4.37; 7.6-8; 10.15). The purpose of Israel's election was service. As such, Israel is constantly reminded that being elected, or belonging to the covenant, is not only a privilege but also involves responsibility. Indeed, Israel was chosen to be a holy people and to keep the commandments (cf. Deut. 7.6-11; 10.15-20). In Second Isaiah election is seen in terms of mission (cf. Isa. 42.1; 43.10). This special responsibility of election was emphasized by the prophets when Israel failed to keep their covenant obligations (cf. Amos 3.1-8).

A significant aspect of the Old Testament concept of election is that Jews were chosen because they belonged to the nation of Israel. Thus election was equivalent to belonging to the nation of Israel. Though some Gentiles were incorporated into the covenant, this only occurred as they joined the nation of Israel. Later, however, when the majority of Israel failed to live up to the covenant obligations set out in the Mosaic Law, a 'remnant-theology' developed. Belonging to Israel no longer guaranteed membership in God's covenant. Covenant membership or privilege can only be claimed when the covenant obligations have been kept.

The Dead Sea Scrolls also place a great emphasis on the concept of election. The idea is based on the Old Testament and especially on the concept of the remnant. The Essenes considered themselves to be the remnant 'converts of Israel' (CD 4.2). Consequently, not every Israelite is elected (1QS 3.13-4.1). We see that election, as in the Old Testament, was closely associated with covenant. 'Only the initiates of their own 'new Covenant' were to be reckoned among God's elect' (cf. 1QS 11.7-9) (Vermes, 1977: 170). Election is also due to God's grace (1QH 10.5-7; 4.34-37). However, the Scrolls have a very closed view of election. 'The doctrine of predestination in the 'Treatise on the Two Spirits' leaves no room for human responsibility' (Murphy-O'Connor and Charlesworth, 1990: 218).

Many scholars see the influence of Iranian Zoroastrianism in the predestination of Qumran (Merrill 1975: ix). Predestination in the Dead Sea Scrolls is seen in terms of a rigid dualism, God has created two spirits, of good and of evil, and all people are assigned, or appointed, either to the one or to the other on the basis of God's will (Merrill 1975: 57). Thus the Qumran view concerning the destiny of human beings is fatalistic. However, the sectarians did not explain how God can still be just and how one can still be responsible for one's actions if one has already been assigned to the spirit of evil (Charlesworth 1990: 79-89).

Election has been a hotly debated issue in Johannine research, and conclusions have often been the result of theological presupposition instead of careful exegesis. There appears to be a contradiction or tension in the Gospel with respect to election. On the one hand election is affirmed in several passages (cf. Jn 3.18, 21, 33-36; 5.24; 6.35-40, 44-47, 65; 8.47; 10.3-5, 14, 25-26; 11.25-26; 12.39-48; 15.16; 17.2, 9, 12, 24; and 18.37). But on the other hand, human freedom is insinuated in some passages (cf. Jn 3.16, 20-21, 33, 36; 4.13; 6.45, 47, 67-69; 12.32; 3.8; 12.36; 14.11; 19.35; and 20.31). The Gospel does not resolve this problem. In the words of Kysar:

> The Fourth Evangelist—if indeed this was his or her position—does not attempt to work out the relationship between these two facts. The author is not like a modern theologian who might attempt a logical exposition of how divine determinism and human freedom are woven together to produce belief. Both kinds of assertions are left side by side in the Gospel with no explanation (much to the frustration of later interpreters like us). The Evangelist may be asserting that there is a mystery about the origin of faith. The reason why some persons are capable of believing and some are not is elusive (1993: 72).

The position of the present study is that John is undoubtedly deterministic.[77] Those who believe Jesus are those whom the Father has given to Jesus. In other words, they believe because they were elected for that purpose. Election is realized within the community. This is similar to the thought presented in the Dead Sea Scrolls. 'The very fact that a man joined the Community proved that he was one of the predestined. He did not do so to become one of the Elect; he did so because he was one of the Elect' (Merrill 1975: 58). Nevertheless, the Gospel also maintains human responsibility and obligation. It is never stated that Jesus' opponents do not believe because they were assigned to this fate, unlike the concept in Qumran. There is no concept of a double predestination in the Gospel, that is, that some are destined for

---

77. See Hoskyns (1940: 591).

salvation whereas others are destined for damnation. In other words, there is a paradox present in the Gospel, and it does not appear that the author ever tries to resolve this paradox. It is wrong to presume that the author was not aware of this paradox as Kysar suggests.[78] The Qumran material, of which the Johannine community was certainly aware, clearly shows that this paradox was a current question of thought.

Probably the most important question that we must ask concerning the Johannine concept of election is, 'What is the function of this concept in the Gospel?' First, it served an apologetic purpose. The community was struggling for its survival. The concept must be understood from the perspective of those who were persecuted and oppressed, not the other way around. Therefore, accusing the Gospel of fatalism loses its significance. It must be understood that the modern reader sees the Gospel from the perspective where Christianity is the dominant and powerful group. Belief in predestination is a very strong source of affirmation and comfort and strength for those who are suffering. In the same way, Onuki sees Johannine determinism as arising from the community's historical experience (1984). Secondly, in John the emphasis on the idea of election, as in the Old Testament, is not on privilege but on obligation. The Gospel's most pertinent statement on election is found in Jn 15.16. The disciples were chosen not for a special privilege but in order to bear fruit, which is to participate in the sending of Jesus. Therefore, instead of being a fatalistic concept, the concept serves to encourage the community to gather others into the community. The same teaching, or use of the doctrine is made in the prayer of John 17. In John 17 the verb describes election in terms of the Father's gift. God gives Jesus his works (Jn 5.36), his disciples (Jn 6.37), his name (17.11), and all things (Jn 3.35).

3. *Part II: Jesus Prays concerning his Disciples (verses 9-19)*

a. *Exegesis*
In the second section of the prayer Jesus is praying for his disciples (vv. 9-19). At v. 9 the attention of the Johannine Jesus shifts away from himself to the community. Jesus is now asking (ἐρωτῶ) concerning

---

78. Kysar suggests that, 'the author was not theologically astute enough to see the contradictions of the work' (1993: 73). Kysar does not recognize that election is a Jewish concept with its roots in the Old Testament.

those the Father has given to him. The present tense indicates Jesus is going to make a number of requests for his disciples. The uniqueness of the disciples is brought out by the statement that Jesus is not asking concerning the world, οὐ περὶ τοῦ κόσμου ἐρωτῶ. The concern is not for the world but only for the community.[79] In fact, as Barrett pointed out, this is required by Johannine theology, for 'to pray for the κόσμος would be almost an absurdity, since the only hope for the κόσμος is precisely that it should cease to be the κόσμος' (1955: 422). This is in contrast with Jesus' preaching of the universal kingdom of God in the Synoptic Gospels. In the concept of the kingdom, all nations and all creation comes into view. Instead, the soteriology of Johannine theology is only concerned with the community of believers and not with the world at large. However, this should not be seen as a direct statement against the created world, since κόσμος in John refers to people as belonging to the sphere of darkness. The ὅτι introduces the causal clause giving the reason why Jesus only prays for them. Jesus prays for the community because they belong to the Father, ὅτι σοί εἰσιν. The present indicates that the community always belongs to the Father.

The demarcation of v. 10 as beginning after ὅτι σοί εἰσιν is unfortunate as v. 10 must be taken together with ὅτι σοί εἰσιν. Therefore, the expression καὶ τὰ ἐμὰ πάντα σά ἐστιν καὶ τὰ σὰ ἐμά must be understood in terms of election.[80] The phrase τὰ πάντα refers to the Johannine community collectively, and does not refer to all created things. Before, the neuter πᾶν was also used in connection with the community (cf. Jn 17.2). And it was in the community that Jesus has been glorified. If the preposition ἐν is taken in a local sense, the glory here may be understood in a soteriological sense, that is, the community glorified Jesus because it believed and received life through him (cf. Jn 17.2). Therefore, Jesus is praying for the community because the community was given by the Father to Jesus, belongs to the Father and Jesus, and glorified (believed) Jesus. We notice then that Jesus prays for the community because it is elected and hence responded to his message. The community's election and response should be seen as two sides of the same coin. It was because it belonged to the Father

---

79. A pronoun, αὐτῶν or ἐκείνων, should be supplied in the expression περὶ ὧν δέδωκάς μοι.

80. Barrett understands this phrase as a parenthesis (1955: 423).

that it believed Jesus' message. The community's favourable response follows logically from its election.

The perfect passive verb, δεδόξασμαι, refers to the time of the community and indicates that the community continues (the sense of the perfect) to glorify Jesus (Thüsing 1975: 62). This can be seen as a positive endorsement of the community by the author. The prepositional phrase ἐν αὐτοῖς can be understood in a number of ways. I have already referred to the local sense of the preposition above. Another possibility is that the preposition ἐν can be taken in an instrumental sense, that is, to designate a personal agent, though this is usually expressed by ὑπό with the genitive. The translation then is,'I have been glorified by them,' in which sense glory probably refers to the disciples continuing the sending of Jesus (cf. Jn 17.18).

Verse 11 begins a new thought and provides the context for the coming requests. The Johannine Jesus is no longer to stay in the world as he is about to go to the Father, but the community is to stay in the world. The present tenses used here describe near future events (Burton 1976: 9).

Jesus then addresses the Father as πάτερ ἅγιε.[81] The adjective ἅγιος is used here only to describe the Father, usually it is associated with the Spirit (Jn 1.33; 7.39; 14.26; and 20.22). The address to the Father as being holy prepares the reader for the request of v. 17. Verses 11b to 16 forms a unit with respect to the protection of the community in the world, and vv. 17 to 19 form a unity with respect to the consecration of the community in the world. First Jesus prays that the Father may keep (τήρησον) the community in the Father's name (ὀνόματί σου) which the Father had given Jesus, in order that the community may be a unity (ἕν) as the Father and the Son are.[82] The idea here is not that the community may be guarded from the world but that the community's unity may be preserved. The neuter ἕν requires us to translate it as 'unity', rather than 'one (person)' which would be masculine, that is, εἷς. This unity is achieved in the name of the Father (ὀνόματί σου). I have already mentioned that 'name' indicates the character of a person, and thus refers to Jesus' revelation of the Father (cf. Jn 1.18). This is equivalent to τὸν λόγον σου or τὰ

81. Cf. Lev. 11.44; Mt. 5.48; 1 Pet. 1.16; and also *Did.* 10.2.
82. R.E. Brown notes that, 'It is interesting that John does not use the abstract noun for 'unity,' *henotes*, found in Eph iv 3, 13, and frequently in Ignatius of Antioch' (1966: II, 759).

ῥήματα ἃ ἔδωκάς μοι. The preposition ἐν is important and it should probably be understood in both an instrumental sense, that is, 'by means of', and in a local sense, that is, 'in (the contents of) the word'.[83] In other words, it is a unity both in the Word and achieved by the Word. Therefore, the unity of the community includes a unity of confession, it is not simply a matter of fellowship. It is possible that we have here the first murmuring of a coming split in the community over certain Johannine teachings. In any case, we again see the importance of the Word in the Johannine community.

The unity that Jesus prays to be among the community is based on the unity between the Father and the Son. The comparative conjunction καθώς is very significant here, and indeed for the understanding of Johannine ecclesiology.[84] Its importance is highlighted by the fact that it occurs 32 times in John,[85] and no less than eight times in the prayer (cf. Jn 17.2, 11, 14, 16, 18, 21, 22, 23). It only occurs three times in Matthew, seven times in Mark, and 16 times in Luke. It is best understood as an explanatory causal and therefore may be translated as 'because'.[86] The usage of this preposition is very important as it is used to describe the close relationship between the Johannine Jesus and the community. It sets up the closest possible parallel between the function of Jesus and that of the community. 1 John 4.17 is very instructive in this respect; as Jesus is, so the community is in this world. In this connection Radl has pointed out that

> In the subject God-Christ-disciples καθώς is used esp. in the Johannine literature (cf. Eph 4.32). Καθώς here describes the agreement between Father and Son (John 5.30; 8.28; 12.50; 14.31; 17.2) and between Jesus and his disciples (13.15, 34; 15.12; 17.14, 16; 1 John 2.6, 27; 3.3, 7, 23; 4.17; cf. 2 John 4.6) and in analogies involving both relationships (John 6.57; 10.15; 15.9, 10; 17.11, 18, 21, 22; 20.21; cf. 17.23) (1991: 226).

There is thus the closest analogy between the Johannine Jesus and the community. The community is a reflection of Jesus in every respect. The community's existence is not only founded on the earthly life of

83. For examples of the latter see Jn 5.39; 6.45; 8.(5), 17, 31, etc.
84. See also Bultmann (1971: 382 n. 2), and de Dinechin (1970: 195-236).
85. Cf. Jn 1.23; 3.14; 5.23, 30; 6.31, 57, 58; 7.38; 8.28; 10.15, 26; 12.14, 50; 13.15, 33, 34; 14.27, 31; 15.4, 9, 10, 12; 17.2, 11, 14, 16, 18, 21, 22, 23; 19.40; 20.21; 19.40; 20.21.
86. Blass and Debrunner say that καθώς 'used to introduce a sentence may have something of the meaning "because"' (1961: 236).

Jesus, but it is also the continuity of Jesus' life in the world. Here we see that the community in its unity acts as a reflection of the Son, and in this case of his unity with the Father.

Verse 12 goes back again to the earthly life of Jesus. When Jesus was (ἤμην) with the disciples, he was keeping (ἐτήρουν) them in the Father's name. The pronoun ἐγώ is redundant here and therefore serves to emphasize the Son's activity of keeping or protecting the community. Jesus has guarded the elected ones (ᾧ δέδωκάς μοι). None of the disciples perished except the son of perdition, in order that the Scripture may be fulfilled. The expression ὁ υἱὸς τῆς ἀπωλείας is a semitism and refers to Judas.[87] It is important to note that the perdition of Judas was not caused by the lack of vigilance on the part of Jesus, but so that the Scriptures might be fulfilled (Hoskyns 1940: 594). The Scripture in question is that of Ps. 41.10, already referred to in Jn 13.18. Schnackenburg makes an interesting point when he says that 'The community is reminded here that separation from the true community of salvation means loss of salvation, a return to the sphere of the 'world' and even a reversion to satanic power (see I Jn 2.18f; 4.3; 5.19b)' (1990: III, 182).

The beginning of v. 13 places the focus again on the return of the Son to the Father, which is part of the Son's glorification. 'The "now" which stands here, is the now of Jesus' "hour"' (Thüsing 1975: 61). As Jesus is to go (ἔρχομαι) to the Father, he is speaking (λαλῶ) these things in the world, in order that the community may have his joy (τὴν χαρὰν τὴν ἐμὴν) fulfilled (πεπληρωμένην) in themselves. Since Jesus will leave his disciples he is speaking these things to them so that they may have a record of the Son's revelation with them.[88] Here the reason why the Johannine Jesus is revealing these things to the community is that their joy may be fulfilled. The joy of the community is therefore to consist in the Word. The perfect of the participle indicates that the joy is to be a lasting characteristic of the community. Before, the Baptist rejoiced at the voice (φωνή) of the bridegroom (Jn 3.29). In Jn 15.11 Jesus has spoken (λελάληκα) these things in order that his joy may be in them and that their joy may be full (πληρωθῇ). In Jn 16.20-22 the disciples' mourning will turn into joy, because Jesus will see them again and no one will be able to take away

---

87. This expression ὁ υἱὸς τῆς ἀπωλείας also occurs in 2 Thess. 2.3.

88. I have already indicated that the verb λαλέω is often used in connection with the revelation the Son brought.

their joy. And in Jn 16.24 the disciples are encouraged to ask in Jesus' name, that is, according to his Word,[89] so that their joy may be full (πεπληρωμένη). Similarly, in 1 Jn 1.4 the author is *writing* these things so that your joy may be full (πεπληρωμένη). Therefore, in the Johannine community joy consists primarily in the revelation or the Word of the Revealer. This is in contrast to the Synoptics where joy springs from the encounter with the resurrected Lord (cf. Lk. 24.41, 52; Mt. 28.8), the discovery the kingdom (cf. Mt. 13.2-10; 13.20, 44; Mk 4.16), the proclamation of the gospel (cf. Lk. 2.10), and the final rest (cf. Mt. 25.21, 23).

Verse 14 continues the theme of revelation. The Revealer has given (δέδωκα) the Word (τὸν λόγον σου) of the Father to the community. ἐγώ is again redundant and is used here for emphasis. The perfect δέδωκα indicates that the Word continues to be in the possession of the community. In other words, the community serves as the depository or the preserver of the Son's revelation.

The world, however, hated (ἐμίσησεν) the community. The aorist is the comprehensive aorist and refers to all the suffering and persecution the community suffered in the past. This is clearly a reference to the antagonism of the synagogue against the Johannine community. The opposition of the synagogue is seen as symbolic of the opposition of the world against the community. At this point we should notice that in John the world is not equated with the Jews but with the synagogue, or the religious leaders of the Jews. The reason for the world's hatred is because the community does not belong to the world (οὐκ εἰσὶν ἐκ τοῦ κόσμου). In this connection the community is the same as Jesus (οὐκ εἰμὶ ἐκ τοῦ κόσμου).[90] Exactly the same expression is used to describe the community and Jesus in relation to the world. The conjunction καθώς does not only make a comparison between the community and Jesus, but should be understood in a causal sense as in v. 2. The community does not belong to the world, because Jesus does not belong to the world. Therefore, the community's existence in the world is determined by the being of Jesus. Just as Jesus can never belong to the world, so too the community can never be a part of the world. In fact, the community can be described as *Christus prolongatus*.

In v. 15, though the world hates the community Jesus does not pray

89. See Hendriksen's comment, 'A prayer in Christ's name is a prayer that is in harmony with whatever Christ has revealed concerning himself' (1961: 274).
90. I have discussed the meaning of the preposition ἐκ before.

that it should be taken out (ἄρῃς) of the world (ἐκ τοῦ κόσμου), but that it should be kept away from the Evil One or evil (ἐκ τοῦ πονηροῦ).[91] The second ἐκ should probably be understood in the sense of ἀπό, 'away from'. The basic idea of the preposition ἐκ is that of separation. This is the best way to understand this sentence since κόσμος and πονηρός are virtually equivalent in John. Twice it is said that the works of the world are evil (cf. Jn 3.19; 7.7), and in Jn 16.33 Jesus has conquered (νενίκηκα) the world, whereas in 1 Jn 2.13, 14 believers have conquered (νενικήκατε) the Evil One. Therefore, the community's expectation in conflict is not towards the final eschatological deliverance but is directed towards the protection of the Father. The community cannot leave the world because it has a crucial role to play in the salvation of the world (cf. Jn 17.18, 20-21). In Hoskyn's words:

> Being thus set for the salvation of the world of the scattered children of God, no prayer for the removal of the disciples from the world is possible; it would obstruct the purpose of God (xiii,1). Jesus therefore solemnly dedicates His disciples to the mission (1940: 595).[92]

Bultmann sees these words directed against two things:

> First, against the primitive Christian expectation of the imminence of the end, and the longing for the glorious Parousia, which will make the community an ecclesia triumphans... Secondly, the words are directed against the temptation that continually threatens the community, viz. of falling back into the world's hands; it must not allow itself to become engrossed in its place in world-history, or regard itself as a factor of cultural importance, or find itself in a 'synthesis' with the world and make peace with the world. It must retain its unworldly character, it must remain 'protected from the evil,' i.e. from the 'world'; otherwise it would lose its essential nature (1971: 508).[93]

---

91. In John the word πονηρός is not used in a personal sense, but is so used in the Epistle (cf. 1 Jn 2.13-14; 3.12; 5.18-19). In the Epistle, Cain was out of the Evil One (ἐκ τοῦ πονηροῦ) because his own works were evil (1 Jn 3.12); the Evil One does not touch those who are out of God (ἐκ τοῦ θεοῦ; 1 Jn 5.18); and the whole world lies under the power of the Evil One (1 Jn 5.19).

92. Also note J. Becker, 'Die Gemeinde kann nicht vorzeitig aus der Welt genommen werden, weil sie in ihr noch eine Aufgabe wahrzunehmen hat' (1991: II, 627).

93. Likewise Barrett sees a polemic here against the expectation of an imminent Parousia, 'It is possible that John intended to correct the apocalyptic view that the Christians would very shortly, at the *parousia*, be caught up from the earth' (1955: 425).

Verse 16 goes on to give the reason for the Son's request. The conjunction καθώς is again to be understood in a causal sense. The community does not belong to the world because Jesus does not belong to the world (cf. Jn 17.14b). Again we see that the community's life is modelled on that of Jesus; what can be predicated to Jesus can also be predicated to the community.

Verse 17 contains the second request of the Son to the Father on behalf of the community. The Johannine Jesus asks that the Father may consecrate the community (ἁγίασον) in the truth (ἐν τῇ ἀληθείᾳ). The preposition has the instrumental usage, that is, the consecration occurs by means of the truth. In this connection Brown comments that

> In common Jewish prayer, it was proclaimed that God sanctifies (consecrates) men through His commandments—an idea that is partially similar to John's thought, since for John 'word' and 'commandment' are virtually interchangeable (1966: II, 765).

We see that truth is equated with the Word, ὁ λόγος ὁ σὸς ἀλήθειά ἐστιν.[94] Later, we will consider the meaning of truth in John more fully.

The idea of holiness is not very prominent in John. The verb ἁγιάζω occurs four times in the Gospel (Jn 10.36; 17.17, 19 [twice]). In Jn 10.36 the Father has consecrated the Son, that is, has set him aside to send him into the world (cf. Jn 3.17). His consecration was for the purpose to save the world. In other words, consecration has a soteriological significance. The noun ἅγιος occurs four times in the Gospel and always in connection with πνεῦμα, that is, the Holy Spirit (cf. Jn 1.33; 7.39; 14.26; 20.22). The word ἁγιάζω also occurs in the Lord's Prayer (cf. Mt. 6.9; Lk. 11.2), but the meaning of the word here is clearly different from that of the Lord's Prayer. In Eph. 5.26 the word is applied to the church.

In John, sanctification or consecration does not refer to the state of being sinless, but it means to be set apart for mission in the world.[95]

---

94. Cf. Ps. 119.142 (LXX).

95. In Paul sanctification is a state, cf. 1 Cor. 1.2; 6.11. This is similar to the Dead Sea Scrolls; cf. 1QH1 1.12:

> For the sake of Thy glory
>> Thou hast purified man of sin
> that he may be made holy for Thee,
>> with no abominable uncleanness
>> and no guilty wickedness

Therefore, the word is better translated into English with the term consecration rather than sanctification. Here in the prayer it is the community's consecration for the purpose of its sending into the world. Therefore, I concur with Balz that holiness here does not refer to a condition but to the church's separation for God (1990: 46). And also with Barrett:

> At 10.36 God is said to have sanctified Jesus, clearly for his mission to the world. This is a normal and a very common use of ἁγιάζειν; a person is set apart for a sacred duty. The setting of the present verse is similar to that of 10.36; as there, the word ἀποστέλλειν is in the context. The disciples in their turn are to be set apart by God for a mission to the world (1955: 426).

This basic idea of consecration for some service is also found in the consecration of the priests in the Old Testament (cf. Exod. 28.41; 29.1, etc.).[96] Van Rensburg underscored this point in his study, 'The consecration of the disciples means that God separates them through Jesus Christ in his property,—but he also separates them for his service' (1958: 80).[97]

Verse 18 describes the purpose of the consecration. Because the Father sent Jesus into the world, Jesus also sent the disciples into the world. The aorist here (ἀπέστειλα) should be understood from the perspective of the community looking back to the commissioning by Jesus (cf. Jn 20.21). The preposition καθώς again is causal in meaning. The sending of the community is analogous to the sending of the Son. 'A characteristic of the Gospel of John is that the sending of the disciples is understood as an image of the sending of the Son' (Lattke

---

Many scholars, I feel, overinterpret the text at this point when they see sanctification here in terms of sacrifice or moral purity. As I have said in the introduction, the interpreter has to ask what is specific in the focus of the text. Though it is possible to see the ideas of sacrifice and purity behind these verses, these ideas are at most secondary. Therefore, though Schnackenburg says, 'It is not possible to exclude the idea of sacrifice from Jn 17.19' (1990: III, 187), it is not specific to the text. Also cf. Lattke (1985).

96. Despite R.E. Brown's comment (1966: II, 224), the basic idea of holiness in Scripture is that of separation (Snaith 1944: 24-26).

97. 'Die heiliging van die dissipels beteken dat God hulle deur Jesus Christus afsonder as sy eiendom—maar ook afsonder vir sy diens. Dit word gesê in Joh. 17.18: "Soos u my in die wêreld gestuur het, het Ek ook hulle in die Wêreld gestuur"' (1958: 80).

1975a: 121). Similarly, Bultmann has said, 'The community has a task analogous to his, and rooted in it' (1971: 510). And the object of both the Son's and community's sending is the world. Therefore, the community's sending, in analogy with the Son's sending, must feature prominently in Johannine ecclesiology. The community has been called into being and exists for the purpose of continuing the sending of the Son (Riedl 1973: 12). Later I shall deal more extensively with the concept of sending in John. Schnackenburg's comment and quote from Bultmann again highlights John's difference from Gnosticism:

> ...the community sees itself as sent into the world with the task of proclamation...it is certainly a fundamentally different attitude from that prevailing in gnostic and esoteric groups, since 'the sending out into the world of the chosen ones by the redeemer has no parallel in myth'... (1990: III, 187).

In v. 19 the consecration (ἁγιάζω) of Jesus refers to his being sent into the world on behalf of (ὑπέρ) the disciples. Jesus was consecrated, that is, set apart and sent into the world for the sake of the disciples. Many commentators have understood his consecration here in a sacrificial sense in view of the preposition ὑπέρ.[98] Though Jesus' death on the cross is included in his sending, I do not think that this idea is prominent here. Instead, it is the whole mission of Jesus that is in view. The present tense (ἁγιάζω) is significant because it shows that the mission (being sent) of Jesus is still continuing. Though the community is now continuing the mission of Jesus it always remains Jesus' mission. We also note in this verse that Jesus' mission or sending is for the benefit of the community. The aim of Jesus' coming into the world, unlike Paul, has a limited reference; it was only for the elected ones. The perfect (ἡγιασμένοι) indicates that the disciples were made holy and are being kept holy for the task of mission. The purpose of Jesus' consecration was that the disciples could be consecrated. In other words, the sending of Jesus was to achieve the sending of the community. Indeed, from the requests in vv. 20 to 23 it appears that the community's *raison de être* is to continue the sending of the Son. Therefore, the sending of the community plays an integral part in God's plan for the salvation of the world. Lastly, we also see that the community is prepared for their sending by means of the Word. The preposition ἐν is best understood instrumentally.

98. See Hoskyns (1940: II, 596-97), Hendriksen (1961: 362), and van den Busche (1967: 457). Randall says that v. 19 'has eucharistic overtones' (1965: 389).

b. *Truth in John*

The term ἀλήθεια, with its cognates, is very prominent in the Gospel of John.[99] Scholars have been preoccupied with the origin of this Johannine concept in the history of religions. Bultmann correctly speaks of a Greek use of truth as opposed to a semitic one (1964b: 238).[100] But his interpretation of ἀλήθεια as 'authenticity', 'divine reality', and 'revelation', probably reflects his own existential philosophy, rather than the meaning of the concept in John (1964b: 239). In Hellenism the term ἀλήθεια has a more abstract meaning, 'truth' or 'reality' is that which is eternal or divine. In Hebrew thought the closest equivalent to ἀλήθεια is the term אמת. The meaning of אמת is more concrete than ἀλήθεια, and is closely associated with the attributes of God. Often the term אמת is used to describe God's nature (Gen. 24.27; Pss. 25.5; 31.5; etc.) and God's words (Pss. 119.142, 151, 160; etc.). Likewise, Dodd says that, '…ἀλήθεια is fundamentally an intellectual category, אֱמֶת a moral category' (1953: 173).

Most scholars have favoured an Old Testament and Judaic origin for the concept in John. The Hebrew has no abstract word for truth that is equivalent to the Greek word ἀλήθεια or the English word 'truth'. The Hebrew word for truth is based on the root אמן, which means 'steadfastness' or 'faithfulness'. As such, truth in the Old Testament is defined in terms of God's promises. God's truth is his faithfulness (אמן) in keeping his promises. Consequently, closely associated with the term אמת in the Old Testament is the term דבר, meaning 'word'. Often God's word and truth are indistinguishable terms. Indeed, Hebrew has no word for 'promise', it simply uses דבר. The word אמת is also often associated with חסד (cf. Pss. 40.11; 61.7; 115.1; 138.2; Isa. 16.5). God is characterized as a God who shows חסד and אמת, cf. 2 Sam. 2.6. And God sends forth his mercy and truth for salvation (cf. Pss. 57.3; 85.10). There is therefore a soteriological aspect associated with the term אמת in the Old Testament.

The concept of truth in the Dead Sea Scrolls depends largely on that of the Old Testament, but one marked evolution is truth as revelation and the emphasis on truth as the quality of the community and its members (Charlesworth 1990: 185). Cross has also pointed out that

99. Cf. Jn 1.17, 17; 3.21; 4.23, 24; 5.33; 8.32, 40, 44, 45, 46; 14.6, 17; 15.26; 16.7, 13; 17.17, 19; 18.37; 38.

100. For Bultmann the New Testament usage is partly determined by the Hebrew term אמת and partly by the non-biblical use of ἀλήθεια (1964b: 238).

truth in the Dead Sea Scrolls has polemical overtones (Charlesworth 1990: 185). The Essenes are a community that opposes Israel and the priesthood. They alone are the 'true' Israel. In the Dead Sea Scrolls truth is also a designation of revealed doctrine, embodying the Law and its interpretation. Emphasis is also placed on truth as a quality of moral behaviour. Those who belong to the group constitute a community or a house of truth (1QS 2.26; 5.6; 8.9). And they are called 'sons of truth' (1QS 4.5). Lastly, truth is also seen as a medium of purification and sanctification (1QS 4.20-21; cf. Jn 17.17-19) (Charlesworth 1990: 197).

Turning to the Gospel of John we notice both similarities and differences from its Jewish context. Most importantly the Johannine characteristic of truth is that it is centred in the event of Jesus (cf. Jn 1.14-17). Truth in John is understood especially in terms of the event of the Redeemer's descent into the world. The Old Testament connection of mercy and truth lies clearly behind the statement in Jn 1.14 (cf. 14.6; and 8.32). Also, in John ἀλήθεια is a soteriological term.[101] For example, Aalen interprets ἀλήθεια in the Gospel in terms of salvation history (1964). And also according to Lindars and Rigaux the term should be understood in connection with the mission of the Son (1974: 148). The Johannine concept of truth is the revelation of God in history in the event of the Redeemer's descent. Moreover, this term must be understood in terms of the polemic of the Gospel.

4. *Part III: Jesus Prays concerning Future Believers (verses 20-26)*

a. *Exegesis*
In the third part of the prayer the Johannine Jesus prays for the future of the community (vv. 20-26). Thus the expression οὐ περὶ τούτων δὲ ἐρωτῶ μόνον signals the third major transition in the prayer (cf. v. 9). The Johannine Jesus does not only pray for present believers but also for those who will believe in the future.[102] The present participle πιστευόντων stands for the future (Burton 1976: 59), and is best translated as 'those who will believe' (J.W. Wenham 1965: 151). We

101. De la Potterie seeks a derivation from the Old Testament and Judaism (1959).
102. Here we may note what R.E. Brown says, 'As for the constituency of the group of those who will believe in Jesus through the word of the disciples, we may recall x 16 and xi 52 where the call is extended to Gentiles as well as to Jews. For John there is a divine selection, but this is not on an ethnic basis' (1966: II, 774).

notice that the concern of the prayer is therefore not just with the past history of the community or with its present situation, but is also directed towards the future. The prayer is comprehensive in scope and is not directed towards a particular situation or *Sitz im Leben*. As such the prayer functions as a programmatic statement concerning the existence of the community. It is intended to serve as a general statement about the Johannine community's place in the world. These observations support my suggestions in Chapter 2 concerning the function of John 17.

The participle πιστευόντων is to be taken with εἰς ἐμέ, which indicates that the object of Johannine belief is not in a system of doctrine (i.e. ἡ πίστις as in the Pastoral epistles) but in Jesus. The preposition εἰς is used in a metaphorical sense. The prepositional phrase διὰ τοῦ λόγου αὐτῶν answers how future disciples will come to believe in Jesus. Διά should be translated with 'through', and indicates the means through which their faith is going to be effected. Future disciples will come to believe in Jesus through the Word (λόγος) of the present disciples. Therefore, we again see the centrality of the Word in Johannine thinking.

Verse 21 gives the reason why the Johannine Jesus is also praying for future believers. Three purpose clauses, introduced by ἵνα with the subjunctive, provide the purpose of Jesus' prayer and progressively ascend to a climax:

ἵνα πάντες ἓν ὦσιν
ἵνα καὶ αὐτοὶ ἐν ἡμῖν ὦσιν,
ἵνα ὁ κόσμος πιστεύῃ οτι σύ με ἀπέστειλας

The first reason is that all believers (πάντες) may be one or a unity (ἕν). It is interesting to note the alteration between the masculine πάντες (i.e. all believers) and the neuter ἕν (i.e. a unity). The neuter ἕν does not simply denote all believers for then it should have been εἷς. Instead, it denotes the community of believers as being a distinct entity in itself.

An important question at this point is, What is meant by the concept of unity? Scholars have suggested several possibilities.[103] Again, I feel

103. The various interpretations of the meaning of unity here have been highlighted by Randall. He writes, 'The unity between the Father and Son is sometimes pictured as a simple unity of will, sometimes as a unity of action, sometimes as a complete unity of nature. Christian unity goes from mere harmony, to unity of faith:

scholars have read too much into the text and have not asked what is distinctive to John. Later, I shall consider this concept in greater detail. However, at this point we may note that the following phrase, explaining the nature of the unity, goes a long way in providing the answer, καθὼς σύ, πάτερ, ἐν ἐμοὶ κἀγὼ ἐν σοί. The unity of the community must be understood in terms of the unity between the Father and the Son. For the unity of the community is a reflection of the unity between the Father and the Son. Thus the unity between the Father and the Son serves as both the ground and the model of the unity in the community. Now this unity between the Father and the Son in John is clearly a unity of words and works. In other words, it is a unity of function, and not a unity in nature or essence.[104] In Johannine language we may call it a 'unity in sending'.

The second purpose clause states that not only should the community be a unity but also that they may be a unity in the Father and the Son (ἐν ἡμῖν). The preposition ἐν indicates that the community should be intimately connected with the Father and the Son. Again, the meaning is not that the community is of the same essence of the Father and the Son, but that the community is intimately connected with the words and works of the Father and Son. In other words, the phrase ἐν ἡμῖν is a prepositional phrase of manner. The third purpose clause expresses the last and final reason for the request of the Son, that is, that the world may believe that the Father sent the Son. Therefore, the ultimate aim of the prayer for unity is so that the world may believe. This supports my suggestion that unity in John refers to a unity in function, or more particularly a unity in sending. It is only by means of the sending of the community into the world, or by the community uniting with the sending of the Son, that the world is going to come to faith. Thus the three purpose clauses provide a progressive order of

faith based on the word; invisible, with no dogmas or organization; visible, for it must be a sign: like the union of the bride with her beloved; unmystical; mystical; eucharistic: a participated unity with God whereby we become the sphere of His activity' (1965: 373). Randall himself opts for a eucharistic interpretation of the unity. However, I do not find his argument convincing, for he argues from the eucharistic passage in *Did.* 9-10 that John has eucharistic overtones. If the *Didache* interprets John in a eucharistic setting, it does not follow that the concept of unity in Jn 17 was referring to the eucharist. Also see R.E. Brown's discussion (1966: II, 775).

104. This does not mean that John would necessarily deny that Jesus and God are of the same essence, but that it is not the important emphasis of John.

intention. The community should be a unity, so that it may be in the Father and the Son, so that finally the world may believe. In other words, the unity of the community, which is always in association with the Father and the Son, leads to the believing of the world. The community should be united with God in the mission to save the world. Therefore, it is not the unity of the community in itself that will lead the world to believe, but it is the sending of the community into the world that will cause the world to come to faith.

The present πιστεύῃ indicates duration of belief, that is, the world should continue to believe. And the object of the belief is ὅτι σύ με ἀπέστειλας. Therefore, the content of belief in Jesus (εἰς ἐμέ) is to believe that the Father sent the Son (ὅτι σύ με ἀπέστειλας).

Verses 22 and 23 are parallel to the thoughts contained in v. 21. They continue the theme of the community's unity. Jesus has given (δέδωκας) the glory the Father had given (δέδωκα) him to his disciples in order that they may be a unity (ἕν), just as (καθώς) the Father and the Son are a unity. The glory of Jesus can be equated with his mission to give life to the world. Concerning this glory, Schnackenburg says that it is 'the culmination and the summary of what Jesus "has given" to the disciples whom he leaves behind in the world and sends out into the world' (1990: III, 192). This mission Jesus in turn gave to the community so that it could be a unity. The preposition καθώς again bases the community's unity on the unity between the Father and the Son. The community is the reflection of that which is above. The close relation between Jesus and the disciples and the Father and Jesus is so that the community may be perfected into a unity, and so that the world may know that the Father sent the Son:

ἵνα ὦσιν τετελειωμένοι εἰς ἕν,
ἵνα γινώσκῃ ὁ κόσμος ὅτι σύ με ἀπέστειλας

Here again the unity of the community is the effective cause for the acknowledgment of the world that the Father sent the Son. The participle τετελειωμένοι is probably another theological passive and the perfect tense underscores the enduring quality of that unity. We also notice here that γινώσκειν is synonymous with πιστεύειν (cf. v. 21). The following two clauses form a parenthesis as they do not follow on logically from what has gone before and set the stage for the conclusion of the prayer:

καὶ ἠγάπησας αὐτοὺς
καθὼς ἐμὲ ἠγάπησας.

Here the conjunction καθώς is again important. The Father loved the disciples because he loved Jesus. The most unique relationship between the Father and the Son, that is, love, is now likewise bestowed on the community. As such, there is no longer any qualitative difference between the Son and the community.

The most extensive studies on love in the Fourth Gospel have been done by Lattke (1975) and Augenstein (1993). For Lattke, love in the Fourth Gospel means unity in the Word (*Einheit im Wort*). Love also denotes a reciprocal subject–object relationship, 'The Father loves the Son and his own, the Son loves the Father and his own, his own love the Son and one another' (1975: 20). And the love of the lower (between believers) is a reflection of the higher (between the Father and the Son). There is also an important relationship between love and unity. Love produces and is reflected in unity. My own exegesis, likewise, has already highlighted the importance of the Word for the Johannine community, and also that the community's existence is a reflection of the Son.

Augenstein also underscores the importance of love for the Johannine community. The love command in the Gospel of John is a characteristic and a condition of discipleship and also a sign of recognition to those on the outside. Augenstein also points out that though the love command functions primarily within the Johannine community, it should not be understood in terms of a very narrow ethic. In spite of the hatred of the world, the disciples are still sent into the world. Therefore, the community of discipleship is an open community. Moreover, the love of Jesus for the community is the basis and model of the love of the disciples for one another. Augenstein's study also showed that the love command in John is related to the Old Testament statements on the electing love of God (1993: 87-88).

Many scholars have pointed out that John's concept of love has a parallel in the Dead Sea Scrolls, where love also functions primarily within the community. John also stresses love for one another within the Christian community (R.E. Brown 1992: 199). But whereas the Qumran community is commanded to love their brothers, they are also commanded to hate those who do not belong to the community. They are commanded to love the children of light and to hate the children of darkness (cf. 1QS 1.3-4, 10 and CD 3.1). This is different from the Johannine Jesus, because the latter never commands hatred for one's enemies.

Verse 24 returns to the theme of glory and ends the inclusion begun at the beginning of the prayer:

24 πάτερ, ὃ δέδωκάς μοι, θέλω
    ἵνα ὅπου εἰμὶ ἐγὼ κάκεῖνοι ὦσιν μετ᾽ ἐμοῦ,
    ἵνα θεωρῶσιν τὴν δόξαν τὴν ἐμήν, ἣν δέδωκάς μοι
        ὅτι ἠγάπησάς με πρὸ καταβολῆς κόσμου.

The final destination of believers is to be with Jesus and to contemplate his glory. Barrett clearly overinterprets the text when he says, 'This means the glory of Christ within the Godhead, his glory as God' (1955: 429). Instead, the text has to be understood in conjunction with John's overall perspective on the descent and ascent of the Revealer. Therefore, Schnackenburg's comment and qualification throws more light on the text:

> The expectation of the fulfilment of salvation which emerges clearly here may also be in many respects close to the gnostic idea of the 'ascent of the soul,' but the Christian character of the Johannine text is preserved by the personal bond with Jesus, in whose glory believers are to share (1990: III, 195).

For Schnackenburg, then, Jesus' statement here has a future orientation.[105] Stimpfle has offered a different interpretation of this verse by arguing that a realized eschatological meaning is intended. Though the statement, ἵνα θεωρῶσιν τὴν δόξαν τὴν ἐμήν, seems to indicate a future event, the words ὅπου εἰμὶ ἐγὼ (present tense), indicate a present reality (1990: 230). The apparent futuristic statement of this verse is an example of Johannine misunderstanding which serves to keep true understanding from the non-elect.[106] In Stimpfle's words, 'The glory of Jesus, which "his own" will see, is the glory of his pre-existence, of his incarnation and of his post-existence' (1990: 230).

The expression πρὸ καταβολῆς κόσμου also occurred at v. 5. This phrase is common in the New Testament (cf. Mt. 13.35; 25.34; Lk. 11.50; Eph. 1.4; Heb. 1.4; 9.26; 1 Pet. 1.20; Rev. 13.8; 17.8), and therefore cannot be seen as a tradition from proto-Gnosticism (cf. 1 Jn 3.1-4).

---

105. Also see Barrett (1955: 499), Wikenhauser (1957: 304 and 311), Lattke (1975: 203), and J. Becker (1991: II, 619, 629-30).
106. Stimpfle's study builds on the work of Leroy (1968).

25 πάτερ δίκαιε, καὶ ὁ κόσμος σε οὐκ ἔγνω,
ἐγὼ δέ σε ἔγνων,
καὶ οὗτοι ἔγνωσαν ὅτι σύ με ἀπέστειλας·
26 καὶ ἐγνώρισα αὐτοῖς τὸ ὄνομά σου
καὶ γνωρίσω,
ἵνα ἡ ἀγάπη ἣν ἠγάπησάς με ἐν αὐτοῖς ᾖ
κἀγὼ ἐν αὐτοῖς.

Verses 25 and 26 conclude the prayer and may be considered as the final justification of the requests contained in the prayer. The Father is addressed as the Righteous One, a term that has legal implications. Because the Father is righteous he will certainly hear the Son's request. In contrast to the world, Jesus and the community have known the Father. And Jesus will continue to make the Father known to the community. 'The second statement, "I will continue to make it known," may refer to the work of the Paraclete (xiv 26, xvi 13)' (R.E. Brown 1966: II, 781). The result of this knowledge will be that the love of the Father for the Son may be in the community. We see that the highest common characteristic of the Father and the Son, that is, love, must be a characteristic of the community. The last phrase can either be translated as 'in them' or 'among them'. As to the meaning, it does not really matter which translation is adopted. Probably, the author intended a double meaning here.

b. *The Oneness Motif in John*

Many scholars have noted the importance of the concept of unity or oneness in John.[107] However, there is disagreement on exactly what is meant by the concept. The term ἕν occurs 36 times in John and five times in the prayer. The mere frequency of the term and its centrality in the narrative underscores its importance for Johannine theology. The religious traditions of the Johannine milieu have failed to provide an adequate context for understanding the oneness motif in John.

The theological importance of oneness in the Old Testament relates primarily to the one God of Israel (cf. Deut. 6.4). The only true God

107. Appold has produced a dissertation on the oneness motif in the Fourth Gospel (1976). He sees the oneness motif deeply imbedded in the structure and orientation of the Gospel. John's Christology is based on the oneness motif, depicting Jesus as God who fulfils his mission in a demonstration of power. 'Jesus' oneness with the Father is the central concern of John's proclamation. It is the content of faith' (1976: 137).

is Yahweh, and he is one. It is interesting to note that the Hebrew word for one used here is אחד, as this term has a plural form as well. 'It stresses unity while recognizing diversity within oneness' (Harris 1980: I, 60). This diversity in unity is seen in the tabernacle whose curtains are joined into one (Exod. 26.6, 11; 36.13), and in the union between Adam and Eve as 'one flesh' (Gen. 2.24). Also in Gen. 34.16 the men of Shechem want to marry Jacob's children in order to become 'one people' (Harris 1980: I, 30). Another tradition that may serve to clarify the Johannine motif of unity is contained within the Old Testament prophecies concerning the gathering of the scattered Israel again into one people (cf. Ezek. 34.17, 22; Hos. 1.11; Amos 3.3; Mic. 2.12). In John 10.16 the Johannine Jesus must bring other sheep also, so that there may be one flock and one shepherd. And in Jn 11.52 the High Priest prophesies that Jesus is going to die for the nation, and gather into one the dispersed children of God.

In the Dead Sea Scrolls, 'unity' (יחד) is a technical term for the community (Reicke 1992: 149). In 1QS 5.2 the members of the Qumran community shall constitute a unity; in 1QS 8.4-10 we read of a community of unitedness; and, likewise in 1QS 9.5 we read of a house of unitedness for Israel. Moreover, the Qumran community plays a central part in God's plan for his people. The Qumran community is seen as a divine planting, and the community is the bearer and guarantor of salvation for all Israel. As such, the knowledge of the eternal truth is achieved only within the community (cf. 1QH 6.25 and 1QS 9.3). The community stays together, eats together, studies together and prays together (cf. 1QS 6.11,12). Nevertheless, only those born of Israel can join the congregation, after an examination (cf. 1QS 7.10). Lastly, the community of Qumran provides defence against enemies (cf. 1QH 6.25-27). Maier also understands יחד as a synonym for the Qumran congregation or community (1960: 149). In most cases it occurs as a *terminus technicus* (1960: 148). Maier further suggests that יחד is used exclusively in the service of the symbolism of the Temple, and consequently signifies the practical representation of the true temple-sanctuary through the community (1960: 166, 178, 181).

Though the Old Testament and the Dead Sea Scroll usage of the terms אחד and יחד may help to clarify the Johannine motif of unity, neither adequately explains the Johannine usage. These are some of the traditions that flow into the Johannine theological prism, yet the centre of the Johannine oneness motif is not to be found in any of these traditions. An adequate understanding of the Johannine motif has to start with the statement in Jn 10.30, ἐγὼ καὶ ὁ πατὴρ ἕν ἐσμεν. The Son and the Father are one. It is important to note that the word for 'one' (ἕν) here is in the neuter case and not in the masculine. In other words, the Son and the Father are not one person, but a unity. Moreover, from the context of the previous verses the Son and the Father are equally active and concerned about the safe keeping of the sheep. Therefore, from the context the unity in mind here is above all a unity in action or function. The work of the Son is equivalent to that of the Father. There is the closest possible analogy between what the Father does and what the Son does. In fact, the work of the Son is identical to that of the Father (cf. Jn 5.17, 19, 30; 6.38; 8.16, 18, 26, 28).

Therefore, I want to conclude by saying that unity in John means the solidarity of two parties in one action or function. There is an absolute unity between the Father and the Son in action. The Son only does what he has seen from the Father. It is not a unity in essence but a unity in function, though the addition of the prologue goes in the direction of a unity in essence (Jn 1.1). In John 17 Jesus' prayer for both the present community and future believers is that they may be one (ἕν) (Jn 17.11, 21). Indeed, the central thrust of the prayer for the community is that they may be one. This unity of believers is a reflection of the solidarity between the Father and the Son in sending. Therefore, the unity of believers does not consist so much of a unity of confession, though it is of necessity included, but consists primarily of a unity in sending.

Similarly, Theron (1987) highlighted two aspects of 'oneness' in John. First, the oneness and solidarity of the Father and the Son, and secondly, dependent on this divine oneness, the solidarity of the Christian community. 'As to content, this prayer is not for unity *per se*, but for that specific unity that grows from a dynamic, confessional solidarity with the salvific mission of the Son of God' (1987: 93).

We see here, therefore, that the Johannine concept of unity is different from that of Paul. In Pauline ecclesiology Jews and Gentiles are joined into one body, or church of Christ (cf. 1 Cor. 12.1-14; Gal. 3.28; Rom. 12.5; Gal. 6.2; and Phil. 1.27; etc.). Oneness in John, however, refers to the Johannine community's unity in their being sent into the world.

5. *Conclusion*

In this exegesis of John 17 we have seen that the author is very interested in the relationship between the community and the Johannine historical Jesus. Indeed, the author sets up the closest possible relationship between the community and Jesus. Throughout the prayer the conjunction καθώς has played a very important role in this respect. Everything that can be said of the community can be said 'because' (or 'just as') it is said of Jesus. This is because the community and the Johannine Jesus are one. The central thrust of the prayer is that the community may be one, and that they may be one with Jesus and the Father. In fact, the concept of unity underlies several aspects of Johannine ecclesiology.

The prayer addressed three very important aspects of the community, which we may call the defining elements of Johannine ecclesiology, namely, the origin of the community, the character of the community and the purpose of the community. The community has its origins in Jesus, and therefore is a community which is from above. It is a community that consists of those who belong to the Father and who were given to Jesus. In other words, it is a community of *given ones*, elected and drawn by the Father. Therefore, the community exists theoretically even before the revelation brought by the Son. The Son called the community into active existence by giving the *given ones* life. As such, the origin of the community is traced to the earthly ministry of Jesus. Because the community belongs to the Father it does not have its origin from the world. In fact, the world hates it.

The nature of the community is characterized in several respects. First, in Käsemann's words it is a community that is under the Word; its existence is based on, and defined by, the revelation of the Son. This primarily consists in acknowledging Jesus' pre-existence with the Father and his being sent into the world. The community also serves as the preserver of the Word, keeping the Word which Jesus gave to them, and having joy in the Word. Secondly, the community is characterized by unity, a unity that exists both within the community and between the community and the Son and the Father. And I have argued that this unity is especially a unity in purpose and function. Thirdly, the members of the community are characterized by love for one another. In the words of Edanad, 'John envisages the Christian community as a community of love having as its model and basis the union of love that exists between the Father and the Son' (1985: 142).

The function of the community is to continue the sending of Jesus into the world. In this way the community functions as the agent of Jesus as it continues his sending. As the Father sent the Son, so the Son is sending the community into the world. Jesus' presence continues in the world through his community. This is in accordance with the Jewish principle that the one sent represents the sender (Lattke 1975a: 121). As such, there is no real distinction between the sending of Jesus and that of the community. The community is the *praesentia Christi,* or better, *Christus prolongatus*. The community's sending is not only analogous to that of the Son, but it is indeed the same sending. The purpose of this sending is for the world also to believe that the Father sent the Son. We see, therefore, that a soteriological or missiological motif underlies Johannine ecclesiology. Indeed, we have seen that the prayer is structured around the concept of glory which is a soteriological motif. I shall discuss the Johannine concept of glory in the next chapter.

In what terms then can we refer to the Johannine ecclesiology? Since there is the closest possible relationship between the community and Jesus, it appears that it is most accurate to refer to Johannine ecclesiology as a *christological ecclesiology* or a *Christ-ecclesiology*. There is a very close relationship between Jesus' origin and the community's, between Jesus' reception of the Father's Word and the community's reception of the Word, and between Jesus' mission and the community's mission into the world. The community, in effect, becomes or plays the role of the Johannine Christ.[108] Indeed, I want to suggest that John 17 as a literary creation of the community reflects the unity between the Johannine Christ and the community. In her insightful article Rosenblatt convincingly argues that the voices of

---

108. Though the term Μεσσίας is used twice in John (Jn 1.41 and 4.25), and John tries to show that Jesus is the Messiah, the Johannine Jesus is certainly rather the Christian Christ who comes to save the world (MacRae 1987: 178). Conzelmann similarly observed that, 'In differentiating the title 'Messiah' from Jewish Messianology, John does not depict the Jewish expectation of the Messiah in historically faithful terms. He already sees it from the perspective of Christian doctrine' (1969: 338). For recent discussions concerning the relationship between Messianology and Christology see Charlesworth (1987: 255-64; 1992a: 3-35), MacRae (1987: 169-85), Dunn (1992: 365-81), Horsley (1992: 276-95), Vermes (1973: 129-91). Also see de Jonge (1973) for a discussion concerning the messianic expectation of the Jews in John.

Jesus and the narrator (i.e. the evangelist or editor) have become conflated in the prayer. She writes:

> The community experiences such identification with Jesus that the resulting atmosphere of faith frees one of its members to pray the Master's prayer on behalf of the community. The lines separating the ones given to Jesus 'out of the world' (John 17.6) and Jesus himself become blurred. The voice of the believer and the voice of the Master who continues to pray in the community's midst can no longer be clearly distinguished (1988: 139-40).

Though the actual literary history of the prayer in John 17 may have been much more complicated than what Rosenblatt seems to suggest in this statement, her basic point is valid: the Johannine community sees itself as continuing the voice and presence of Jesus in the world.

Chapter 5

THE JOHANNINE CONCEPT OF GLORY

1. *Introduction*

I have already noted that the concept of glory plays a central role in John 17. The prayer begins with the Son's request for his own and his Father's glorification. It is also said in the prayer that the Son is glorified by the disciples (v. 10), that the Son has given his glory to the disciples (v. 22), and that the disciples may see the Son's glory (v. 24). Glory also plays a prominent part in the rest of the Gospel. In Jn 1.14 the incarnation is seen in terms of a revelation of glory; the first sign (σημεῖον) is understood as a revelation of glory (Jn 2.11); and throughout the first part of John Jesus frequently refers to his glory (Jn 7.18; 8.50; 11.4, 40, etc.). My concern in this chapter is to ascertain what is meant by the concept in John, and then how the concept relates to Johannine ecclesiology. Moreover, closely related with John's usage of the terms δόξα and δοξάζω is the role of Johannine eschatology. In comparison with the Synoptic Gospels and the Dead Sea Scrolls, the concept of glory is not only much more pronounced in John, but also reflects a different eschatological orientation. Therefore, another concern of this chapter is to point out the realizing eschatological orientation of glory in John as opposed to a futuristic eschatology in the Synoptic Gospels and the Dead Sea Scrolls, and what that means for ecclesiology. Numerous studies have already dealt with the philological aspects of the terms δόξα and δοξάζω in John.[1] Most scholars have understood the terms in a Hebrew or Jewish context, rather than in terms of a Greek or Hellenistic context. My own research will support this preference, especially as we consider the similarities of the concept between the Dead Sea Scrolls and John.

---

1. See Kittel and von Rad (1964), Hegermann (1990: 832-43), Caird (1968: 267).

However, we will note that the eschatological orientation in the Dead Sea Scrolls and John is different.

2. *Johannine Eschatology*

Since the beginning of this century New Testament scholars have become increasingly aware of the discrepancies between the eschatological expectation of the Synoptic Gospels and John (Beasley-Murray 1946: 97-108). In Mark especially, but also in the other Synoptic Gospels, the expectation of the reader is directed towards the future coming of God's kingdom in power,[2] whereas in John the reader is encouraged to make a present decision to believe in Jesus for eternal life. Recently scholars have also become aware of the discrepancies in John,[3] and among the Synoptic Gospels.[4] Some scholars have tended to ignore these discrepancies. Bultmann, for example, explained away the futuristic eschatology in Jn 5.39 by saying that this verse was a later addition to the Gospel of John. Stimpfle takes these references more seriously and understands them in terms of Johannine misunderstanding (1990). Various approaches have been attempted to solve these discrepancies between the Synoptics and John, and within them (Ladd 1974: 215). It is not the purpose of this chapter to criticize the solutions that have been proposed by different scholars. I shall, however, contribute to the debate by trying to explain the general difference in the eschatological perspectives between John and the Synoptics in terms of the glory motif. Though John is not always consistent, the focus shifts from the future in the Synoptics to the present in John; the coming of a future kingdom is replaced with the present possession of eternal life.[5] Important questions that have to be asked concerning John's eschatological orientation include the following: 'Why is John's eschatological orientation different from that of the Synoptics? Are

2.   Cf. Mt. 24; Mk 13; and Lk. 21.

3.   See Jn 5.25-29 and Jn 6.39-40. In these verses Jesus refers to a future resurrection which is similar to the future eschatological expectation of the Synoptic Gospels and Paul. I have already noted Stimpfle's argument that John has a consistent realized eschatology, and that the futuristic statements have to be understood in terms of Johannine misunderstanding (1990).

4.   See Mk 9.1; cf. Mt. 19.28 and Lk. 9.27. In this tradition the kingdom as a present reality is emphasized.

5.   There is no reference to a future coming of the kingdom in Jn 3.5, the only time where the kingdom is mentioned in John.

the differences between the Synoptics and John irreconcilable? What are the reasons for John's eschatological reorientation?' The answer to these questions will also help us not only to appreciate John's usage of the glory motif, but also assist us to place John in its proper *religions-geschichtliche* context.

3. *John, the Synoptic Gospels and the Dead Sea Scrolls*

A cursory glance at a concordance reveals that the term 'glory' (δόξα in the gospels, and כבוד in the Scrolls) is much more prominent in both John and in the Scrolls than in the Synoptics.[6] This observation supports the view that there was Qumran influence on the Johannine community. On the other hand, however, John's realizing eschatology differs from the imminent and futuristic eschatologies of the Synoptics and the Scrolls. The threefold relationship, therefore, between the Synoptics, John, and the Scrolls is an interesting question that deserves closer examination.[7]

The results of the research on the Scrolls so far have convinced most New Testament scholars that the Gospel of John was produced in a community that knew and interacted with the traditions of Qumran.[8] If we proceed on this assumption, which appears to be the *consensus communis*, a comparison of the differences and similarities between the Scrolls and John will enable us to draw valuable conclusions regarding the theological orientation of the Johannine community. A concluding question of Scrolls research for the New Testament scholar should be, 'How do the Scrolls, if at all, improve our understanding of the context and text of the New Testament documents?'

Comparisons between the Scrolls and the New Testament documents must be conducted with caution, however, since both traditions share the common background of the Old Testament and the Jewish world. Therefore, in this chapter I shall briefly survey the Old Testament usage of the term כבוד and shall examine the usage of the term in the

---

6.   The noun δόξα and the verb δοξάζω occur 15 times in Matthew, four times in Mark, 22 times in Luke, and 41 times in John.

7.   Although the Scrolls have enjoyed a tremendous amount of scholarly attention in the last 30 years, there remains a wealth of unexplored treasure for the New Testament scholar. With the free availability of all the Scrolls now we can look forward to an even greater industry in Qumran research.

8.   See R.E. Brown (1990: 1-8) and Charlesworth (1990: 76-106).

Scrolls. Furthermore, I shall limit my discussion to the major, and well-researched, Qumran Scrolls, namely the *Rule of the Community*, the *Zadokite Document*, the *Thanksgiving Hymns*, and the *War Scroll*—a full examination of all the Qumran material would demand far more space than is possible in this chapter. Lastly, I shall turn my attention to the material in John.

4. *Glory in the Old Testament and Pseudepigrapha*

The Hebrew word כבוד is frequently used in a variety of ways in the Old Testament. The basic meaning of the word כבוד is 'to be heavy' (Harris 1980: I, 420).[9] From the basic idea 'to be heavy' the meanings of honor, riches and glory are derived. In my survey of the Old Testament usage I am concerned only with the term as it applies to God, namely, that which is expressed by the phrase כבוד יהוה. The term כבוד in relation to God indicates what makes God impressive to, and distinct from, the human (Kittel and von Rad 1964: 238).

a. *The Exodus*

The first mention of the כבוד יהוה in the Hebrew Bible occurs in Exod. 16.7-10 in the context of the Exodus. God responded to the murmurings of Israel by a revelation of his כבוד. The כבוד is here depicted as something visible; it would be seen (וראיתם) on the following morning, it appeared (נראה) in the cloud.[10]

In Exod. 24.16-18 the כבוד יהוה is associated with the visible phenomenon of the cloud. Subsequently the cloud metaphor is often used by the biblical writers for God's glory (e.g. Exod. 40.34, 1 Kgs 8.11). In v. 17 the כבוד יהוה appeared like a consuming fire (כאש אכלת). The connection of כבוד יהוה with אש casts the reader's mind back to the burning bush episode in Exodus 3: the commissioning of Moses. In the fire יהוה made his presence visible, and revealed himself as אהיה אשר אהיה.

A very interesting passage concerning כבוד יהוה appears in Exod. 33.18-22. Moses explicitly requests to see the כבוד of God. If we interpret the answer of Yahweh to Moses affirmatively we have a

---

9. Also see Caird (1968, 267) and F. Brown (1952: 457).

10. Keil and Delitzsch in their commentary on Exodus understand that Jehovah's glory was not only experienced in seeing the glory in the cloud, but also in their eating of the gift of bread (1975).

correlation of goodness with the כבוד of God. God says to Moses, 'I will make all my goodness (כל טובי)[11] pass before you,' (v. 19). Therefore, when God says in v. 22, 'When my glory (כבוד) passes by...', the כבוד is parallel with the טובי of v. 19. God's כבוד, therefore, is seen in his goodness; and in the book of Exodus God's goodness is his saving activity on behalf of his people.

At the end of Exodus the tabernacle becomes the habitation of the כבוד יהוה (Exod. 40.34-38). Before the erection of the tabernacle God was present with his people in the cloud by day and in the fire by night (cf. Exod. 16.10). But when the tabernacle was erected we read, 'Then the cloud covered the tent of meeting, and the glory of the LORD filled the tabernacle' (Exod. 40.34).[12] The tabernacle became the dwelling place of God with his people, which was in accordance with God's promise to Moses (cf. Exod. 33.12-17).

Later Solomon's Temple became the place where the כבוד יהוה resided (1 Kgs 8.11; cf. 2 Chron. 5.13, 11; 7.1-3). In the 2 Chronicles passages the writer again associates כבוד with God's goodness.

The symbolism of the tabernacle and Temple, God dwelling in the midst of his people, goes back to the glory-cloud imagery of the Exodus, which symbolized the presence of God with his people and revealed his saving activity on behalf of the Israelites. The כבוד יהוה had thus become a technical term already in early biblical tradition to denote the presence and revelation of God.

b. *Ezekiel*
In the visions of Ezekiel, the כבוד יהוה attained a more sophisticated spiritual, if not apocalyptic, meaning. In Ezek. 1 the prophet is overwhelmed by a transcendent vision of God, which reached its highest point with the figure like a man on the throne (vv. 26-27). At the end of the chapter the prophet says, 'This was the appearance of the likeness of the glory of the LORD' (Ezek. 1.28).[13] This description of the כבוד יהוה is doubly significant. First, the כבוד is dissociated from a connection with the Temple—the vision appears to the prophet in Babylon. Secondly, the prophet alone experiences the revelation of the

11. It is interesting to note the reading of the LXX in this verse: Ἐγὼ παρελεύσομαι πρότερός σου τῇ δόξῃ μου. The LXX translates טובי with τῇ δόξῃ μου.

12. The Hebrew passage reads: ויכס הענן את אהל מועד וכבוד יהוה מלא את המשכן.

13. In the Hebrew the passage reads: הוא מראה דמות כבוד יהוה.

כבוד in contrast to the people as a whole (Kittel and von Rad 1964: 240).

In chs. 9 and 10, the prophet sees the כבוד יהוה departing from the Temple on account of Israel's apostasy (cf. Ezek. 7.20). God's כבוד in the cloud is the sign of his presence with his people, but since he cannot dwell with an unholy people the כבוד departs. Ezekiel's prophecy, however, does not end without an anticipation: in ch. 43 the prophet sees that the כבוד יהוה returns again to fill the Temple.

Solomon's Temple was destroyed by the Babylonians in 585/6 BCE and was rebuilt when the exiles returned under Zerubbabel. But the prophetic literature[14] dealing with that time nowhere relates a fulfillment of Ezekiel's vision of the returning כבוד יהוה. As Feinberg observes, 'The Shekinah glory is never mentioned in connection with the (Zerubbabel's) temple, so that temple cannot be the fulfillment of what is predicted here' (1969: 251). These visions of Ezekiel, with their future anticipation, provided the fertile soil for the development of the כבוד imagery in later Jewish literature.

In our survey so far we have seen that כבוד יהוה refers to the presence and self-revelation of God in his saving activity for and with his people. We must now focus our attention on two other factors that are associated with the term כבוד as it applies to God.

c. *Glory, Power, and Judgment*

Closely related with God's כבוד is his power or strength (כח, עז, גבורה, etc.). This is seen especially in the poetry of the Psalms where כבוד is often conjoined with the idea of power. In Ps. 63.2 the psalmist expresses a longing to see God's עז and כבוד in the sanctuary. Ps. 78.61 speaks of the ark as being God's power (עזו) and glory (ותפארתו). Another example is Ps. 145.11 in which the author speaks of God's כבוד and might (גבורה). These examples show that in speaking of God's כבוד the psalmist is also reflecting on God's power. God's power, in other words, is an expression of his כבוד.[15] The obvious background of this idea is the saving activity of God in the Exodus: to save his people from their oppressors there needs to be a display of his power (cf. Ps. 21.5).

Another factor associated with the concept of כבוד in the Old Testament is the idea of judgment. In ch. 2 of Isaiah we read that on the

14. The prophecies of Haggai and Zechariah.
15. See also Pss. 3.3; 12.9; 29.1; 96.7.

Day of the Lord people will flee 'from the terror of the Lord and the glory (כבוד) of his majesty' (vv. 10, 19, and 21). The כבוד יהוה will be revealed when he judges. People will see his כבוד as a consuming fire and will flee from it. Again we can see how this idea is related to כבוד as the goodness of God in his saving activity. Since God's judgment means the deliverance of his people, judgment is a manifestation of his glory. The Egyptians were judged at the Red Sea so that Israel could be saved.[16]

d. *The Pseudepigrapha*

This idea of כבוד יהוה as a revelation of judgment becomes more prominent in postexilic Jewish literature. When we look at the post-exilic Jewish literature, especially the apocalyptic literature, we find that the term glory is used in a variety of ways. For the purpose of this study I shall note only that the term takes on a decidedly futuristic orientation. The future revelation of glory becomes a crucial event in Salvation History. In the garden Adam was alienated from God's glory (*Apoc. Mos.* 20-21); the aim of Salvation History is the restoration of this glory so that the righteous may contemplate the glory of Yahweh (*4 Ezra* 7.97; *2 Bar.* 51.10-11). We also see that the Messiah's coming will be in glory (*2 Bar.* 30.1), and that there will be a future manifestation of glory at judgment (*4 Ezra* 7.42). In the apocalyptic material, then, we observe that there has been an expansion of the glory concept in the Old Testament. The concept of glory has become an important factor of Salvation History and the final blessing of the righteous consists primarily in the contemplation of the glory of Yahweh. On the other hand, we may note that the Old Testament idea of glory as the goodness of God in his saving activity does not receive much emphasis.[17]

e. *Summary*

The survey of the Old Testament shows that כבוד is an important term used to denote the presence and revelation of יהוה. In Exodus the כבוד יהוה, which later found its habitation in the tabernacle, is a display of the saving activity (his goodness) of God on behalf of his people.

---

16. Calvin very aptly says, 'When you hear the glory of God mentioned understand that his justice is included' (1983: III, XXIII, 8).

17. I am primarily dependent on Kittel for this paragraph (Kittel and von Rad 1964: 247).

Later in the Psalms and Prophets God's power and judgment are subsumed under the concept of כבוד. In order to deliver his people there needs to be a demonstration of God's power, which inevitably issues into the judgment of his people's oppressors. This Old Testament background is crucial for an understanding of glory in the Scrolls and especially in John.

5. *Glory in the Dead Sea Scrolls*

I shall now turn my investigation to the material of the Scrolls. As already mentioned I shall limit my investigation to the *Rule of the Community* (1QS), the *Zadokite Document* (CD), the *Thanksgiving Hymns* (1QH), and the *War Scroll* (1QM). I shall treat each document independently but will note the differences or development of the כבוד concept from document to document.

a. *Glory in the* Rule of the Community
The word כבוד is used in a variety of ways in the *Rule of the Community*. We find it in the sense of the original meaning of the word in the phrase וכבוד אוזן (1QS 4.11)—heaviness or dullness of ears. It also appears to denote the idea of purity (1QS 4.5). Most commonly, however, the word has the meaning of glory. Everything was made and planned according to God's glorious design (1QS 3.16). God has also appointed a term for perversity in his glorious wisdom, ובחכמת כבודו (1QS 4.18). In these two cases כבוד is used as an adjective of amplification to show the majesty of God.

The remaining occurrences of כבוד are more significant for our present study. Rule(a) 2.14-21 has a section describing the position of the members of the community in accordance with their glory. Each member will receive glory according to his standing in the community. In 1QS 4.7 one of the rewards of those who walk in the ways of the spirit of truth is a crown of glory (וכליל כבוד). In 1QS 4.23 the partners of God's covenant will have all mortal glory (כול כבוד אדם). Following this idea of a future reward of glory the *Rule of the Community* concludes with a contemplation of the final glorious habitation of the righteous (1QS 10.3, 9, 12 and 11.7, 20). The obvious background of this future כבוד of the righteous is the apocalyptic literature of the time. In the *Rule of the Community*, then, כבוד is a term with a decidedly futuristic orientation.

I conclude that in the *Rule of the Community* the idea of the final כבוד of the righteous is most prominent, especially as a description of the future reward of the righteous, which is also a prominent idea in the apocalyptic literature. The term is applied to describe God, but we do not find glory in terms of the goodness of God in salvation as is the case in the Old Testament. In this connection we may note that the Rule and the apocalyptic literature correspond in their similarities and differences in relation to the Old Testament.

b. *Glory in the* Zadokite Document
The term כבוד is much less frequent in the *Zadokite Document* than in the Rule, it occurs only three times. The reward of the righteous is 'all mortal glory' (CD 3.20). It is also used to describe the festivals (CD 3.15).

The reference in CD 20.26 is more important for our study since here כבוד refers to the future judgment. Those who have been unfaithful in the community will be judged 'at the time when God's glory (כבוד) is made manifest to Israel.' Here כבוד is connected with a time of future judgment, a connection that we have already seen in Isaiah.

The use of כבוד in the *Zadokite Document*, then, is very similar to the *Rule* except that the *Zadokite Document* also makes the connection between כבוד and judgment.

c. *Glory in the* Thanksgiving Hymns
In the *Thanksgiving Hymns* the concept of כבוד is much more frequent and complicated than in the *Rule* and in the *Zadokite Document*. (The term occurs 48 times in the *Thanksgiving Hymns*, 17 times in the *Rule*, and three times in the *Zadokite Document*.) There has clearly been a further development of the term in the *Hymns* in comparison to the *Rule*. As in the latter כבוד is used as an attribute of God (1QH 5.20; 9.16; 10.11, 12; 16.9), and as a reward of the righteous (1QH 7.24; in this passage the psalmist receives the same glory of God upon suffering); 9.25 (the reward of suffering for the psalmist will be a crown of glory, cf. 1 Pet. 5.4); 11.27; 13.11; 17.15). In 1QH 13.11 the כבוד is a present reward; in 1QH 17.15 the כבוד was the reward of the Old Testament saints. The dwelling place of God and the angels is described as a place of כבוד (1QH 12.30; cf. *Liturgy of the Angels*, 'the angels that minister in the presence of God's glory.').

In addition to the *Rule*, כבוד in the *Hymns* is used to describe the works of God displayed in creation (1QH 1.10; 13.6; this is common

in the Old Testament; cf. Ps. 19.1.) Here כבוד is brought into association with the power (כוח) of God, as his works in creation are a display of his power (cf. 1QH 2.24; 6.12; 15.20; also see 5.20; 9.16). As
I have observed above, the equation of כבוד with power is frequent in
the Psalms of the Old Testament. The other Old Testament connection
of כבוד with judgment is also common in the *Hymns*. God's future
display of כבוד will mean the judgment of the wicked (1QH 2.24;
3.35; 9.24 [כבוד supplied]; 15.20).

A significant difference in the *Hymns* from the *Rule* and the
Zadokite Document, however, is the emergence of the idea of salvation in connection with כבוד (1QH 6.12, 14; 12.15, 22; 16.9). In 1QH
6.12 God has acted for his כבוד that 'the Law may come to
fruition...that all nations may know your truth and all peoples your
glory (כבוד).' Of further importance is the observation that the connection of כבוד with the idea of salvation is especially made in relation
with the Teacher of Righteousness. In 1QH 12.15 the Teacher says,
'You have put an end to my [darkness], and the splendor of your glory
(כבוד) has become unto me as a light everlasting.' Again in 1QH 16.9
the Teacher says, 'Behold, you have granted mercy to your servant
and shed upon him your grace, your ever-compassionate spirit and the
splendor of your glory (כבוד).' Note that the author has experienced
or seen the כבוד of God. Thus the revelation of the כבוד of God does
not lie totally in a future day—the author is already experiencing the
revelation of כבוד. There is a shift from the futuristic use of כבוד to
the present. Thus we see a difference in the use of the term כבוד in the
Hymns as compared to its use in the *Rule* and the *Zadokite Document*.
This leads to the conclusion that there is also a realizing 'eschatology'
in the *Thanksgiving Hymns*.

The כבוד of God's work in salvation, however, is not so obvious as
that of creation. It is a 'hidden' כבוד; only the enlightened are able to
see it (1QH 3.4 [in this passage כבוד is in parallel construction with
truth] 18.22; 15.17). This כבוד is found in the presence of God (1QH
7.15). Since the author has been illumined to see the glory of God he
describes himself as the revealer of that glory to men (1QH 4.29; in
this passage power is again connected with כבוד). Lastly, others who
have also gained insight into God's truth are exhorted to tell forth his
כבוד which is displayed in his counsel and deeds for their salvation
(1QH 1.30; 6; 12, 14; 10.27; 11.6, 8). In one passage the community
together as a group glorifies God (1QH 8.5).

In summary, כבוד in the *Thanksgiving Hymns* is a term to denote the work of God; it may be in creation, salvation or judgment. As in the Davidic Psalms there is a close connection between God's power and his כבוד. God's כבוד, however, is not only understood in terms of a future revelation of 'glory', there is a 'glory' that the enlightened Qumranite has already experienced. Finally, in the *Hymns* the community is exhorted to proclaim the כבוד of God, that is, his great acts in salvation.

d. *Glory in the* War Scroll

As in the *Thanksgiving Hymns*, כבוד in the *War Scroll* is used to describe the abode of God and the angels (1QM 12.2), and as an attribute of God (1QM 12.6; 12.7). In this writing כבוד has also become an attribute of God's people (1QM 4.6, 8; 12.10, 15). This can be seen as a development of the idea in the *Hymns* where God's people are illuminated to understand God's כבוד and receive כבוד as a reward. We have already seen that in the above documents כבוד begins to have a futuristic orientation, in the *War Scroll* this orientation becomes even stronger (1QM 1.9; 12.12; cf. 19.4). The final battle between God and Belial will usher in the era of כבוד. In 1QM 13.8 כבוד is a synonym for God's acts in the history of his people. We may summarize these observations by saying that in the *War Scroll* the term כבוד has come to denote the future revelation of God's majesty and power in the battle against Belial. It has also become an attribute of God's people.

e. *Summary*

The Hebrew word כבוד is seen both as an attribute of God and as an attribute of God's people. It is also given as a reward for the righteous; in this respect the Righteous Teacher features prominently in the *Thanksgiving Hymns*. God's work is described as a revelation of his כבוד. As in the postexilic Jewish literature there is a predominant futuristic use of the term in nearly all the documents I have examined. There will be a future day of כבוד in which God's judgment will be revealed. The Qumran community looked forward to a coming day of glory. This expectation becomes stronger through the development of the Scrolls which we have examined. The Old Testament association of כבוד with God's goodness in salvation emerges only in the *Thanksgiving Hymns*, and then it is mostly a 'hidden' כבוד which only the illumined can see. God's people are also exhorted to tell forth his glory.

6. *Glory in the Gospel of John*

As I have noted at the beginning, the concept of glory features prominently in the Gospel of John, especially when we compare John with
the Synoptics. John uses δόξα sometimes in the sense of honor or
praise, which corresponds with a similar usage of כבוד. We will not
concern ourselves with passages in which δόξα is used in this sense.[18]
Many commentators have interpreted the Gospel's literary structure in
terms of glory. Bultmann divides the Gospel according to 'The Revelation of δόξα before the World' (chs. 2–12) and 'The Revelation of
δόξα before the Community' (chs. 13–20) (1941: 77). Kysar divides
the Gospel into two parts: 'Jesus Reveals Glory' and 'Jesus Receives
Glory' (1993: 18). I agree with the emphasis that these commentators
have placed on the glory of Jesus in their analysis of John, since my
own observations concur with their assessment of the importance of
glory in John. The following questions, however, remain to be
answered, Why does the concept of glory receive so much attention in
John? And what is the context in which the theological meaning of the
term is to be understood? We must now turn our attention to these
important questions.

a. *The Glory of Jesus in the Prologue*
The concept of glory occupies a central place in the Prologue[19], which
could also be read as a summary of the Gospel,[20] it is stated (Jn 1.14):

κὰι ὁ λόγος σάρξ ἐγένετο
καὶ ἐσκήνωσεν ἐν ἡμῖν,
καὶ ἐθεασάμεθα τὴν δόξαν αὐτοῦ,
    δόξαν ὡς μονογενοῦς παρὰ πατρός,
    πλήρης χάριτος καὶ ἀληθείας.

---

18. These occurrences are in Jn 5.41, 44; 7.18; and 8.54. Ibuki refers to these as
the profane usage of the term (1988: 45-55).

19. For a discussion on the Prologue as a Logos hymn see Schnackenburg
(1990: I, 224-25).

20. Most probably this Logos hymn is a later addition to the Gospel to combat
Docetism. Its location at the beginning of the Gospel ensures the superiority of Jesus
over his adversaries and guards his full humanity against Docetic tendencies. Harrison says, 'The language will not fit the docetic idea that the λόγος came upon a man,
identified with him for a season, and then abandoned the human form prior to the
crucifixion by a return to a spirit existence (1978: 26).

And the word became flesh
and tented (tabernacles) among us,
and we beheld his glory,
> glory as of the Father's only-begotten [Son],
> full of grace and truth.

The suggestion of this chapter is that δόξα in John is to be understood in terms of the כבוד concept as developed in the Old Testament and the Dead Sea Scrolls.[21] Cook's statement certainly applies to John, 'There is no question that the New Testament usage of *doxa* keys from the LXX rather than from secular Greek' (1984: 292). I disagree with Bultmann who says that John comes from a Hellenism that is saturated with Gnosticism and 'avoids expressions that stem from Jewish apocalyptic' (1951–55: II, 6). For when John says, 'And the Word became flesh and tented (ἐσκήνωσεν) among us, and we beheld his glory...' he links the δόξα of Jesus with the כבוד יהוה as it was revealed in the Old Testament tabernacle.[22] The verb ἐσκήνωσεν (aorist of σκηνόω) can be literally translated 'he tabernacled' (Grimm 1890: 578), the reader is brought right back into the sanctuary of the tabernacle where the כבוד יהוה was manifested (Harrison 1978: 26-27). Behind this expression lies the rich Old Testament idea of the presence of כבוד with his people, and also the pregnant futuristic connotations of כבוד as developed in the Dead Sea Scrolls. I shall therefore proceed to examine the usage of δόξα in terms of its Jewish context in the concept of כבוד יהוה.

Before we proceed, however, I need to point out the importance of the Prologue in John. The Prologue (Jn 1.1-18) introduces and summarizes the main themes of the Gospel which, inter alia, include the theme of glory (Westcott 1955: xliv). In the following narrative these themes are progressively worked out as the story unfolds.[23] Verse 14 then, as part of the Prologue, is a summary and an anticipation of the story which will follow; the Prologue is the window through which

21. It should be noted that the Classical Greek usage of δόξα differs from the Hebrew כבוד. In Homeric and Herodian literature δόξα is related with the verb δόκεω which has the basic meaning 'to think'. So in the subjective sense δόξα has come to mean 'expectation' or 'opinion'; in the objective sense 'reputation' or 'renown'. According to Josephus and Philo δόξα has four meanings, namely 'opinion', 'honor', 'splendor', and 'divine radiance' (Kittel and von Rad 1964: 233).

22. Riga (1963: 412) and Harrison (1978: 26) made the same connection.

23. For a recent discussion on plot development in John, see Culpepper (1983: 89-98).

the author or later editor intends the reader to see the Gospel. According to the writer, the earthly life of Jesus was the manifestation of the כבוד יהוה. How that δόξα was manifested is worked out in the following narrative (Smith 1986: 34). 'Step by step the Gospel of St John lays open the progress of this manifestation' (Westcott 1955: xlvii).

I am now in a position to continue my discussion of the δόξα of Jesus in John. What summary does the author give the reader of the δόξα of Jesus in Jn 1.14? Apart from a difference of emphasis the picture of Jesus' δόξα is similar to that of the כבוד יהוה in the Old Testament.

The δόξα of Jesus like כבוד יהוה refers to the presence of God with his people for salvation. The Word, which is identified with God (Jn 1.1), became flesh and tabernacled among the disciples. The verb σκηνόω associates the earthly ministry of Jesus with the presence of יהוה with his people at the exodus, which meant the salvation of his people. Harrison writes:

> In the Old Testament the presence of God as indicated by means of the pillar of fire and cloud is noted for the first time in connection with the exodus (Exod 14.19, 24), and this served to express at once the power of God to safeguard his people and to deal effectively with their enemies (1978: 29).

As such the concept of glory may have an apologetic purpose for the Johannine community as they struggled with the synagogue.

In the words καὶ ἐθεασάμεθα τὴν δόξαν αὐτοῦ we have the confession of the believing community, the whole ministry of Jesus was characterized by δόξα.[24] The transition from the inclusive πάντες (v. 7), πάντα (v. 9) and κόσμος (v. 10) to the exclusive 'we' in ἐθεασάμεθα indicates that only the disciples, those who believed in Jesus, comprehended the δόξα of Jesus (Smith 1986: 33; Riga 1963: 41). Verse 14 goes on to explain the phrase δόξαν αὐτοῦ by two epexegetical declarations δόξαν ὡς μονογενοῦς παρὰ πατρός and πλήρης χάριτος καὶ ἀληθείας. In the first declaration the particle ὡς serves to define the δόξα of Jesus more precisely.[25] With the use of the phrase μονογενοῦς παρὰ πατρός the author stresses the source

---

24. See Zerwick's discussion on the global aorist (1963: 83).
25. See Blass and Debrunner (1961: 219), and Grimm (1890: 680-82).

(origin) of the δόξα.[26] It is a δόξα that is not from this world, but of the only-begotten from the Father. The δόξα of Jesus is thus fitted into the dualistic paradigm of the Gospel. Schnackenburg states that it is also possible to translate this phrase as 'the only-begotten (Son), coming from the Father' in the context of the Prologue (Schnackenburg 1990: I, 271). This would indicate that the author had the earthly mission of Jesus in mind by these words. Jesus' glory is seen in his whole earthly life, including his death. If this is correct, the idea conveyed is that of the Son's mission to execute a special work (Westcott 1955: 12). By comparing Jn 1.14 with Jn 3.16, de Kruijf has made a connection between μονογενής and sacrifice. He writes that, 'the term as used in the Fourth Gospel is more of a soteriological than a christological nature' (1970: 123).

The next declaration defines the character of the δόξα of Jesus. The word πλήρης is often indeclinable, as here, and so can refer to λόγος (nominative), δόξαν (accusative), or μονογενοῦς (genitive). Contrary to Schnackenburg, who connects πλήρης with μονογενοῦς, I take it as referring to δόξαν, which corresponds with the Old Testament idea that God's goodness in salvation is an expression of his כבוד. The δόξα of Jesus is one of 'grace and truth'. This syntactical interpretation would further support the argument that δόξα in John is to be interpreted in terms of the Hebrew כבוד.[27]

The concept of δόξα which we find in the Prologue, therefore, is similar to that of כבוד יהוה. We may note that the presence of God as salvation and grace is most prominent in the thought of the author. In this the idea is closer to the כבוד יהוה of the exodus than the later emphasis on judgment which we find in the literature of Qumran.

From this introductory or summary statement in Jn 1.14 the author has prepared the reader for the further development of the δόξα of Jesus in the Gospel.

---

26. De Kruijf warns that there has been a 'tendency of conforming too easily with later Christology' (1970: 112) in the interpretation of the term μονογενής.

27. Painter also writes on this verse, 'John sets out to make clear the character of the divine glory from the beginning. It is the self-giving love of Jesus, who gave himself for the world, and this is understood as the self-giving of God (3.16; cf. 1 John 4.7ff.). The glory is revealed in humiliation, suffering and unswerving faithfulness to the world which refused to know him' (1975: 58).

b. *The Glory of Jesus Revealed in his Signs*
The first revelation of Jesus' δόξα in the Gospel proper occurs at the
narration of the first sign, the changing of the water into wine, in
Cana of Galilee (Jn 2.11):

> ταύτην ἐποίησεν ἀρχὴν τῶν σημείων
> ὁ Ἰησοῦς ἐν Κανὰ τῆς Γαλιλαίας,
> καὶ ἐφανέρωσεν τὴν δόξαν αὐτοῦ,
> καὶ ἐπίστευσαν εἰς αὐτὸν οἱ μαθηταὶ αὐτοῦ.

> Jesus did this, the first of the signs, in Cana of Galilee,
> and revealed hs glory,
> and his disciples believed in him.

Here we have the first 'sign' of the seven recorded in the Gospel. It
has been suggested that these seven signs of Jesus have been incorporated into John from a signs source (Fortna 1970). Though I shall not
enter into a discussion of sources at this point, we may observe that
v. 11 above does not belong to the miracle story itself, it is an addition
that serves to interpret the significance of the miracle. When we
examine the remaining 'signs', except for the raising of Lazarus in ch.
11, we find that the term δόξα does not occur. This may suggest that
the association of 'sign' with δόξα in v. 11 is the work of the author,
again showing the importance that he attached to the concept of δόξα.

The author tells the reader that Jesus performed this sign in order
to reveal his glory. In other words, the sign points the reader to the
δόξα of Jesus. More specifically then, how does the author understand
this sign as a revelation of Jesus' δόξα? Changing water into wine
reveals the power of Jesus over nature; it is a power miracle. Schnackenburg says:

> The δόξα revealed by Jesus through the change of water into a munificent
> gift of wine, is primarily his divine and creative power, the δύναμις
> which is proper to him as God (1990: I, 335).

The signs in John are extraordinary, even in comparison with the
Synoptics. Jesus heals the nobleman's son without even being in his
presence (4.46-54); he heals a man who had been lame for 38 years
(5.1-15); Jesus walks on the water (6.6-21); he is able to heal a man
who had been born blind (9.1-5); and he raises a man who had been
dead for four days (11.1-44). In the signs of John, then, the power of
Jesus is revealed—the salvation of God arrived in power (in the Synoptics the power of Jesus is further demonstrated in his ability to

perform exorcisms). Pamment's comment on Jn 2.11 that '*doxa* is used with associations not of power, but of selfless generosity and love' (1983: 12), misunderstands that a revelation or demonstration of power is necessary for the accomplishment of salvation in biblical literature. In other words, the expression of power by God, or Jesus in this case, is also an expression of 'selfless generosity and love'.

As I have mentioned δόξα also features in the seventh sign, the raising of Lazarus (Jn 11.1-44). When Jesus heard that Lazarus was sick he responded by saying, 'This sickness is not unto death, but for the glory of God, that the son of God may be glorified through it' (Jn 11.4). Jesus then goes to Bethany and raises Lazarus from the dead. In this story the apprehension of the δόξα of God is explicitly linked with belief. Jesus mildly rebukes Martha objecting to the opening of Lazarus' tomb, by saying (Jn 11.40):

οὐκ εἶπόν σοι
    ὅτι ἐὰν πιστεύσῃς
    ὄψῃ τὴν δόξαν τοῦ θεοῦ.

Did I not tell you
    that if you would believe
    you would see the glory of God?

This aspect of the 'hidden' δόξα in the ministry of Jesus was already alluded to in the prologue.

I conclude that the signs of Jesus in John must be understood in the framework of his δόξα, the first and the seventh being closely related to the revelation of δόξα. In the signs of John the author shows that the power of God is revealed through Jesus for salvation, which is the outworking of Jn 1.14. Therefore Cloete correctly states that in all seven miracles, '...occurs the revelation of his glory (2.11, 11.4) and the works of God (9.3). And the essence of it is grace and truth' (1980: 73). Again, these observations point to the Old Testament as the best source for understanding the Johannine usage of the term glory. Riga in his study has made similar observations:

> The glory of God is the divine power which multiplies miracles, and which thereby manifests God's presence and power of salvation... And just as the events of the Old Testament (creation, crossing the Red Sea, the manna in the desert, the water from the rock) revealed the presence and power of God, St John put the *semeia* of Christ in relation to these miracles or signs of the Old Testament, proving that Christ was God's envoy and that the presence of God was in the incarnate Christ (1963: 411).

c. *The Glory of Jesus in the Cross*
The latter half of ch. 12 (vv. 12-41) deals extensively with the δόξα of Jesus. The noun δόξα and the verb δόξαζω occur no less than eight times in the latter half of the chapter. Here the reader comes to the heart of the concept in John. The concept of δόξα is introduced to the reader in v. 16:

ταῦτα οὐκ ἔγνωσαν αὐτοῦ οἱ μαθηταὶ τὸ πρῶτον,
ἀλλ' ὅτε ἐδοξάσθη Ἰησοῦς
    τότε ἐμνήσθησαν,
    ὅτι ταῦτα ἦν ἐπ' αὐτῷ γεγραμμένα
    καὶ ταῦτα ἐποίησαν αὐτῷ.

His disciples did not understand these things at first
but when Jesus was glorified
    then they remembered,
    that these things had been written about him
    and that these things had been done to him.

The natural question that this verse suggests to the reader is, When was Jesus glorified? The reader does not need to wait long for an answer—it is supplied in the following narrative. Upon the inquiry of certain Greeks to see Jesus, he made the statement (v. 23), ἐλήλυθεν ἡ ὥρα ἵνα δοξασθῇ ὁ υἱὸς τοῦ ἀνθρώπου.

In these words Jesus is referring to the cross. For in what follows it is seen that ἡ ὥρα is pointing to the hour of his death: the ear of wheat must die before it can bring forth fruit (Lightfoot 1956: 240).

According to the author of John, therefore, Jesus is also glorified in the death of the cross. Though Stimpfle has correctly noted that Jesus' glory does not only refer to his death on the cross (1990: 228), the cross nevertheless remains the primary revelation of his glory (Onuki 1984: 174-75).[28] The idea that Jesus' glory consists in his death on the cross is notably different from the concept of Jesus' glory found in 1 Peter. For the author of 1 Peter, Jesus suffered first and then entered into his glory (cf. 1 Pet. 1.11; 4.13). John equates the suffering of Jesus with his glory. This paradox must be understood in terms of Jn 1.14—if his glory was 'full of grace and truth', then surely the

28. Though Pamment has written a perceptive article on the meaning of glory in John, and has correctly understood glory in terms of God's love (1983: 15), her insistance that Jesus' glory only refers to his death on the cross is not supported by the Gospel. Jesus' life on earth was also a manifestation of glory (cf. Jn 1.14; 2.11; 17.4; etc.).

cross was the pre-eminent manifestation of that glory. In this the δόξα of Jesus in John is similar to the Old Testament יהוה כבוד, that is, God's goodness in salvation. At this point I shall quote the eloquent Calvin, 'The glory of God shines...never more brightly than in the cross...' (1959: II, 68).

It is significant to note that it was upon the inquiry of certain Greeks—Gentiles—to see Jesus that he is made to speak of his δόξα.[29] Did the author of John associate δόξα with the mission of salvation to the Gentiles? It appears that this was indeed the case. Moreover, this ties in very well with the Old Testament concept of יהוה כבוד which means God's goodness in salvation. I therefore disagree with Barrett who contended that, 'They speak as representatives of the Gentile Church to which John and his readers belonged' (1955: 351). Kysar accurately captures the meaning of John when he says:

> John introduces the Greeks at this point for purely symbolic reasons, it appears, for they do not figure in the narrative or in the following discourse (at least directly). Their function here (as well as perhaps their indirect access to Jesus through the disciples) prefigures the coming of the Gentile world to the Christian faith in the life of the early church (1984: 60).

Verse 32, with the emphasis on mission, further supports this view. Verses 31 and 32 refer to the cross in terms of judgment and salvation. The cross means judgment for the world, but salvation for those who believe. Here the ideas of judgment and salvation are brought together in the glorification of Jesus.[30] The pericope ends with the statement (v. 41):

> ταῦτα εἶπεν Ἡσαΐας
>   ὅτι εἶδεν τὴν δόξαν αὐτοῦ,
>   καὶ ἐλάλησεν περὶ αὐτοῦ.

> Isaiah said these things
>   because he saw his glory
>   and spoke concerning him.

The pronoun ταῦτα refers not only to the immediate quotation from Isaiah but to the chapter as a whole, especially to the hour of Jesus'

---

29. I agree with Hoskyns that these men were not Hellenistic Jews but Gentiles of Greek birth (1940: 423).

30. We may speculate whether the author had Haggai in mind when he prophesied that God will fill the rebuilt Temple with כבוד at the time all nations will come with their wealth, Hag. 2.7.

glorification, for he says Isaiah εἶδεν τὴν δόξαν αὐτοῦ. The reference is to Isaiah 6 where the prophet had the vision of Yahweh sitting on the throne in the temple. It is interesting to note here that the author may be reflecting on the *Targum Onqelos* which reads in Isa. 6.5, 'My eyes have seen יקר שכינת מלך עלמא' (Kittel and von Rad 1964: 245). Isaiah saw the Lord in the temple, the place where his כבוד was manifested, and the temple was 'filled with smoke', which evidently came from the burning altar. It may be that the author saw that burning altar as anticipating the sacrifice of Jesus on the cross, for herein, he says the prophet saw his δόξα. Also in 2 Chron. 7.1-3 it appears that the glory cloud which filled the temple came from the smoke of the sacrifices which were ignited by the fire from heaven. This imagery may have provided the background of John's association of Jesus' cross with his δόξα. Therefore, the suffering that the Johannine Jesus endured is an important element of his mission (being sent) into the world.[31] Since his elected ones will obtain salvation through his suffering, it constitutes a crucial element of his glory. Therefore, in Riga's words:

> When the Jews seemed about to extinguish and destroy the work of Christ, at that moment, St John tells us, comes the very moment of his *glorification* (death, resurrection, and ascension as one whole, one 'entity' of salvation) as the Son of God (1963: 424).

This aspect of suffering in the glory of Jesus is significant for Johannine ecclesiology. The community's struggle is the moment of glorification. As such the community's struggle is crucial for being *Christus prolongatus*. The *Sitz im Leben* of the Johannine community may well have shaped this understanding of glory.

In ch. 12, then, the δόξα of Jesus resides in his crucifixion. With this idea John's development of the theme introduced in Jn 1.14 reaches its climax. Through the cross of Jesus God accomplished the salvation of his people—the fulfillment of grace and truth in salvation history. Jesus' death on the cross, therefore, is not simply his return to the Father, but is the completion of his mission and means the salvation of the elected community. This soteriological understanding of Jesus' mission (John's *Sendungschristologie*) in the historical event of the cross makes John a Christian Gospel and not a Gnostic one. Ibuki

---

31. The prayer in Jn 12.27 shows that even the Johannine Jesus was not immune to suffering.

likewise understands the death of Jesus as the fulfilment of his mission of salvation for the world (1988: 72). Jesus' death on the cross is therefore a revelation of his glory.

d. *The Glory of Jesus in his Mission*

Another aspect alluded to in Jn 1.14 is associated with δόξα in the prayer of Jesus (Jn 17.1-5), namely, that of 'mission'. First, Jesus' mission from the Father is seen in terms of δόξα, and then the disciples' mission is also subsumed under the concept of δόξα. Jesus prays (Jn 17.1-5):

πάτερ, ἐλήλυθεν ἡ ὥρα·
    δόξασόν σου τὸν υἱόν,
        ἵνα ὁ υἱὸς δοξάσῃ σέ,

ἐγώ σε ἐδόξασα ἐπὶ τῆς γῆς
    τὸ ἔργον τελειώσας ὃ δέδωκάς μοι
    ἵνα ποιήσω·
καὶ νῦν δόξασόν με σύ, πάτερ, παρὰ σεαυτῷ
    τῇ δόξῃ ᾗ εἶχον πρὸ τοῦ τὸν κόσμον εἶναι παρὰ σοί.

The basis of this prayer is Jesus' conviction that he received a mission from the Father. In his prayer Jesus prays that the Father may glorify him, that is, accomplish the mission for which he has been sent: the laying down his of life for the sheep. As we have seen the glorification of the Son consists especially in his death on the cross, which he boldly approaches (Jn. 12.23-28). The subordination of ἵνα ὁ υἱὸς δοξάσῃ σέ to δόξασόν σου τὸν υἱόν indicates the total dependence of the Son on the Father and is a particular Johannine thought. Jesus, then, is in fact praying for his death, which is in sharp contrast to his prayer in the Synoptics (Mk 14.36; Mt. 26.38-39, 42; Lk. 22.42), because in John Jesus did not come to do his own will but the will of the Father who sent him (cf. Jn 6.38). Therefore the Father is called upon to bring about the hour of his crucifixion so that the prince of this world may be judged and all be drawn to the Son. We also see here that the glorification of the Father means the glorification of the Son, and vice versa. Therefore, the glory of the Father and the glory of the Son are identical.[32]

In v. 4 Jesus equates δόξα with the work (ἔργον) which the Father

---

32. In the words of Stimpfle, 'Die δόξα des Gesandten ist identisch mit der δόξα des Senders. Verherrlichung—sei es des Vaters, sei es des Sohnes—meint Offenbarung der δόξα—sei es des Vaters, sei es des Sohnes' (1990: 226).

has given him. Jesus has glorified the Father on earth by finishing the work the Father assigned him, identifying δόξα with his mission from the Father.[33] The contrast in vv. 4 and 5 between ἐπὶ τῆς γῆς and παρὰ σεαυτῷ should be seen in terms of the protology, and hence dualism, which we find in John. This fact has been well expressed by Schnackenburg:

> The glory that Jesus possessed 'before the world was made' characterizes not the pre-mundane, but the supra-mundane existence of the Logos, and ultimately the superiority of the divine revealer to and his transcendence over the world (1990: III, 174).

Following on from the connection of Jesus' δόξα with his mission is that the disciples receive δόξα as they participate in the mission of Jesus. In v. 10 Jesus prays, καὶ δεδόξασμαι ἐν αὐτοῖς. He can pray that he is glorified in his followers because he gave his δόξα to them, κἀγὼ τὴν δόξαν ἣν δέδωκάς μοι δέδωκα αὐτοῖς (v. 22). According to the context of the prayer, the δόξα here is to be understood as the mission Jesus received from the Father. The δόξα that Jesus gives to his disciples is the sharing in his mission. As the Father sent him, so he sends the disciples to bring salvation to the world (cf. Jn 4.36; 12.24; 20.21). As Jesus' life was directed according to the mission he received, so his followers' lives become redirected according to the mission of God (cf. Jn 12.26 and 21.18, 19). The disciples' δόξα then is to continue the divine mission of Jesus. Again this ties in well with the idea of יהוה כבוד as essentially God's goodness in salvation. Leon Morris says, '...just as His true glory was to follow the path of lowly service culminating in the cross, so for them [i.e. His disciples] the true glory lay in the path of lowly service wherever it might lead them' (1971: 735). For Peter this 'true glory' in the path of lowly service leads to death (cf. Jn 21.18, 19).

This idea that the believer's δόξα consists in his or her sharing of the mission of salvation is also expressed in Jn 15.1-8. At the end of this parabolic discourse it is stated that the disciple glorifies God in fruit bearing (v. 8):

33. In the author's mind the work of Jesus was already finished, for he was fully determined to do the will of God. According to Schnackenburg it is not the exalted Christ who is speaking here, 'This is the prayer of the departing Christ, who is certain of the fulfillment of his work and of his own fulfillment' (1990: III, 173).

ἐν τούτῳ ἐδοξάσθη ὁ πατήρ μου
ἵνα καρπὸν πολὺν φέρητε
καὶ γένησθε ἐμοὶ μαθηταί.

In this my Father is glorified
    that you bear much fruit
    and be my disciples.

The phrase ἐν τούτῳ is forward looking[34], referring to the fruit bearing of the disciple. The aorist here (ἐδοξάσθη) is also used proleptically.[35] Therefore, to glorify God (i.e. to be a disciple) a person must 'bear fruit'. In the other New Testament documents, especially in Paul, the figure of fruit generally denotes the presence of spiritual virtues (cf. Gal. 5.22). However, in John the figure is used in a different sense. Before the illustration of the vine it occurs twice in Jn 4.36 and Jn 12.24, and in both these cases the figure is used in terms of harvest. It is in enlarging the number of believers in Jesus that the disciple bears fruit. It is interesting to note that both these passages allude to the salvation of the Gentiles. Jesus' words to the disciples in Jn 4.36 follow on from his conversation with the Samaritan woman, and in Jn 12.24 the context is the inquiry of the Greeks to see Jesus. This supports my earlier conclusion that δόξα in John is linked with the mission of salvation to the Gentiles.

Finally, the reference to δόξα in Jn 17.24 refers to the future reward of those who have served and followed Jesus (cf. Jn 12.26). They will be able to enjoy the fullness of the Son's salvation, which means inter alia the incorporation of the elected ones into the community, in the presence of the Father. About this verse Uprichard aptly says, 'God's glory in God's Son is revealed in the consummation of the Church' (1984: 6).

e. *Summary*

The preceding study shows that the concept of δόξα was important for John and presumably also for the Johannine community. The concept occupies a central place in the Prologue and features prominently

34. This agrees with Morris (1971: 672). I differ from Westcott who says 'ἐν τούτῳ' looks back. The reason I have adopted the view of Morris is on the basis of the use of this phrase 'ἐν τούτῳ' in 1 John where the phrase is used nine times (1 Jn 2.3, 5; 3.16, 24; 4.2, 10, 13, 17; 5.2). In seven of these occurrences the phrase looks forward. In 2.5 the phrase looks back, and in 4.17 the orientation is unclear.

35. See Blass and Debrunner (1961: 171); and also E. Burton (1976: 23).

throughout the Gospel narrative. In the Prologue the δόξα of Jesus is seen in terms of the Old Testament כבוד יהוה which loads the term with soteriological significance. This statement characterizes Jesus' ministry as a revelation of δόξα.

His ministry (ἔργον) is the mission he received from the Father to save those the Father has given to him. Therefore, his signs, as a demonstration of power, and then, ultimately and pre-eminently, his suffering and death on the cross, is seen as a revelation of δόξα. This δόξα of Jesus is only appreciated by those who believe in him. Their eyes have been opened to comprehend the δόξα of Jesus. They also share in his δόξα by participating in his mission. The revelation of δόξα in John consists primarily in the saving ministry of Jesus and not in a future event. For the author of John, the eschatological day of glory has dawned, first in the ministry of Jesus and now in the mission of the disciples. I suggest, therefore, that the concept of glory has a very concrete meaning in John. In short, it describes the revelation or realization of the grace and power of God's salvation in the life of the community. To use a German term, glory in John refers to the *Heils-offenbarung* of God in Jesus and in the community of disciples. We should reject, therefore, any metaphysical or abstract interpretation of the concept, as for example 'splendor', 'majesty', 'brightness', and so on (Fry 1976: 421-25).[36] In John, glory is a soteriological concept and not an ontological one.

7. Conclusion

My examination above makes a strong case for the view that the δόξα of Jesus in John should be understood against the background of the כבוד concept of the Old Testament. I have noted that the frequency and significance of the term δόξα in John is in sharp contrast with the Synoptics. I can explain this contrast by proposing that the Johannine

36. Many scholars have suggested an interpretation of glory in John. For Schnackenburg glory equals the fullness of divine life (1990: III, 192). For Thüsing glory equals the 'splendour and power of divine love'; but also see his comment where he understands 'glory' as a summary term for Johannine salvation (1975: 89). Zahn and Tillmann regard glory merely as miraculous power. Wikenhauser understands glory as the revelation of the word, and for Loisy glory has to do with the Eucharist. For Caird glory refers to the mutual indwelling of the Father and the Son (1968: 271). And lastly, for Käsemann Jesus' glorification means his return to the Father (1978: 19-20). I regard all these interpretations as inadequate.

community which produced the Gospel was influenced by the Dead Sea Scrolls. The idea of glory as judgment and salvation in the period of Hillel and Jesus is found in the Dead Sea Scrolls and John. I want to propose, therefore, that John inherited his concept of δόξα from the Dead Sea Scrolls, and modified it to emphasize salvation corresponding to his Christology, which emphasizes the descent of the heavenly Revealer.

To support the proposal above I shall point out the similarities between John and the Dead Sea Scrolls. The idea of glory as the revelation of God's judgment and salvation of God is found in both the Scrolls and John. In both sets of documents the revelation of glory is a crucial event of salvation history. For the Scrolls the revelation will take place in the future; for John the revelation took place in the ministry of Jesus. In John the eschatological day of glory has come with Jesus. Although the concept of 'glory' is significant for salvation history in the Old Testament prophets, the idea did not have such prominence as in the Scrolls. Moreover, in the Scrolls the association of כבוד with salvation is made in relation with the Teacher of Righteousness. The revelation of God's glory is seen as coming through an individual. In John, Jesus is the person through whom the revelation of glory occurs. Therefore, when John sees the ministry of Jesus in terms of glory, he may be interpreting the event in terms of Qumran thought. Another similarity between the Scrolls and John, which is absent from the Old Testament, is the idea of a 'hidden' glory. In the Scrolls only the enlightened are able to see the glory of God's revelation; in John only those who believe can see the glory of Jesus. Lastly, in both documents an apprehension of glory is a future reward.

The differences between the Scrolls and John, however, should also be pointed out. The first difference is that of emphasis. In the Scrolls the future day of glory is primarily seen as a day of judgment, whereas in John, though the idea of judgment is present, the emphasis is on salvation: the glory of Jesus was full of grace and truth (Jn 1.14). The second difference is more profound, that is, in John the glory of Jesus lies prominently in his crucifixion. Jesus' hour of glorification was when he was lifted up on the cross, thereby casting out the prince of this world and drawing all people to himself. The last difference I want to point out is the important eschatological distinction between the Scrolls and John.[37] For the Scrolls the day of

37. Strictly speaking we should not talk of 'eschatology' in the Dead Sea Scrolls,

glory lay in the future[38]; in John the day of glory has come with Jesus. Jn 1.14 is in sharp contrast to the predominant futuristic 'eschatological' use of כבוד in the literature of Qumran. For the Johannine community the eschatological complex of the revelation of God's salvation and judgment has occurred in the events of Jesus. We notice then that an eschatological reorientation has occurred in the Johannine community.

Therefore, the research shows that though there are close ideological similarities between the Scrolls and John, there are also major differences. I explained the similarities by proposing that the Johannine community was influenced by the Scrolls.[39] It remains to be asked, however, 'How do we account for these differences between the Scrolls and John?' My answer is that the Johannine community inherited their concept of glory from Qumran, but they modified the concept corresponding to their Christology. Since Jesus came so that those who believe in him may have everlasting life, the soteriological element of glory is emphasized. The glory of Jesus was not to condemn the world but to save it. In this John is a Christian Gospel with a strong missionary intention: the disciples now share in the glory of Jesus as they continue the mission begun by him.

Another question that I should address is, 'How do my observations help us to understand the discrepancy between the futuristic eschatological expectation in the Synoptics and predominant realizing eschatology in John?'[40] For the Synoptics (and 2 Pet. 1.16-18) glory lay in the future manifestation of the kingdom, for John the ministry of Jesus, especially the cross, reveals his glory. John wants his readers to comprehend the glory of Jesus' mission from the Father and share in

since it is a Greek term used to denote the doctrine of the *eschaton* in the New Testament documents.

38. H. W. Kuhn (1966) identified three different types of eschatology present in the Dead Sea Scrolls: (1) Realizing Eschatology; (2) Imminent Eschatology; and (3) Futuristic Eschatology. The predominant eschatological orientation of the Scrolls, however, is future.

39. How that influence took place is not my concern here, although Brownlee has made some suggestions in this connection (1990: 166-94).

40. The futuristic eschatology which we find in Jn 6 is determined by the tradition with which the author is working. The Gospels are both literary creations and a compilation of traditions. The New Testament scholar should be sensitive to the tension which we find in the Gospels between the historical tradition of Jesus and the literary intentions of the author.

the same by participating in that mission. To me it seems that John is intentionally trying to shift the futuristic orientation of the traditions of Jesus to the present. Because, according to John, Jesus has come so that those who believe in him may have life. Attaching a futuristic eschatology to the tradition (the future establishment of the kingdom of God) makes it incomplete, and therefore diminishes the significance of Jesus' life, death and resurrection. Appreciating the Qumran influence—a community which had a strong futuristic 'eschatological' orientation—upon the Johannine community, I suggest the following theory to help us to understand the eschatological shift of John. John was written with the background of the disappointed 'eschatology' of the Qumran community.[41] The Johannine school does not want to substitute another eschatology for that of Qumran, instead it presents a realizing eschatology. That which was expected, the revelation of the eschatological day of glory, has happened in the ministry of Jesus and is in the process of happening in the mission of the disciples.[42] The reader does not need to put his hope in a future event that may not occur. The tension in John is not between the now and the not yet, but between that which is from above and from below.

What I have said above has important implications for Johannine ecclesiology. In the prayer of John 17, which describes Johannine ecclesiology, the glory motif occurs at the beginning (vv. 1-5), in the middle (v. 10), and at the end of the prayer (vv. 22 and 24). The eschatological hour of both Jesus and the community is the hour of glory. Therefore, the significance of the community's present time is that it is the time of salvation. Moreover, we notice in the prayer that Jesus gave his glory to the community, that is, the Son has committed his mission (being sent) to save the world to the community. The community, therefore, becomes the agent of the Son's mission as it carries on his mission in the world. Therefore, the Johannine community is not a closed or inward-looking community, but instead understands itself as existing primarily for the salvation of the world. Though the community has experienced conflict and suffering, its

---

41. The community was destroyed by the Romans shortly before CE 70.

42. Of course, Johannine eschatology should also be understood in the context of the disappointed hope of the early Christians at the end of the first century, i.e. the delay of the *parousia*. To this, Stimpfle has also added the influence that split in the Johannine community and the death of the Beloved Disciple had on the community's eschatology (1990).

ecclesiology still wants to empower the community for a continued mission into the world. The final destiny of the community is to see the Son's glory, that is, to see the completion of the Son's mission when all the elected ones have been brought into the salvific community. In this way Johannine ecclesiology may also be described by the German term as a *Herrlichkeitsekklesiologie*.

Lastly, the understanding of glory in terms of suffering has an added significance for the Johannine community. Their glory is the suffering they experience while remaining in the world for the sake of the salvation of the world. Therefore, the suffering that the Johannine community experiences is indispensible for accomplishing their task in the world, because it is their suffering that leads the world to salvation. We therefore see that there is a close relationship between the concepts of glory and sending (*Sendungschristologie*) (Ibuki 1988: 68-69). And it is to the consideration of the latter concept that I now turn in the next chapter.

Chapter 6

THE JOHANNINE CONCEPT OF SENDING

1. *Introduction*

This chapter will attempt to point out the significance of the concept of sending for placing John in its proper *religionsgeschichtliche* context and for understanding Johannine ecclesiology. The importance of the concept of sending[1] for Johannine theology achieved recognition with Kuhl's monograph, *Die Sendung Jesu und der Kirche nach dem Johannes-Evangelium*, which was published in 1967. Yet, the meaning and origin of the concept remain disputed questions among scholars today. The words of Schweizer still apply: 'It is still unclear from where the presentation of the sending of God's Son from heaven derives' (1966: 199). Scholars have found the origin of the concept in different traditions,[2] and have interpreted its meaning in different ways.[3] Attempts at a solution to the problem have often been unsatisfactory because of the failure to deal with all the questions involved.[4] Three questions, at least, have to be examined before a satisfactory answer can be given: (1) Is there any difference between the two verbs employed, ἀποστέλλω and πέμπω? (2) What is the historical

---

1.   Closely related to 'sending' is the 'mission' motif of the Gospel, which is receiving considerable scholarly attention. See Okure (1988); Ruiz (1987); Waldstein (1990); and Popkes (1978).

2.   In his article Schweizer examines several Greek and Hellenistic-Jewish sources for a possible solution, and finds it in the Jewish Wisdom tradition (1966: 207). Miranda, on the other hand, understands John's concept of sending in terms of the prophetic tradition (1977: 90-92).

3.   An important question is whether the concept of sending should be understood from a christological perspective (e.g. Bühner, Miranda) or a soteriological-ecclesiological perspective (e.g. Kuhl, Okure, Ruiz).

4.   Haenchen's examination of the formula 'the Father, who sent me' is weak in that it does not consider the *religionsgeschichtliche* context of John (1962–63).

origin of the concept? And, (3) What is the theological meaning of the concept? The answer to the last question must take into account the sociological context of the Johannine community.[5]

2. *The Johannine Vocabulary for 'Sending'*

A variety of terminological expressions are used to describe the sending concept in the Fourth Gospel. Kuhl has listed 18 terms used in the Gospel that relate either directly or indirectly to the Johannine theology of sending (1967: 53-57).[6] In this chapter, however, I shall focus only on the two terms that refer directly to the sending of the Son by the Father, namely, ἀποστέλλω and πέμπω. Other terms that deal indirectly with the concept of sending will be discussed only when it becomes necessary.

The verb ἀποστέλλω, a compound of στέλλω with the preposition ἀπό, is a common word in both Classical and Koine Greek. It has the basic meaning of 'to send forth', and can be used of persons or things. When the object of the verb is a person, ἀποστέλλω often has the connotation of a commissioning, which transfers the authority of the sender to the person being sent.[7] It is used in this sense in legal as well as religious literature. In Cynicism ἀποστέλλω is used in a technical sense of the divine authorization of the Cynic (Rengstorf 1965: 399). In the LXX ἀποστέλλω regularly translates the Hebrew שלח. The verb ἀποστέλλω is also used extensively in the Greek literature of early

5. See Meeks (1972). In discussing the relationship between Johannine Christology and Gnostic myths, Meeks demonstrates the importance of discerning the function which concepts served within the Johannine community.

6. Verbs that relate directly to the concept of sending are πέμπω and ἀποστέλλω; analagous to these are ἔρχομαι, ἐξέρχομαι and καταβαίνω; prepositions that are used with the sending concept are ἀπό, ἐκ and παρά; other terms that relate to the concept are ἁγιάζω, δίδωμι, σφραγίζω and ἐντέλλομαι; verbs that describe the return of the emissionary to the Father are ὑπάγω, πορεύομαι, ἀφίημι, ἀναβαίνω, μεταβαίνω and ἀπέρχομαι (Kuhl 1967: 53-57).

7. There is a good example of this usage from an inscription dating from the second century BC cited in *Pan du désert* (Bernard 1977: 253).

Σωτήριχος Ἰκαδίωνος Γορτύνιος, τῷ[ν]
ἀρχισωματοφυλάκων, ὁ ἀπεσταλ-
μένός ὑπὸ Παῶτος...

Bernard's comment is to the point: 'Le verbe ἀποστέλλω ... est d'usage courant pour désigner l'envoi d'un subordonné par son supérieur' (1977: 256).

Judaism, in Philo, and in Josephus. The noun ἀπόστολος is much more important or popular as a religious term in the Hellenistic period (Rengstorf 1965: 407-45). In the Fourth Gospel, however, the noun occurs only once in the form of a Synoptic logion, and refers interestingly not to Jesus but to his disciples (cf. Jn 13.16).

Apart from the exception mentioned above, ἀπόστολος never occurs in the Fourth Gospel. As such the concept of sending is entirely a verbal one in John. Later I shall explore the significance of this phenomenon. The verb occurs 28 times in John,[8] and, according to Bühner (1990: 141), 19 of those relate to Christology. The verb is common in all the Synoptic Gospels: it occurs 21 times in Matthew, 21 times in Mark, and 26 times in Luke.

The verb πέμπω is also a common term in both Classical and Koine Greek, though it is not used in the same technical sense as ἀποστέλλω in Greek religion. It is commonly translated as 'to send', but, whereas in ἀποστέλλω the emphasis falls on the relationship between the sender and the person being sent, in πέμπω the emphasis falls on the act of sending (Rengstorf 1965: 398). πέμπω is rare in the LXX,[9] but more common in the Greek literature of early Judaism, in Philo and in Josephus.[10]

The verb πέμπω occurs 33 times in the Fourth Gospel.[11] As compared to the Synoptic Gospels the term is much more frequent in John; it occurs four times in Matthew, once in Mark, and 10 times in Luke. Of special significance is the formula ὁ πέμψας με which occurs

8.   Jn 1.6, 19, 24; 3.17, 28, 34; 4.38; 5.33, 36, 38; 6.29, 57; 7.29, 32; 8.42; 9.7; 10.36; 11.3, 42; 17.3, 8, 18, 21, 23, 25; 18.24; 20.21.

9.   πέμπω occurs 26 times, but only in six instances does it translate the Hebrew שׁלח, cf. Gen. 27.42; 1 Sam. 20.20; Ezra 4.14; 5.17; Neh. 2.5 (Rengstorf 1965: 400).

10.   In Josephus ἀποστέλλω and πέμπω are used interchangeably: *Ant.* 20.37: ...τοὺς μὲν ὁμηρεύσοντας μετὰ τέκνων εἰς τὴν Ῥώμην ἐξέπεμψε Κλαυδίῳ Καίσαρι, τοὺς δὲ πρὸς Ἀρταβάνην τὸν Πάρθον ἐφ' ὁμοίαις προφάσεσιν ἀπέστειλεν.

Life 51: ...μὴ ὑποστρέψαντος δὴ τοῦ ἐξελευθέρου Φίλιππος ἀπορῶν τὴν αἰτίαν δεύτερον ἐκπέμπει μετ' ἐπιστολῶν πάλιν τὸν ἀπαγγελοῦντα πρὸς αὐτὸν τί τὸ συμβεβηκὸς εἴη τῷ ἀποσταλέντι, δι' ὃ βραδύνειεν. This usage shows how the merging of the two terms in John could have occurred quite easily.

11.   Jn 1.22, 33; 4.34; 5.23, 24, 30, 37; 6.38, 39, 40, 44; 7.16, 18, 28, 33; 8.16, 26, 29; 9.4; 12.44, 45, 49; 13.16, 20; 14.24, 26; 15.21, 26; 16.5, 7; 20.21. Ritt and Kuhl counted 32 times (1993: 68; 1967: 53).

23 times in John.[12] In Jn 1.33 the same formula occurs in connection with John the Baptist.

According to the frequency of ἀποστέλλω and πέμπω it appears that both verbs are of equal importance to the Johannine concept of sending.[13] An important question is whether or not the terms are synonymous or have different meanings. Most scholars hold to the opinion that the two terms are synonymous in John.[14] According to Kuhl the πέμπω statements express the unity between the sender and the one sent, and the ἀποστέλλω statements express the authority of the one sent in virtue of his relationship with the sender. Kuhl concludes, however, by saying that one should not make a sharp distinction between the two verbs.[15]

In this chapter, however, I shall suggest that a distinction needs to be maintained between these two terms. Granted, in many instances in the Gospel the terms are used interchangeably or synonymously. Yet, this should not prevent us from appreciating the different traditions that lie behind the usage of these two terms. I shall argue that it is probable that ἀποστέλλω and πέμπω are remnants of two distinct sending traditions. With the passage of time these two distinct traditions have become merged in the final redactions of the Fourth Gospel. It should be kept in mind that the Fourth Gospel was composed over an extented period of time.[16] Though Kuhl's analysis for

12. Ritt counted the formula 22 times in John (1993: 68).

13. At the conclusion of this chapter I need to discuss what I mean by the 'Johannine' concept of sending. Does Johannine refer to the final edition of the Gospel or to the thought of the original author or community?

14. For Haenchen 'there is no difference in meaning' between the two verbs (1984: I, 96). Also for Barrett, 'The two verbs seem to be used synonymously in this gospel' (1955: 473). Likewise for Okure, 'It is not evident that a different shade of meaning is intended in the use of each of these two verbs' (1988: 2). See also Mercer's article, which wants to revise 'the recent trend of seeing no difference' (1990: 619).

15. 'Alles in allem wird man den Bedeutungsunterschied zwischen beiden Verben nicht zu stark betonen dürfen. Auffallend ist z.B., daß im Kap.17, das doch ganz geprägt ist vom Geiste der Einheit und Verbundenheit zwischen dem Gesandten und dem sendenden Vater, nie πέμπειν gebraucht ist, dafür aber 7 mal ἀποστέλλειν zur Bezeichnung der Sendung Jesu' (1967: 54).

16. Some scholars would date the signs source, which is probably the earliest source of the Fourth Gospel, to as early as the CE 40s. This would mean that the Gospel incorporates material streching over a period of more than 50 years. See R.T. Fortna (1970).

the final edition of the Gospel may be sound, it is still important to recognize the role of two distinct sending traditions in John in order to understand the *religionsgeschichtliche* context of the Gospel.

3. *The* Religionsgeschichtliche *Context of Sending in John*

The concepts embodied by the ἀποστέλλω and πέμπω statements in John represent two distinct early traditions about sending. The ἀποστέλλω statements in the Synoptic Gospels represent an Old Testament prophetic tradition about the prophet as the emissary of God. The origin of the πέμπω statements, on the other hand, should be located in the early Gnostic myth about the sending of the Redeemer.[17] It should be pointed out, however, that in the New Testament, including the Fourth Gospel, such a distinction is difficult to maintain across the board. The lines of demarcation have already been blurred, and there is no longer a sharp distinction between these two terms. Yet we are still able to detect remnants of two separate sending traditions in the Fourth Gospel. In the following section I shall first attempt to isolate the ἀποστέλλω tradition of early Christianity and then the πέμπω tradition that has been 'borrowed' from an early form of Gnosticism.

a. *The Old Testament, Apocrypha and Pseudepigrapha*
It is the present study's contention that we can talk of a prophetic ἀποστέλλω tradition, with its roots in the Old Testament, current in first-century Palestine. The sending of the prophet by God is a concept that occurs regularly in the Old Testament. The origins of this concept can be traced back to the tradition of the pre-eminent prophet, Moses, who was sent (שלח) by Yahweh (יהוה) to deliver the Israelites from slavery in Egypt. In Exod. 3.10-14 God appears to Moses and sends him to Pharaoh to bring the Israelites out of Egypt. The term שלח is used three times in this passage—the same word used to describe the office of the prophet (cf. Jer. 26.12, 15) (North 1966: 40).

We should also note that divine revelation was closely associated with the sending of Moses. When Moses asked what he should say,

---

17. I am not assuming that there was a preChristian Gnostic Redeemer myth, but only a preJohannine Gnostic Redeemer myth. The final edition of John appeared at the end of the first century; by then there was ample evidence for the existence of such a Redeemer myth.

God said to Moses, 'I am who I am. This is what you are to say to the Israelites: "I am has sent me to you"' (Exod. 3.14).[18] Moses' sending by Yahweh not only entails deliverance from Egypt, but is also a self-revelation of Yahweh to his people. Moses is the great prophet and becomes the model of later prophets (cf. Deut. 18.15). There is evidence that the tradition that Moses was sent by God was current in Palestine in the first century CE. In 2 Esd. 14.3, 4 the Lord says to Ezra, 'When my people was in slavery in Egypt, I revealed myself in the bush and spoke to Moses, sending him to lead Israel out of Egypt.'[19]

In the Latter Prophets God often sends (שלח) his prophets as representatives on special missions (cf. Isa. 6.8; Jer. 1.7; 25.4; 26.5, 12, 15; 35.15; 44.4; Ezek. 2.2-3). The main qualification of a prophet is that he is being sent by God (cf. Jer. 14.14-15). In Jer. 23.21 false prophets are rebuked in that they were not sent by God, 'I did not send these prophets, yet they run with their message; I did not speak to them, yet they have prophesied.' In this verse God's self-revelation (i.e. speaking), following the tradition about Moses, is in parallel construction with sending. When God sends someone it means that he has revealed himself to the one being sent. The prophetic message therefore gains its authority in being sent by God (cf. Isa. 9.8; Zech. 7.12).[20] Later on the fulfillment of the prophet's message became the evidence that the prophet was sent by God (cf. Zech. 2.9, 11; 4.9; 6.15).

Another aspect of the Old Testament prophetic tradition is that the prophet is often rejected by those to whom he is sent. The origin of this tradition can also be traced back to Moses who was often rejected or scorned by the Israelites (cf. Exod. 5.20, 21; 6.9; 14.11, 12; 16.3; 17.2). The call of Isaiah in Isa. 6.8-10 reinforces the same idea; the prophet is sent to a nation that will not receive his message.

Therefore, I want to highlight three important ideas in connection with the Old Testament concept of the sending of the prophet: (1) the

18. 'I am', of course, is also a Johannine expression.
19. Most of 2 Esd. was written at the end of the first century CE. See Myers (1974). 2 Esd. 10.20 refers to the destruction of Jerusalem in CE 70.
20. Müller, following Westermann and Koch, sees a connection between the sending concept of the Old Testament and the Mari prophets (1986: 148). It is interesting to note the occurrence of 'I' statements and the predominance of 'the way' in the Mari prophecies.

prophet is a bearer of God's authority, the term שׁלח denoting the authority of the prophet's commission; (2) the prophet's message is a revelation of, or from, God; and (3) the prophet is often rejected by those to whom he is sent.

In the Apocrypha and Pseudepigrapha the Old Testament prophetic tradition, described by the verb שׁלח, continues to play an important role.[21] However, a different emphasis is that angels are often pictured as being sent by God to reveal the message.[22] Angels stand in God's presence and are therefore perfect messengers of his will. In Tobit, Raphael, one of the seven angels who stands in the presence of God, reveals that he was sent by God to test and cure Tobit and Sarah (Tob. 20.13, 14). In 2 Macc. 15.22 Maccabees recollects '...that in the days of King Hezekiah of Judah you sent your angel and he destroyed as many as a hundred and eighty five thousand men.' In 2 Esd. 4 Uriel the angel is sent to Ezra to reveal the ways of this world. In 5.31 an angel is sent to Esdras to give instruction. In 6.33 the angel is sent with revelations and a message. And in 7.1 the same angel is again sent to Esdras. In the *Life of Adam and Eve* angels are frequently sent (ἀποστέλλω) by the Lord in response to prayer (cf. 6.2; 9.3; 13.1, 2; 40.7).[23] In the *Testament of Abraham* the angel Michael is sent (ἀποστέλλω) by God to Abraham (cf. 2.6; 7.11, 12; 8.11).[24] In the *Testament of the Twelve Patriarchs* we again find that angels are sent (ἀποστέλλω) by the Lord (*T. Levi* 5.3). In *3 Bar.* 1.4 the Lord sent (ἀποστέλλω) his angel to reveal all the things of God. God also sends humans to bring a revelation. In Judith, Judith is sent by God to bring a message to Holophernes. She says, 'I have been given foreknowledge of this; it has been revealed to me, and I have been sent to announce it to you' (Jdt. 11.19; cf. 11.16, 22). Therefore, like the Old Testament tradition, sending involves the bringing of certain revelation. It is also

21. In the Greek translations (LXX) πέμπω is used too, though less often, but with no particular significance that is distinct from ἀποστέλλω.

22. In the Old Testament angels were also sent by God: cf. Gen. 24.7, 40; Num. 20.16. But the idea is not so prominent as in the Apocrypha and Pseudepigrapha.

23. I am here referring only to the Greek text (*Apoc. Mos.*). Most scholars believe that the Greek and Latin texts are translations from an original Hebrew document (Johnson 1985: 251) and that the date of composition is between 100 BCE and CE 200, with a preference towards the end of the first century (Johnson 1985: 252).

24. The *Testament of Abraham* probably dates from c. CE 100 (Sanders 1985: 875).

significant to note that the word here used for 'send' in the Greek is ἀποστέλλω.

The idea of the rejection of the prophet also occurs. In 2 Esd. 1.32 we read, 'I sent my servants the prophets to you, but you took them and killed them and mutilated their bodies.'[25] The idea of the rejection of the prophet who was sent by God is also found in *1 Enoch*, which talks about the slaying of the sheep that the Lord sent (ἀποστέλλω) to his people (cf. 89.45, 51-53).[26]

We also find the idea of transition along vertical space in the sending event on a few occasions. Raphael says to Tobit, 'I am about to ascend to him who sent me' (Tob. 20.20). In the *T.Abr.* 7.8 we read, 'And the light-bearing man which came down from heaven, this is the one sent from God, who is about to take your righteous soul from you.' In the *T.Abr.* (Recension B) 4.9, 'The archangel answered and said, Lord, you sent me to Abraham to say to him, Depart from the body and leave the world; the Lord calls you.' These references, however, cannot be taken as the origin of John's dualism. They are rare, and do not occur in such a pronounced dualistic demarcation of above and below as we find in John.

The concept of sending also occurs once in connection with wisdom. In the Wisdom of Solomon, Solomon prays, 'With you is wisdom, who is familiar with your works and was present when you created the universe, who is aware of what is acceptable to you and in keeping with your commandments. *Send* (ἀποστέλλω) her forth from your holy heaven, and from your glorious throne bid her come down, so that she may labour at my side and I may learn what is pleasing to you' (Wis. 9.9, 10).[27] A little further on Solomon says, 'Who ever came to know your purposes, unless you had given him wisdom and sent your holy spirit from heaven on high?' (Wis. 9.17). There is a similar passage in 2 Esd. 14.22 where Ezra asks, 'If I have found favour with you, send into me your holy spirit.' Again, however, we cannot attribute the origin of John's dualistic sending concept to the

25. Myers's view that verse 32 is dependent on Lk. 11.49 is doubtful; cf. 2 Chron. 36.15, 16 (1974: 155).

26. The Greek text of *1 Enoch* 89.51-53 has not been preserved, but since ἀποστέλλω is used in 89.45 one would assume that ἀποστέλλω occurred in 89.51-53 as well.

27. The italics are mine.

Jewish wisdom tradition.[28] The concept of sending does not play an important role in the wisdom tradition.

In concluding my discussion of sending in the Apocrypha and Pseudepigrapha I want to highlight two points: (1) angels are sent to reveal messages of revelation; while (2) prophets are sent, and as in the Old Testament, are often rejected. In some instances sending also occurs in a dualistic framework and in connection with wisdom, but these are isolated references and not significant to explain John.

The Apocrypha and Pseudepigrapha were popular in Palestine during the first century CE. Indeed many of these documents were written during this period. This material provides evidence that a prophetic sending tradition, rooted in the Old Testament concept of שׁלח, was current in the first century CE. In Greek this tradition was described with the verb ἀποστέλλω. More evidence for the existence of a prophetic sending tradition is provided by the existence of the Jewish institution of the שׁליח, and by the Synoptic Gospels.

b. *The Institution of the* שׁליח

That there was a prophetic sending concept current in first-century Palestine is also borne out by the existence of the Jewish institution of the שׁליח. Though the history of the institution can be traced back to the time of the exile, it is only during the first century CE that it became an official institution (Rengstorf 1965: 414-15). This institution 'is expressed briefly in the principle found in the Mishnah, 'A man's agent (s[h]alûah) is like himself' (*Ber.* 5.5) (von Eicken and Lindner 1975: 127-28). Rengstorf pointed out that 'the designation שְׁלוּחִים is neither description of the fact of sending nor indication of the task involved but simply assertion of the form of sending, i.e., of authorisation' (1965: 415). Therefore, we see that some aspects of the sending concept of the Old Testament (i.e. of authorization) took on concrete shape in the שׁליח during the first century.

---

28. This is against the view of Schweizer, 'Die Stellen, an denen das Schema "Gott sandte seinen Sohn, damit..." erscheint, finden sich bei Paulus und Johannes. Bei beiden steht eine Christologie im Hintergrund, die Jesus in den Kategorien der Sendung der präexistenten Weisheit, bzw. des Logos, zu erfassen sucht' (1966: 206-10). Schweizer confuses the origin of the christological Logos concept with that of sending. Of course, these two concepts are closely related in John, but do not originate in the same location.

c. *The Early Christian Tradition*
Turning to the Synoptic Gospels we find that several pericopes refer
to the Old Testament sending motif of God's emissary in terms of
ἀποστέλλω.

(1) John the Baptist (Mk 1.2-6; Mt. 3.1-6; 11.10; Lk. 3.1-6; 7.27). In
these pericopes the coming of John the Baptist is explicitly set against
the Old Testament promise of a coming prophet. Specifically in Mk
1.2 several Old Testament passages with an explicit sending motif are
combined to introduce the ministry of the Baptist. The quotation is a
combination of Mal. 3.1 (Hebrew), Exod. 23.20 (LXX), and Isa. 40.3.[29]
In Matthew and Luke the ἀποστέλλω tradition is also associated with
the Baptist in Mt. 11.10 and Lk. 7.27. In both instances the quotation
is from Mal. 3.1.

(2) The Parable of the Wicked Husbandmen (Mk 12.1-12; Mt. 21.33-
46; Lk. 20.9-19; *Gos. Thom.* (log. 65). The concept of sending is central to the parable of the wicked vine-dressers.[30] It is not my concern
to discuss the nature of the allegory of this parable.[31] Whether it is
true allegory or not, it is clear that in this parable Jesus[32] sees his
mission in terms of the Old Testament prophet who is sent by God.[33]
According to Jeremias, 'In these two missions Matthew sees the earlier
and the later prophets, and the mention of stoning has special reference to the fate of the prophets (2 Chron. 24.21; Heb. 11.37;
Mt. 23.37; Luke 13.34)' (1972: 72). In both Mark and Matthew

29. There is disagreement among scholars as to the exact handling of these passages by the Markan author. But it is generally recognized that these verses formed
'part of a whole series of *testimonia* associated with John the Baptizer' (Mann 1986:
195). Therefore, it is not a Markan creation. Johnson thinks that the quotation from
Mal. 3.1 was added later (1972: 33).
30. In the Old Testament the symbol of the vineyard/vine is often used for Judah
or Israel; cf. Ps. 80.8-16; Isa. 5.1-7; Song 1.6.
31. This has been a hotly debated question among scholars. See Fitzmyer (1985:
II, 1280).
32. This parable probably goes back to Jesus (Fitzmyer 1985: II, 1280).
33. Albright and Mann, in comparing Matthew with Mark and Luke, say, 'The
Matthean plural clearly calls for equating the slaves with the prophets, sent as God's
representatives' (1971: 264). Also note Taylor's statement, 'The term δοῦλος
Κυρίου is used of Moses (Jos. xiv. 7, Psa. civ. (cv.) 26), Joshua (Jos. xxiv. 29),
and David (2 Kgdms iii. 18), and then regularly of the prophets (Am. iii. 7, Zech. 1.
6, Jer. vii. 25, etc.)' (1966: 474).

ἀποστέλλω is used for sending. The alteration of ἀποστέλλω with πέμπω in Luke is to be explained by Luke's practice of substituting synonyms for Markan material, and is therefore not significant in terms of *Religionsgeschichte*. Probably, the ἀποστέλλω tradition is not as frequently highlighted in Luke because of its non-Jewish concerns. It is probable that the version of Thomas is the more original and that Mark may have had access to similar material.[34] The Coptic ⲭⲟ, 'to send forth', is probably a translation of the Hebrew/Aramaic root שׁלח. In any case, having discounted Luke's version, it is significant to note that sending is seen in terms of ἀποστέλλω and not πέμπω. Charlesworth has underscored the early origin of this parable in Jesus within Judaism, 'The details of the parable reflect Jesus' time, not Mark's or that of any writer after 66 CE, the beginning of the Great revolt against Rome and too early a date for the composition of Mark' (1988: 145). This parable also captures an important theme attached to the Old Testament sending tradition, namely, the rejection of God's emissary.

(3) Jesus' Lament over Jerusalem (Mt. 23.34-39; Lk. 11.49; 13.34-35). The theme of the rejection of the one sent by God is explicitly taken up in Matthew and Luke in these pericopes, probably from Q material. Its absence from Mark shows that the sending concept was widespread, and that its prominence in early Christianity was not only dependent on Mark. In both Matthew and Luke ἀποστέλλω is used. The addition of crucifixion in Matthew should be attributed to the church as it knew that Jesus was crucified and not stoned. The Lucan version, then, appears closest to that of Q. The Lucan form is significant in that it appears in the form of a saying, implying a long-standing tradition behind the words. Jesus' lament over Jerusalem also appears to be an original saying of Jesus, as shown by Charlesworth (1988: 143-45), and is therefore further evidence of a prophetic sending tradition current in Palestine at the time of Jesus.

The passages discussed above are the most important, demonstrating the existence of a prophetic sending concept with its roots in the Old Testament in early Christianity. However, there are still a number of passages in the Synoptic Gospels that relate to the sending concept of early Christianity. I shall now turn my attention to these.

---

34. See Mann's discussion in his commentary (1986: 458-63). See also J. Jeremias (1972: 70-77).

(4) The Syro-Phoenician Woman (Mt. 15.24; cf. 10.6).[35] In this passage Jesus' mission, in accordance with Matthew's overall purpose, is exclusively directed to the house of Israel. Here again the verb ἀποστέλλω is used. This Matthean passage should be understood against the Old Testament background which considers the Jews as the particular people of God (cf. Mt. 8.12).

(5) The Coming of the Son of Man (Mk 13.24-27; Mt. 24.29-31; cf. Mt. 13.41). These apocalyptic passages in the early Christian tradition also employ the verb ἀποστέλλω.[36] The non-Markan characteristics of the passage in Mark betray that the author is working with a distinct saying of early Christianity.[37] It is interesting to consider whether John knew this apocalyptic tradition 'he will send his angels' and transformed it to apply to the mission of the disciples at the present time, as 'angels' can also be 'messengers'?

(6) True Greatness (Mt. 10.40; Lk. 10.16; cf. Mk 9.37; Lk. 9.48). In this saying, probably from Q, Jesus refers to the Father as τὸν ἀποστείλαντά με, 'the one who sent me'. 'The disciples, therefore, speak and act in the name of Jesus, just as he speaks and acts in the name of the one who sent him' (Fitzmyer 1985: I, 857). This sounds very much like the Johannine Jesus, yet this expression is never found in John. In John the Father is always ὁ πέμψαντας με (cf. Jn 5.23; 12.44, 45; 13.20). Did John know this saying from Q and then deliberately change it?

(7) Jesus' Preaching at Nazareth (Lk. 4.18). In Luke Jesus' mission is interpreted at the outset in light of the messianic passage in Isa. 61.1-3.

(8) The Mission of the Disciples (Mk 6.7; 3.14; Mt. 10.5, 16; Lk. 9.2, 52; 10.1-3). Lastly, in the Synoptic Gospels Jesus sends his disciples on the mission to preach. In all these commissioning passages the verb ἀποστέλλω is used. In John both ἀποστέλλω and πέμπω are used in the commissioning of the disciples (cf. Jn 17.18; 20.21).

35. See Davies for a discussion on the origin of this logion (1991: 550-51).
36. Cf. Isa. 13.10; 24; 23; 34.4; Joel 3.4; 4.15; 4 Esd. 5.4; 1 En. 80.4-7; *T. Levi* 4.1; *Ass. Mos.* 10.5; *Sib. Or.* 3.976-77.
37. See Mann (1986: 531).

d. *Summary*

There is clear evidence from the materials that I have discussed that there was an early Christian tradition about God's sending of his prophet, and that this tradition stems from the Old Testament. This concept occurs frequently in the Synoptic Gospels. The Greek term used to convey this Old Testament concept of שלח was ἀποστέλλω. This concept may be summarized as follows: the prophet is sent, that is, authorized by God, to announce God's message or revelation; as such the prophet represents God in the fullest sense; those who reject the prophet reject God; those who accept the prophet accept God—more often than not, however, the prophet is rejected and suffers. The absence of πέμπω from this early tradition makes its frequent occurrence in John significant.

e. *The Gnostic Tradition*

It is the present study's contention that there was also a πέμπω tradition current in Palestine during the first century CE that was associated with the development of the Gnostic Redeemer myth.[38]

1. *A Gnostic Sending Tradition in Paul*

There are a number of differences between the sending concept of Rom. 8.3 and that of the Synoptic Gospels. The sending concept in the Synoptic Gospels stands squarely within the salvation history perspective of the Old Testament. Sending in the Synoptics is against the background of the Old Testament prophetic movement, and is situated in the context of rejection. The idea of *Heilsgeschichte* is prominent behind the Synoptic concept. The sending formula of Rom. 8.3, however, is akin to a Gnostic influence.[39] Here in Rom. 8.3 the orientation of the sending is ethical, and is set in the context of the incarnation, that is, the descent of the Redeemer. The context is no longer that of *Heilsgeschichte*, but that of the radical difference between the old and the new. Though Paul's emphasis here falls on the salvific act of the crucifixion, the πέμπω statement still refers to the incarnation of the pre-existent Son (Käsemann 1980: 217). The pre-existent Christology

---

38. On the existence of a Gnostic Redeemer Myth see Bultmann (1925), Haenchen (1952), Adam (1959), Rudolph (1983, 56-57), and Schnackenburg (1990: I, 544-48) .

39. For Paul under Gnostic influence see Schmithals (1972; 1978: 385); also see Pagels (1975).

of Paul has its root in the early Gnostic idea of the pre-existent Redeemer from above.[40] As further investigation will point out, this verse betrays a Gnostic tradition of sending.

Paul's statement in Gal. 4.4 where ἐξ-απόστελλω is used, recalls the Jewish expectation of the Messiah at the appropriate time. Paul is evidently familiar with the Synoptic sending tradition. However, Burton is probably right when he says that this verse has to 'be interpreted as having reference to the sending of the Son from his pre-existent state (ἐν μορφῇ θεοῦ, Phil. 2.6) into the world' (1975: 217). We see here then a combination of different sending traditions in Paul.

2. *Gnosticism*

(a) *Irenaeus.* Irenaeus's description of Menander, Simon's successor, in *Adversus haereses* (1.23.5) makes an interesting contribution to our discussion:

> Simon's successor was Menander, a Samaritan who also attained the pinnacle of magic art. He said that the First Power was known to none. *He himself was the man sent down as Redeemer by the invisible (Aeons) for the salvation of men.* The world was made by the angels which in his doctrine, as in Simon's, were emitted by Ennoia (Thought). Through the magic taught by him, he transmits the knowledge of how to overcome the angels who created the world. Through their baptism unto him, his disciples receive (the gift of) resurrection, and therefore can no longer die; and do not age, but remain immortal.[41]

In Irenaeus's summary of Menander's teaching the latter regarded himself as being sent down as Redeemer. Assuming that the above passage is an accurate summary of Menander's teaching, it appears that the idea of 'being sent' occupied an important place in Menander's teaching. It is also possible that as Simon's successor, he is echoing a view of Simon himself. Assuming the reliability of Irenaeus's record, this is the earliest indication extant for the existence of a Gnostic sending tradition. Where this Gnostic sending tradition originated, either in Greek or Oriental thought, is not of concern for the present study. Suffice it to say that Irenaeus's reference is evidence that a Gnostic sending tradition existed around Palestine, and more particularly in Samaria and Antioch, during the first century.[42]

---

40. See Schmithals (1978: 402-406).

41. The italics are mine.

42. The traditional location for Simon's activity is Samaria, and for Menander's, Antioch.

It is unfortunate that the Greek of this passage has not survived. However, a good case can still be made that the Greek word here used for sent was πέμπω and not ἀποστέλλω, since the verb πέμπω is often used (eight times) in *Adversus haereses*,[43] κατά-πέμπω occurs in 33.4, whereas ἀποστέλλω does not occur in the extant Greek sources. Therefore, it may be concluded that πέμπω, or probably κατά-πέμπω, was used in refering to Menander as being sent down as Redeemer.

Irenaeus's description of Menander's teaching has other important similarities to John, which argues strongly that John's πέμπω concept has its origin in Gnosticism: the dualism behind being 'sent down'; the emphasis on knowledge for salvation; and the presence of a realizing eschatology, that is, the disciples already receive the resurrection life. It may also be noted that Menander is chronologically closer to John than Simon. Later I shall return again to these points.

(b) *The Hermetic Writings.* The *Hermetica* is the body of literature that was composed around the second century in Egypt and ascribed to Hermes Trismegistus.[44] We find that in this body of Gnostic literature πέμπω is the term used to describe the idea of sending. In the *Corpus Hermeticum* πέμπω is used in the sense of 'to offer' speech or praise (Lib. 3.21; cf. Scott 1968: I, 252). However, the compound κατα-πέμπω is more frequent and is used for the sending motif. It is used to describe the Creator's (δημιουργός) sending of the original man to earth at creation:

> κόσμον δὲ θείου σώματος κατέπεμψε τὸν ἄνθρωπον—'(for) an orna-
> ment of the divine body (i.e. the earth) he sent down the man'[45] (cf. Lib.
> 4.2; Scott 1968: I, 150).[46]

43. Cf. 1.53.54; 9.86; 10.20; 18.77.82; 24.17; 30.216; 33.4.

44. 'That the literature arose in Egypt is commonly accepted' (Grese 1979: 35). However, there is a variety of scholarly opinion as to when the *Hermetica* were written. The question is complicated in that the material was written over a long period of time. Petrie dates the literature between 500–200 BCE (1908: I, 195-98). Scott's view that most of the *Hermetica* were written in the third century seems too late (1968: I, 10). According to Koester, 'Most of the tractates were probably written in second century CE by different authors, whose religious and philosophical position varies' (1987: 389).

45. The following translations are my own.

46. Grese says, 'The word κατέπεμψε shows that the writer holds the Platonic doctrine that human souls existed ἄνω before they were embodied on earth' (1979: 138).

The term is also used to describe God's sending of mind (νοῦς) to the earth. According to the writer God imparted speech to all men but not mind. In order to become complete, man has to recognize the purpose for which he was made, and believe that he will ascend to the one who sent the basin (filled with mind) down to the earth. It is important to note that the Gnostic is to believe that God sent down the basin:

> Κρατῆρα μέγαν πληρώσας τούτου κατέπεμψε—'Having filled a great basin, he sent it down' (cf. Lib. 4.4; Scott 1968: I, 150).

> ‹καὶ› [ἡ] πιστεύουσα ὅτι ἀνελεύσῃ πρὸς τὸν καταπέμψαντα τὸν κρατῆρα[47]—'and the one believing (fem.) that you will ascend (fut. mid.) to the one who sent the basin down' (cf. Lib. 4.4; Scott 1968: I, 150).

Believing that God sent Jesus is an important emphasis in John. It is also important here to note that God is the ὁ καταπέμψαντας τὸν κρατῆρα, that is, God is identified by the articular participle of πέμπω. Again, in John the Father is frequently refered to as ὁ πέμψας με.

The compound ἀνα-πέμπω occurs in a passage concerning astrology:

> ὅσον ἀναπέμπει ἐκ τοῦ θατέπου μένους τοῦ πρὸς οὐρανὸν βλέποντος —'that is, he sends up [light] from the part of . . . that [is] facing toward heaven' (cf. Lib. 16.8; Scott 1968: I, 266).

God controls the heavenly bodies with light he sends upwards. Since this is an astrological passage, it is not important for the present study.

The participle καταπεμπομένη and verb καταπέμπονται occur in the *Anthologium of Stobaeus*. The author here is discussing the origin of the kingly souls (βασιλικαὶ ψυχαί). The souls of the kingly ones were sent from a higher place than the souls who are in other men:

> ἡ γὰρ εἰς αὐτὸν καταπεμπομένη ψυχή [ἐξ ἐκείνου] ἐστι ‹ν ἐκ› [τοῦ] χωρίου ὃ ὑπεράνω κεῖται ἐκείνων ἀφ' ὧν εἰς τοὺς ἄλλους καταπέμπονται ἀνθρώπους—'for the soul being sent down into him from him, is from the region that lies far above those regions from where [souls] are being sent down into other men' (Exc. 24.3; cf. Scott 1968: I, 496).

> καταπέμπονται δὲ ἐκειθεν εἰς τὸ βασιλεύειν διὰ δύο ταῦτα αἱ ψυχαί—'And the souls are sent there to reign for these two reasons' (Exc. 24.4; cf. Scott 1968: I, 496).

---

47. The repetition of τὸν κρατῆρα is redundant here according to Scott (1968: II, 143), but I prefer to hold to the text as the awkward reading is usually to be preferred.

Here the divisions of the upper zones are discussed. The souls which are sent down from the highest regions are the kingly souls, and when the body dies they return (ἀνέρχονται) to the same zones, or even to a place yet higher. It is possible for these souls to do something contrary to their own nature and transgress God's commandment. They are banished to the lower regions:

> αἱ μὲν οὖν τὸ ἄρχειν καταπεμπόμεναι, ὦ τέκνων˙Ὤρω, ἐκ τῶν ὑπεράνω ζωνῶν καταπέμπονται·—'Those souls then being sent down to rule, O my son Horus, are sent from the highest zones...' (Exc. 26.2; cf. Scott 1968: I, 514).

The verb ἐξεπέμπετο occurs in Lib. 1.4, meaning 'to come forth' (cf. Scott 1968: I, 114). We may point out that the verb ἀποστέλλω does not occur in the *Hermetica*.

Therefore, in the *Hermetica* πέμπω, or κατα-πέμπω, is used in a dualistic framework. The term is used to describe descent of the soul to the earth and the journey of the soul to ultimate salvation. God is also identified in terms of πέμπω with the participial expression τὸν καταπέμψαντα τὸν κρατῆρα. It is significant that πέμπω is used throughout and not ἀποστέλλω. The more elaborate metaphysical system built around the use of πέμπω reflects the earlier Gnostic tradition of the Redeemer sent down by God for the salvation of men, which we saw in Ireneaus. The *Hermetica* provided evidence for the importance of the sending motif in Gnosticism and that the verb πέμπω, with its compounds, was used to describe the sending motif in Greek.[48]

(c) *The Nag Hammadi Library*. The discovery of the Nag Hammadi Library in Upper Egypt has made an important contribution to Johannine studies. However, the Nag Hammadi library has not influenced Johannine research to the same extent as the Dead Sea Scrolls have. By and large, the Nag Hammadi material has been neglected in Johannine research.[49]

In this section I shall examine the concept of sending found in the Nag Hammadi library. I shall only concern myself with documents of

48. The identification of Hermes in terms of ἀποστέλλω in Cornutus (cf. Lang 1981: 20) is a second-hand description and is not true to the material itself (Schweizer 1966: 199).

49. See Kysar, 'Recent scholarship has seen notice given that the Coptic gnostic materials must be studied and compared carefully...' (1975: 145).

the first and second century that have a proximity to John. In other words I shall focus on the Christian Gnostic documents of the first and second centuries from the library.

1. *The Gospel of Thomas.* The *Gospel of Thomas* does not belong to the same category as the other documents that I shall discuss. It is earlier and though it has a Gnostic tone it is closer in character to the Synoptic Gospels. The word xooⲩ, meaning 'to send forth', occurs in NHC II,2 45,4.10.11 (i.e. in The Parable of Wicked Vine-dressers), to which I have already referred (cf. Layton 1989: 79).

2. *Sophia of Jesus Christ.* The *Sophia of Jesus Christ* is based on an earlier document, *Eugnostos the Blessed*, which, according to Parrott, 'cannot be considered gnostic in any classic sense' (1990: 221). The *Sophia of Jesus Christ* can therefore be considered as a Gnosticization of of an earlier philosophical text. It is interesting that the concept of sending does not occur in *Eugnostos the Blessed*, but is quite prevalent in Sophia. This again argues that the sending concept occupied an important place in Gnosticism. The verb ⲧⲛ̄ⲛⲟⲟⲩ, meaning 'to send' is used seven times in Sophia.

> 'But to you it is given to know; and whoever is worthy of knowledge will receive (it), whoever has not been begotten by the sowing of unclean rubbing but by First Who Was Sent (ⲁⲗⲗⲁ ϩⲛ ⲡⲉ2ⲟⲏ ⲉⲓⲧ ⲉ‹ⲧ›ⲁⲩⲧⲛ̄ⲛⲟⲟⲩ̄ⲍ), for he is an immortal in the midst of mortal men' (NHC III, 4 93, 16-24; cf. Parrott 1991: 49).

In this verse the origin of the true Gnostic is described. Those who attain to knowledge were begotten by the One Who Was Sent, that is, the Saviour. Here 'send' is used in a technical sense for the Saviour. The same usage occurs in John.

> '... that through that immortal man they might attain their salvation and awake from forgetfulness through the interpreter who was sent (2ⲓⲧⲛ̄ ⲑⲉⲣⲙⲏⲛⲉⲩⲧⲏⲥ [ἑρμήνευτής] ⲛ̄ⲧⲁⲩⲧⲛ̄ⲛⲟⲟⲏϥ), who is with you until the end of the poverty of the robbers' (NHC III, 4 101,9-15; cf. Parrott 1991: 87).

In this verse the Gnostic might attain salvation through the Immortal Man (i.e. God), and awake from forgetfulness through the interpreter who was sent. The revealer is identified with the expression 'the one who was sent'.

'All who come into the world, like a drop of light, are sent by him to the world of Almighty (Almighty is the god of this world), that they may be guarded by him (ⲉⲃⲟⲗ ϩⲓⲧⲟⲟ̄ϥ ⲙ̄ⲡⲁⲓ̈ ⲉⲩⲧⲛ̄ⲛⲟⲟⲩ ⲙ̄ⲙⲟⲟⲩ ⲉⲡⲕⲟⲥⲙⲟⲥ [κόσμος] ⲙ̄ⲡⲡⲁⲛ ⲧⲟⲕⲡⲁⲧⲱⲡ)' (NHC III, 4 106, 24-107, 4; Parrott 1991: 129).

Here the Gnostic has come from the invisible world to this world by being sent by 'Saviour' or 'Sophia' (i.e. Seth). Being guarded (Sophia, Seth) is also a Johannine theme (cf. Jn 6.38; 10.28-29). We see here that not only the Saviour is sent down to this world, but also that the Gnostic is sent to this world. This verse emphasizes the different origin of the Gnostic, that is, the Gnostic is not of this world.

'I have wakened that drop that was sent from Sophia, that it might bear much fruit (ⲁⲉⲓⲧⲟⲏⲏⲟⲥϥ̄ ⲝⲉⲕⲁⲁⲥ ⲉϥⲛⲁⲧ ⲕⲁⲣⲡⲟⲥ [καρπός]' (NHC III, 4 107,15-19; cf. Parrott 1991: 133).

Here Jesus (the Great Saviour) has awakened the drop that was sent from Sophia. The Gnostic is again seen as being sent by Sophia.

'And you were sent by the Son, who was sent that you might receive Light and remove yourselves from the forgetfulness of the authorities (ⲁⲉ ⲛ̄ⲧⲁⲩⲧⲛ̄ⲛⲟⲟⲩ ⲧ ϩⲟⲩⲧⲛ̄ ϩⲓⲧⲙ̄ ⲡϣⲏⲣⲉ ⲛ̄ⲧⲁ ⲏⲧⲛ̄ⲛⲟⲟⲩϥ)' (NHC III, 4 108, 4-11; cf. Parrott 1991: 135).

Both the Son and the Gnostic can be described as 'being sent'. This language has remarkable similarity to the language of the Fourth Gospel. We find this same paradigm in John. It is probable that John has influenced Sophia, rather than that the Sophia has influenced John.[50] Here the Gnostics were sent in order to receive light, which is a symbol of salvation. In John too, the disciples' sending is an integral part of experiencing eternal life. I shall later again return to these points.

'I came from First Who Was Sent (ⲛⲧⲁⲩⲧⲛ̄ⲛⲟⲟⲩϥ), that I might reveal to you Him who is from the beginning' (NHC III, 4 118, 16-19; cf. Parrott 1991: 176).

Here Christ came, was sent, to reveal Him who is from the beginning.

---

50. Which document has priority does not matter for our present concern. I just want to show that there was a Gnostic sending concept. That this concept began to develop before John can be seen in Menander, and so on. John may have played a part in this development.

3. *Apocryphon of John*. The *Apocryphon of John* is an important document for understanding Gnostic thought, especially Valentinian Gnosticism. '*The Apocryphon of John* in its present form, it is certain that the main teachings of the tractate existed before 185 CE, the date of Irenaeus' work *Against Heresies*.' (Wisse 1990: 104). In this document Christ is sent down to save the world by reminding people of their origin (Wisse 1990: 104). The concept of sending is therefore prominent:

> '...why was he sent into the world... And who is his father who sent him, and of what sort is that aeon to which we shall go? (ⲁⲩⲱ ⲭⲉ ⲉⲧⲃⲉ ⲟⲩ ⲁⲩⲧⲛ̄ⲛⲟⲩⲋ ⲉⲡⲕⲟⲥⲙⲟⲥ [κόσμος] ⲉⲃⲟⲗ ϩⲓⲧⲛ̄ [ⲡⲉⲋⲉⲓⲱⲧ ⲁⲩⲱ ⲛⲓⲙ ⲡⲉ ⲡⲉⲋⲉⲓⲱ]ⲧ ⲉⲧⲁ[ⲋⲧⲛ̄ⲛⲟⲩⲋ])' (NHC II, 1 47,22; cf. Giversen 1963: 46-47).[51]

Here Christ was sent into the world, and the Father is described as the one who sent him. John uses exactly the same language.

> 'He did not send them any of that power of light which he had received from his mother' (NHC II, 1 59, 8-9; cf. Giversen 1963: 66-67).

Here sending occurs in an ethical context. Ialtabaoth installs rulers but does not give them any of the power he inherited from his mother.

> 'And he sent (ⲁⲋⲧⲛ̄ⲛⲟⲟⲏ ⲉⲃⲟⲗ ϩⲓⲧⲛ̄ ⲡⲉⲋⲡⲛ̄ⲁ̄ [πνεῦμα]) out from his spirit which is beneficent and rich in his grace a helper to Adam, an Epinoia of light which is from him' (NHC II, 1 68,14-18; cf. Giversen 1963: 84-85).

In the *Apocryphon of John* the Saviour's mission is seen in terms of sending. Both Christ and the Father are described in terms of sending.

4. *The Gospel of Truth*. This document also belongs to the Valentinian school of Gnosticism, dating from the middle of the second century CE (Attridge and MacRae 1990: 38). The document refers to the sending concept in *Gos. Thom.* 41.24-27: '...For the place to which they send their thought, that place, their root, is what takes them up in all the heights to the Father' (cf. Attridge 1985: 114-15). Attridge says that, 'The soteriological process envisioned here is described in detail at *Tri. Trac.* 77.37-78.7 and 78.23-28, where the paradigmatic experience of the Logos is recounted' (1985: 131). In this passage salvation is again set in the context of an ethical dualism.

---

51. This passage has largely been reconstructed.

5. *Dialogue of the Saviour.* This document is a complex compilation of various traditions which may go back as early as the end of the first century (Koester and Pagels 1990: 244). Koester and Pagels observed that 'The form of these brief dialogue units parallels the dialogues found in the Gospel of John' (1990: 244). There is also a reference to Jn 1.18 in the opening section. For Koester and Pagels this document 'resembles the Gospel of John in its attempt to reinterpret the sayings of Jesus in the horizon of gnostic thought' (1990: 246). Sending is mentioned in this document:

> 'And the Greatness remembered it and he sent the Word to it. It brought it up into his presence (ⲁϥⲧⲛ̄ⲛⲟⲟⲏ ⲙ̄ⲡⲗⲟ[ⲅⲟⲥ {λόγος} ϣⲁ]ⲣⲟⲥ ⲁϥⲉⲓⲛⲉ ⲙ̄ⲙⲟϥ ⲉ2ⲣⲁⲓ̈ⲛ̄)' (NHC III, 5 135, 21-22; cf. Emmel 1984: 70-71).

This is a rare yet significant reference to the Word (λόγος) being sent down by God. Before, the Word is identified with the 'Son of Man'. He was sent down to save a seed that was deficient. The term also occurs elsewhere (NHC III, 5 126,5; cf. Emmel 1984: 52), but the passage is not well preserved.

6. *The Apocryphon of James.* This document, originally in Greek, dates back to the beginning of the second century (Williams 1990: 29-30). It also resembles the dialogues of the Fourth Gospel, and contains similar themes. In the opening passage it is repeatedly stated that James sent a book to the addressee:

> '...you asked that I send you a secret book which was revealed to me (ⲁⲧⲣⲁⲧⲛ̄ⲛⲁⲩ ⲛⲉⲕ ⲛ̄ⲟⲩ-ⲁⲡⲟⲕⲣⲩ̄ⲫⲟ(ⲛ) [ἀπόκρυφον])' (NHC I, 2 1, 9-11; cf. Attridge 1985: 28-29).[52]

> 'I also sent you, ten months ago, another secret book which the saviour had revealed to me (ⲁ2ⲓ̈ⲧⲛ̄ⲛⲁⲩ ⲁⲉ ϣⲁⲡⲁⲕ 2ⲁⲑⲏ ⲙ̄ⲙⲏⲧ ⲛ̄ⲉⲃⲁⲧ· ⲛ̄ⲕⲉ-ⲁⲡⲟⲕⲣⲩ̄ⲫⲟⲛ [ἀπόκρυφον])' (NHC I, 2 1, 29-32; cf. Attridge 1985: 28-29).

> 'I have written it in the Hebrew alphabet and sent it to you (ⲙⲙⲛ̄ⲧ2ⲉⲃⲣⲁⲓⲟⲓⲥ [ἑβραῖος] ⲁⲛⲓ̈ⲧⲛ̄ⲛⲁⲟⲩ̄ⲫ ⲛⲉⲕ), you alone...' (NHC I, 2 1, 15-17; cf. Attridge 1985: 28-29).

The following reference is more important:

> 'Verily I say unto you, had I been sent to those who listen to me, and had I spoken with them, I would never have come down to earth (†ⲭⲟⲩ

---

52. Attridge says, 'This is a common epistolary formula' (1985: 7).

ⲙ̄ⲙⲁⳉ ⲛ̄ⲏⲧⲛ̄ ⲭⲉ ⲉⲛⲉⲛⲧⲁⳉⲟⳋⲧ̄ⲡ̄ⲛⲁⲟⳋⲧ)' (NHC I, 2 10, 14-20; cf. Attridge 1985: 42-43).

The Lord's sending is set in a dualistic context, 'had I been sent... I would never have come down to earth.' Attridge thinks that the author is criticizing orthodox Christians at this point (1985: 25).

Again in the following passage the dualistic context stands out:

> 'Woe to those for whose sakes I was sent down (ⲛ̄[ⲧⲁ]ⳉⲟⳋⲧ̄ⲡ̄ⲛⲁⲟⳋⲧ) to this place; blessed will they be who ascend to the Father!' (NHC I, 2 13, 9-11; cf. Attridge 1985: 48-49).

7. *The Tripartite Tractate.* The *Tripartite Tractate* dates probably from the third century and may be a response to the criticism of ortho-dox theologians (Attridge and Pagels 1990: 58). The work appears to be a revision of traditional Valentinianism.

> 'The creator also sent down souls from his substance' (ⲡⲉⲧⲁⳋⲙⲓϭⲉ ⲙ̄ⲙⲁϥ ⲁϥⲧⲛ̄ⲛⲟⲟⲏ ⳉⲱⲱϥ ⲁⲏ ⲁⲡⲓⲧⲛ̄ ⲛ̄ϭⲓ ⲡⲓⲡⲉϥϭⲱⲛⲧ) (NHC I, 5 105, 35-37; cf. Attridge 1985: 284-85).

This passage is an interpretation of Gen. 1-3. The soul of the first human being emanates from the Father.

> '... when he (the Saviour) was sent (ⲓ ⲛ̄ⲛⲟⲟⲏϥ) as a service to them, they received, in fact, the essence of their being' (NHC I, 5 120, 13 14; cf. Attridge 1985: 308-309).

Here the Saviour is described as being sent.

From the above analysis it is clear that sending plays an important role in the teaching of the second-century Gnostic documents of the Nag Hammadi Library. In the sending concept of Nag Hammadi dual-ism plays an important role: the Saviour was sent down to the earth. At times this dualism also takes on an ethical dimension. The Gnostics are described as those who are sent from above to identify their ori-gin, that is, they are aliens in this world. They are also sent by the Saviour. Sending is consequently used as a technical expression to identify the Saviour and the Gnostic. Lastly, it is important to note that the Nag Hammadi sending concept occurs in dialogues similar to that of John.

At this point I am not arguing that John was influenced by the Nag Hammadi sending concept or that John influenced the Nag Hammadi documents. My aim is to show the existence of a Gnostic sending con-cept during the first and second centuries CE that is different from that of early Christianity as represented in the Synoptic Gospels.

(d) *The Hymn of the Pearl.*[53] The original language of the hymn is probably Syriac. In this brief survey therefore, I shall concentrate on the Syriac text. The hymn dates from the second century CE, and is probably a reflection of the Bardaisan Gnostic tradition, though it almost certainly reflects earlier tradition. The Hymn describes the descent and ascent of the soul in terms of a nobleman's son who is sent to Egypt (the symbol of evil) to recover a pearl. The importance of this document for early Gnostic thought is well brought out by Filoramo:

> Symbolic of the wanderings of the soul lost in worldly pleasures and forgetful of its divine origin, the story has often been interpreted as a poetic model of that process of Gnosis fundamental to gnostic myths, based on the word of a divine messenger, whose task is to reawaken in the Gnostic the memory of his origin and thus to communicate the true Gnosis to him (1990: 8).

Sending (ܫܕܪ) features prominently in the hymn. After having being equipped, the parents send the son:

ܗܢܘ ܐܒܗܝ̈ ܟܕ ܫܕܪܘܢܝ—'My parents, having equipped me, sent me forth' (3b; cf. Poirier 1981: 329).

The reader is constantly reminded of the origin or purpose of the son's journey by the following phrases:

ܕܠܗ ܐܒܗܝ̈ ܫܕܪܘܢܝ (οἱ πατέρες μου ἀπεστάλκασίν με)—'For which my parents had sent me' (34b; cf. Poirier 1981: 331).

ܕܠܗ ܠܡܨܪܝܢ ܐܬܫܕܪܬ (κατεπέμφθην εἰς Αἴγυπτον·)—'For which I had been sent to Egypt' (57b; cf. Poirier 1981: 333).

ܠܬܡܢ ܐܒܗܝ̈ ܫܕܪܘܢܝ—'My parents sent thither' (73b; cf. Poirier 1981: 334). And again in 99b: ܘܡܢ [ܕܠܗ] ܕܐܟܪܙ ܗܘܐ ܠܝ ܫܕܪܬ (τοῦ ἀποστείλαντός μοι ταύτην)—'who had sent me to it' (cf. Poirier 1981: 336).

The Greek text contains extra references to sending:

εἰς Αἴγυπτον ἀπεστάλης—'which you sent to Egypt' (45; cf. Poirier 1981: 354).

κινήσεις ἐξεπέμποντο γνώσεως—'the motions of knowledge were stirring' (88; cf. Poirier 1981: 355).

---

53. The *Hymn of the Pearl* is found in *The Acts of Thomas* (108-13), though originally it was not part of The Acts. The Hymn of the Pearl is preserved in both Syriac and Greek texts. See Bornkamm (1933) and Poirier (1981).

σὺν αὐτῷ ἀποσταλεῖσθαι—'with him I should be sent' (104; cf. Poirier 1981: 356).

The Greek translator used both ἀποστέλλω and πέμπω, with ἀποστέλλω used more often.[54] The two terms are used interchangeably, and both translate the same Syriac word, ⲧⲗⲝ. It appears that on one occasion the translator uses the terms synonymously (57b). The date of the Greek translation is considerably later (third century) than the composition of the original and is therefore not very relevant for the present study. The translator may not have been familiar with the Gnostic πέμπω tradition. Most probably the early Gnostic sending tradition had already been merged with the term used for the Jewish Old Testament sending tradition.

(c) *Mandaeism and Manichaeism.* In his important article that appeared in the 1920s, Bultmann argued that the Redeemer figure of the Fourth Gospel can best be understood against the background of the Gnostic Redeemer myth (1925). Bultmann proceeded to use Mandaean and Manichaean sources to reconstruct that myth under 28 points. His second point is that the Redeemer had been sent by the Father into the world and numerous Mandaean and Manichaean references are listed to support the thesis. Bultmann's analysis is exhaustive and impressive and provides clear evidence of the Gnostic concept of sending in Mandaean and Manichaean sources, but since Bultmann's sources appear to be too late I shall ignore them for the present discussion.

f. *Summary*

There is evidence that two distinct sending traditions existed around Palestine during the first century, and that these belonged to Judaism and Gnosticism respectively. The sending concept of early Christianity, as represented in the Synoptic Gospels, belonged to that of Judaism, and can be described as the prophetic sending tradition which stems from the Old Testament. In the Synoptic Gospels this concept uses the term ἀποστέλλω. The ἀποστέλλω concept describes the sending of God's emissary which often results in the rejection and suffering of the emissary; this sending takes place in a historical perspective. On

---

54. The word ⲧⲗⲝ occurs five times in the Syriac text. In the Greek text ἀποστέλλω occurs five times, and πέμπω occurs twice.

the other hand, my investigation shows the existence of a Gnostic sending concept, which differs from the prophetic sending concept. The Gnostic sending concept describes the ascent or descent of a Redeemer figure, and is seen in a dualistic, or sometimes in an ethical, perspective. The Saviour is sent down to rescue the true Gnostics, or to awake in them the knowledge of their origin. There is evidence that the word πέμπω was used to describe this concept in Greek. It should be noted that I have argued for the existence of a Gnostic sending tradition not only on the basis of the occurrence of πέμπω, as distinct from ἀποστέλλω, in Gnostic literature, but also on the basis of the different concept based on that term in comparison with ἀποστέλλω. I have also noted that the ἀποστέλλω tradition, that is, the prophetic sending concept, is much older than the πέμπω tradition—the Gnostic sending concept, which only appears in the first century.

It is not probable that John conceived the Gnostic sending tradition described above, since it already appears in Paul (cf. Rom. 8.3). Also, the teaching of Simon and Menander, which included the Gnostic concept of sending, is before John. Furthermore, we find the Gnostic sending tradition in documents from a wide variety of locations, from Egypt, across Palestine, to Syria. Lastly, I want to make the observation that a well-defined sending concept does not play an important role in the Dead Sea Scrolls and the *Odes of Solomon*.

4. *The Sending Concept in John*

a. *Common Patterns*

As I have already mentioned, the two main terms that John uses with respect to the concept of sending are ἀποστέλλω (28 times) and πέμπω (32 times). An important question is whether or not these terms are synonymous or distinct. There has been a view that these terms are used interchangeably in John and therefore are synonymous. I want to argue, however, that this is not entirely correct. The two terms represent distinct sending traditions whose origins lie in the Old Testament prophetic tradition and the Gnostic Redeemer tradition respectively. When we look carefully how John uses these terms we shall find that some interesting patterns emerge. If the two terms tend to occur within particular expressions, it would seem to indicate that they are not synonymous but have developed in different contexts. We do find that there are some patterns distinct to each term, which argues that these terms are not synonymous and may have different meanings reflecting different traditions.[55]

1. *The* ἀποστέλλω—εἰς τὸν κόσμον *pattern.* ἀποστέλλω is the term used to describe Jesus' sending into the world, and also the sending of the disciples into the world. The verb with the object εἰς τὸν κόσμον indicates the place to which Jesus and the disciples are sent (Bauer 1952: 98). The full force of the preposition εἰς should be maintained in view of John's dualism of above and below. Jesus is commissioned and sent *into* the sphere of this world. God (ὁ θεός) is the one who sent Jesus into the world. And Jesus is the one who sent the disciples into the world. Here 'ἀποστέλλω denotes commissioning and authority from God' (Bühner 1990: 14), or Jesus vis-à-vis the disciples. The verb is always in the aorist tense, and should be understood as a historical or comprehensive aorist. Jesus' whole missionary activity is here viewed in terms of a single fact without reference to its progress (Burton 1976: 19-20).

3.17   οὐ γὰρ ἀπέστειλεν ὁ θεὸς τὸν υἱὸν εἰς τὸν κόσμον
10.36   ὃν ὁ πατὴρ ἡγίασεν καὶ ἀπέστειλεν εἰς τὸν κόσμον
17.18   καθὼς ἐμὲ ἀπέστειλας εἰς τὸν κόσμον, κἀγὼ ἀπέστειλα
        αὐτοὺς εἰς τὸν κόσμον·

2. *The* πιστεύω— ἀποστέλλω *pattern.* ἀποστέλλω is often used in connection with believing (πιστεύω). The disciples should believe that God sent (ἀπέστειλεν) Jesus. The emphasis here again is to recognize that Jesus was commissioned by God, and did not come of his own volition. In this context ἀποστέλλω is used in parallelism with γινώσκω:

6.29   ἵνα πιστεύητε εἰς ὃν ἀπέστειλεν ἐκεῖνος
11.42   ἵνα πιστεύσωσιν ὅτι σύ με ἀπέστειλας
17.3   ἵνα γινώσκωσίν σε... καὶ ὃν ἀπέστειλας Ἰησοῦν Χριστόν
17.8   ἐπίστευσαν ὅτι σύ με ἀπέστειλας
17.21   ἵνα ὁ κόσμος πιστεύῃ ὅτι σύ με ἀπέστειλας
17.23   ἵνα γινώσκῃ ὁ κόσμος ὅτι σύ με ἀπέστειλας
17.25   οὗτοι ἔγνωσαν ὅτι σύ με ἀπέστειλας

55. Tarelli's suggestion, that John's usage of these terms depends not on different meanings, but simply on his preference for using particular verbs with certain grammatical forms (1946), has been correctly criticized by Mercer, in that grammatical forms are 'simply ways to express particular meanings' (1990: 620).

However, πέμπω also occurs on one occasion:

5.24   ὁ ... πιστεύων τῷ πέμψαντί με ἔχει ζωὴν αἰώνιον

Yet, the frequency of the connection between πιστεύω and ἀποστέλλω would still argue that it represents a distinct religious milieu. The reference in Jn 5.24 could be an alteration of the tradition for the sake of consistency. Just before, in Jn 5.23, the Father is referred to as τὸν πέμψαντα αὐτόν. But as I have noted before, there is a connection between πιστεύω and πέμπω in the *Hermetica*.

3. *The πέμπω—θέλημα pattern*. In connection with θέλημα, πέμπω is used. Jesus must do the will of the one who sent him (τοῦ πέμψαντός με):

4.34   ἵνα ποιήσω τὸ θέλημα τοῦ πέμψαντός με
5.30   ἀλλὰ τὸ θέλημα τοῦ πέμψαντός με
6.38   ἀλλὰ τὸ θέλημα τοῦ πέμψαντός με
6.39   τοῦτο δέ ἐστιν τὸ θέλημα τοῦ πέμψαντός με

4. *The ὁ πέμψας με pattern*. The Father is frequently referred to by Jesus as 'the one who sent me', ὁ πέμψας με. The Father is never described as ὁ ἀποστείλας με, though the expression occurs in Mt. 10.40. This fact argues that the expression ὁ πέμψας με was fixed and used as a technical term to refer to the Father in the community where it originated. If there is no distinct tradition behind this usage of πέμπω, it is difficult to explain why the Father is never ὁ ἀποστείλας με, especially when we consider the frequency of the expression, ὁ πέμψας με:

1.33   ὁ πέμψας με βαπτίζειν ἐν ὕδατι
4.34   ἵνα ποιήσω τὸ θέλημα τοῦ πέμψαντός με
5.23   οὐ τιμᾷ τὸν πατέρα τὸν πέμψαντα αὐτόν
5.24   ὁ... πιστεύων τῷ πέμψαντι με ἔχει ζωὴν αἰώνιον
5.30   ἀλλὰ τὸ θέλημα τοῦ πέμψαντός με
5.37   ὁ πέμψας με πατήρ, ἐκεῖνος μεμαρτύρηκεν περὶ ἐμοῦ
6.38   ἀλλὰ τὸ θέλημα τοῦ πέμψαντός με
6.39   τοῦτο δέ ἐστιν τὸ θέλημα τοῦ πέμψαντός με
6.44   ἐὰν μὴ ὁ πατὴρ ὁ πέμψας με ἑλκύσῃ αὐτόν
7.16   ἀλλὰ τοῦ πέμψαντός με
7.18   τὴν δόξαν τοῦ πέμψαντος αὐτόν
7.28   ὁ πέμψας με
7.33   τὸν πέμψαντά με
8.16   ὁ πέμψας με πατήρ

8.18	ὁ πέμψας με πατήρ
8.26	ὁ πέμψας με
8.29	ὁ πέμψας με
9.4	τοῦ πέμψαντός με
12.44	τὸν πέμψαντά με
12.45	τὸν πέμψαντά με
12.49	ὁ πέμψας με πατὴρ
13.16	τοῦ πέμψαντος αὐτόν
13.20	τινα πέμψω ἐμὲ ... τὸν πέμψαντά με
14.24	τοῦ πέμψαντός με πατρός
14.26	ὃ πέμψει ὁ πατὴρ
15.21	τὸν πέμψαντά με
16.5	τὸν πέμψαντά με

The four patterns that I have isolated above show that the two terms ἀποστέλλω and πέμπω are not used randomly in the Fourth Gospel. There are specific contexts in which only one of these terms occurs. Therefore, it is misleading to say that John uses ἀποστέλλω and πέμπω interchangeably. At times this may happen, but not always. Therefore, to understand the sending concept of John we do need to distinguish between the traditions represented by ἀποστέλλω and πέμπω respectively. By the time of the final redaction of the Gospel these separate traditions have been merged, yet they are still evident in the Gospel.

b. *'Sending' and the Origin of Jesus*
John's concept of sending is used to stress the place of Jesus' origin. The Gospel emphasizes that Jesus comes from above. It is in this context that his equality with the Father is to be understood: Jesus belongs to the same category as the Father. In other words, the sending concept is used to identify Jesus. It answers the question, 'Who is Jesus?'

1. *The Formula* ὁ πέμψας με. The articular participial construction with the first-person pronoun, ὁ πέμψας με, occurs not less than 24 times in John. In all cases the reference is to the Father. And in all cases but one (i.e. Jn 1.33), the expression is on the lips of Jesus. In the majority of cases the expression occurs in the revelatory discourses of Jesus when he is making an apology in confrontation with the Jews. This may indicate the possible origin of the use of the expression within the Johannine community.

In four instances Jesus comes to do the will (θέλημα) of τοῦ πέμψαντός με (Jn 4.34; 5.30; 6.38, 39). In Jn 4.34 the disciples urge him to take some food, but he refuses and says that his food is 'to do the will of the one who sent me.' Jesus indicates that his sustenance is not from this world. In this verse the Father's will is parallel with Jesus' work (ἔργον), which is to die on the cross (Jn 17.4, 6). The will of the Father, then, has soteriological implications for the world. According to R.E. Brown, 'to do the will of God' has a more general connotation in the Synoptics; in John it is a description of the nature of Jesus' ministry (1966: I, 173). In Jn 5.30 Jesus summarizes his previous argument. He does not seek his own will but the will of 'the one who sent me.' Jesus identifies himself with the will of the Father who sent him. He can do nothing of himself. In other words, the will of Jesus and the Father is the same. In opposing Jesus, therefore, the Jews are opposing God. In Jn 6.38 and 39 Jesus again states that he came not to do his own will but the will of 'the one who sent me.' Jesus then identifies what the will of the Father is, namely, 'that of all he has given me I should lose nothing, but should raise it up at the last day.' The will of the Father has a salvific intention. The future eschatological expectation here is not characteristically Johannine. According to Bultmann this is an addition by the ecclesiastical redactor, but for R.E. Brown such a dichotomy is unwarranted (1966: I, 220).

In Jn 5.37 Jesus states that the Father, the one who sent him, is testifying concerning him. The Father is the best person to testify to Jesus because Jesus comes from the Father, and the Father knows Jesus.[56] In Jn 7.16 Jesus states that the teaching is not his, but belongs to the one who sent him. The teachings of Jesus derive from the Father (cf. 7.27). In Jn 7.28-29 the Jews do not know the origin of Jesus. The question under discussion is, who is Jesus and where is he from? Jesus came from God (Jn 1.14; 6.46; 16.27; 18.8). R.E. Brown pointed out that 'In a primitive civilization without family names, the place of origin is equivalent to an identifying name, e.g. Joseph of Arimathea, Jesus of Nazareth' (1966: I, 313). Therefore, again the formula ὁ πέμψας με occurs in the context of the question concerning Jesus' identity. In Jn 7.33 Jesus states that he will go back to the one who sent him. This world always remains a foreign place to Jesus, because he is not of this world. R.E. Brown says that '…the theme of Jesus as divine Wisdom is very strong here and underlies many of the

---

56. *When* the Father testified to Jesus is not our concern. Some scholars think Jesus is referring to the Old Testament (Hendriksen 1961: 208). R.E. Brown thinks of the Father's testimony in the hearts of men (1966: I, 227).

statements' (1966: I, 318). In Jn 8.16, 18, 26, and 29 Jesus defends himself against the accusations of the Jews. In the discourse Jesus strongly identifies himself with the Father, or 'the one who sent me.' In Jn 8.16 Jesus is not alone (in judging) but with the Father who sent him. In v. 14 Jesus stresses his knowledge of his origin. In Jn 8.18 the Father, the one who sent him, bears witness to Jesus. According to Dodd, in saying 'I and the One who sent me,' Jesus is using a form of the divine name and implying his solidarity with the Father (1953: 194). In Jn 8.26 the context is that Jesus speaks to the world the things he has heard from the one who sent him. Again the place of Jesus' origin from the Father is highlighted. Jesus only speaks the things which the Father has taught him. And even now the one who sent Jesus is with him, for Jesus always does what pleases him (Jn 8.29). In Jn 9.4 Jesus must do the work of the one who sent him (cf. Jn 4.34).[57] In Jn 12.44-50 the identification between Jesus and the Father is complete. To believe in Jesus is the same as to believe in the Father. To see Jesus, is the same as seeing the Father. Jesus only speaks on the authority of the Father. He and the Father are one (Jn 10.30). In Jn 13.20 the identification between Jesus and the Father is again complete. The one who receives Jesus receives the one who sent him.[58] 'The thought is that no matter who it is that is sent by Jesus, he must be accepted; and this for the simple reason that he was thus divinely commissioned' (Hendriksen 1961: 240).

2. *'Sending' in the Farewell Discourses* Again the origin of Jesus is highlighted with the sending concept in the Farewell Discourses. In Jn 14.24 Jesus states that his words do not belong to him but to the Father who sent him. This idea occurs frequently in Jesus' apologetical confrontations with the Jews (cf. Jn 7.16; 8.26, 28; 12.49-50; 15.22-23) (Schnackenburg 1990: III, 82). In Jn 15.21 Jesus predicts that his disciples will be ill-treated because of his name[59] and because they do not know the one who sent him. Those who oppose Jesus do so because they do not know God. In Jn 16.5 Jesus goes back (ὑπάγω) to the one who sent him. Jesus stays in the world only temporarily. In

57. Haenchen says here that, 'The "we" is intended to indicate that the saying applies to the disciples as well' (1984: II, 38).

58. According to some commentators v. 20 does not belong here.

59. The words 'because of my name' echo Synoptic tradition (Schnackenburg 1990: III, 115).

several passages sending is also connected with the coming of the Spirit. In Jn 14.26 the Holy Spirit will be sent by the Father. In Jn 15.26 the Holy Spirit will be sent by Jesus from the Father. And in Jn 16.7 the Holy Spirit is again sent by Jesus.[60]

In the above survey it appears that the sending concept is used to identify Jesus over against the world or his enemies. As such it serves a christological function in the Johannine discourse. The formula, 'the one who sent me', is much more descriptive than 'Father'—the one expression identifying both the Father and Jesus at the same time. As such it underscores the unity of Jesus with the Father. The formula also implies that Jesus does not belong to this world, but has come from the Father. This usage of the concept gives John its strong dualistic character. Therefore, the expression ὁ πέμψας με is eminently a christological one.

Therefore, I disagree with Ritt's analysis that 'In John the actual historical sending of the Son by the Father is expressed in Jesus' own words in the formula ὁ πέμψας με' (1993: 68). The function of the aorist participle is not the indication of a past event, but that the action is perceived as a simple event or fact. This formula is a christological one and refers to the class to which Jesus belongs. The expression identifies Jesus as not belonging to this world, and sets him over against his opponents. This dualistic aspect of John's concept of sending is undoubtedly derived from the Gnostic sending tradition that I have identified earlier.

c. *'Sending' and the Mission of Jesus*
The sending concept is also employed to indicate the sphere in which Jesus' mission takes place, and the purpose of his mission. In Jn 3.17 God sent (ἀποστέλλω) his Son into the world (εἰς τὸν κόσμον) in order to save the world. This verse indicates both the place and purpose of Jesus' mission (cf. Jn 10.36; 17.18). The mission takes place in the world, the place of darkness which is in opposition to God (cf. Jn 1.5, 10). The usage of ἀποστέλλω here is different from the prophetic sending tradition of the Synoptic Gospels. For John, Jesus is sent to the world; for the Synoptics Jesus is sent to Israel (Mt. 15.24; Lk. 4.43). In the prophetic sending tradition the prophet is sent to deliver God's message. The purpose of Jesus' sending is here expressed as saving (σώζω) the world. To be saved means to receive eternal life

---

60. The idea of the sending of the Spirit may depend on Jewish Wisdom tradition.

(R.E. Brown 1966: I, 134). According to Jewish teaching, especially in the Dead Sea Scrolls, the coming of the Messiah would mean the condemnation of the world or the heathen. For John, God's salvation is not only for the Jews, but is universal in scope.[61] Therefore in this usage of ἀποστέλλω the sending concept in John also has a soteriological function.

The idea of commissioning or authorization, that is important in the prophetic sending tradition, also appears in John. The mission of John the Baptist is also seen in terms of sending (cf. Jn 1.6). In Jn 1.33 John the Baptist refers to God as the one who sent him. On the usage of πέμπω here Bauer observes that 'The idea of moving from one place to another, which is inherent in "sending", can retreat into the background, so that π. takes on the mng. instruct, commission, appoint' (1952: 647). In Jn 3.28 John the Baptist is sent (ἀποστέλλω) ahead of Christ (cf. Mk 1.2, 3). In Jn 3.34 the Baptist identifies Jesus as the one God has sent (ἀποστέλλω). In Jn 5.36 Jesus says that his work will testify that the Father has sent (ἀποστέλλω) him. The work of Jesus and the purpose of his mission is to save the world. In this verse Jesus' sending again has soteriological implications. In Jn 5.38 the Jews are charged that they do not believe in the one that was sent (ἀποστέλλω). For Bühner 'ἀποστέλλω denotes commissioning and authorisation from God. The sending discloses the unique manner in which the Son is bound to the Father; a believing acknowledgment of the phrase 'that you have sent me' therefore constitutes the goal and content of confession (11.42; 17.3, 8, 21, 23, 25)' (1990: 142).

The soteriological function of Jesus' sending is further illustrated in that the world must believe the sending of Jesus. In Jn 5.24 the one who believes in the one who sent Jesus will pass from death to life. In Jn 6.29 the work of God is to believe in him whom he sent. In Jn 11.42 Jesus prays in public that the people might come to believe (ingressive aorist) that the Father sent him. In Jn 12.44 the one who believes in Jesus, believes not in Jesus but in the one who sent him. In Jn 17.3 eternal life is to know God and the one he sent.[62] In Jn 17.8 the disciples believed that Jesus came from the Father and that Jesus

61. The verb ἀποστέλλω in v. 17 is parallel to ἔδωκεν in v. 16. We find the same pair, 'send' and 'give', used of the Paraclete in Jn 14.16 and 26.

62. 'This verse is clearly an insertion into the text of Jesus' prayer, an insertion probably reflecting a confessional or liturgical formula of the Johannine Church' (R.E. Brown 1966: II, 741).

was sent by the Father. In Jn 17.21 and 23 Jesus prays that the world may believe that the Father sent him (cf. Zech. 2.12-13). And in Jn 17.25 Jesus says that the disciples have known that the Father sent him.

Therefore, the ἀποστέλλω statements in John define the mission of Jesus and indicate the place and the purpose of that mission. As such they also recall the Gnostic sending tradition, in which the Saviour is sent to rescue the disciples. It follows that sending is also used as a soteriological concept. The sending of salvation is a common theme in the Old Testament and in Jewish literature. In Isaiah God will send a Saviour (Isa. 19.20; 61.1). In the *T. Benj.* 9.2, 'But in your allotted place will be the temple of God, and the latter temple will exceed the former in glory. The twelve tribes shall be gathered there and all the nations, until such time as the Most High shall send forth [ἀποστέλλω] his salvation through the ministration of the unique prophet.' Finally, I noted that the ἀποστέλλω statements still contain the idea of authorization from God.

d. *The 'Sending' of the Disciples*
In John also the disciples of Jesus are sent on a mission into the world. In Jn 4.38 Jesus sends the disciples to reap the harvest. In Jn 13.20 the one who receives the one Jesus sent receives Jesus. In Jn 17.18 as the Father sent Jesus into the world, so too Jesus sent the disciples into the world.[63] The aorist of the sending of the disciples may refer to the commissioning in Jn 20.21. In other words the present history of the community is represented by Jesus and the disciples in the Gospel.

In Jn 20.21 as the Father has sent Jesus, so Jesus sends his disciples.[64] 'The disciples...enter into the office and position of Jesus' (Haenchen 1984: II, 211). The alteration between ἀποστέλλω and πέμπω is interesting here. Is it so that the disciples can refer to Jesus

63. See R.E. Brown, 'The consecration in truth is not simply a purification from sin, but is a consecration to a mission; they are being consecrated inasmuch as they are being sent' (1966: II, 762).

64. See Ritt, 'The continuation of this sending by Jesus involves the believing disciples (cf. the "Synoptic" logion in 13.20); the Jewish legal principle that the messenger bears the same authority as the one who sent him comes into play. Juxtaposed with passages expressing the same idea with ἀποστέλλω (4.38; 17.18), the logion 20.21 is to be considered primary and has (in the pres.!) the resurrected Lord transmit the authoritative power of divine redemptive activity to the community of disciples' (1993: 68).

as ὁ πέμψας με? But here the terms are most probably used interchangeably.[65] Therefore, an interesting sending paradigm appears in John.[66]

God/Father is	'he who sent' Jesus
Jesus is	'he who was sent'
the disciples are	'they who are being sent'

Therefore, the Johannine community is by no means disinterested in the world.[67]

5. *Conclusion*

John's concept of sending serves two primary functions: (1) it identifies who Jesus is; and (2) it describes the purpose of Jesus' mission. Sending in John is therefore both a christological and a soteriological concept. The Johannine concept is basically taken from the Gnostic sending tradition. Remnants of a prophetic sending tradition, however, are still noticeable. The usage of ἀποστέλλω and πέμπω should be understood in this light. The meaning of ἀποστέλλω, the prophetic sending tradition, is being assimilated to that of πέμπω, the Gnostic sending tradition. Πέμπω in John may represent an earlier stage in the history of the Johannine community than does ἀποστέλλω. Though the ἀποστέλλω concept is older than the Gnostic πέμπω concept.

This differs from Bühner's view, who writes that 'The doctrine of the messenger, connected with the vbs. ἀποστέλλω and πέμπω, does not take its orientation from Gnostic mythology but from Jewish teaching concerning the prophet and the saliah (Borgen 1968; Bühner 1977): the Father who sends legitimizes the Son who is sent and directs him in descent and ascent into the prescribed paths of a

65. See R.E. Brown, 'The verbs, respectively ἀποστέλλω and πέμπω, stand in parallelism here with no visible sign of distinction' (1966: II, 1022).

66. This paradigm also occurs in Gnostic literature (cf. CH XIII), 'The God who has chosen Hermes and regenerated him now wills to use Hermes in order to regenerate Tat' (Grese 1979: 98).

67. As Onuki has pointed out: 'Die johanneische Gemeinde versteht sich zwar als eine von der Welt befreite Gemeinde, als von der Welt abgesonderte Transzendenz und eschatologische Neuschöpfung Gottes, aber sie ist keine von der Welt endgültig entrückte Existenz, sondern durch den Auferstandenen immer neu dazu beauftragt, gerade aus der gerichteten Welt neue Glieder zu gewinnen. Das ist der Grund der Sendung der johanneischen Gemeinde in die Welt' (1984: 91-92).

messenger's course' (1990: 146). Legitimization, or authorization, plays only a secondary role in John's concept of sending.

Moreover, in the concept of sending of John, the close relationship between Jesus and the community is again prominent. The Johannine Jesus always refers to himself as the one the Father sent, in other words, he characterizes his mission in terms of sending. In Jn 17.18 the Johannine Jesus in turn sent the community, as the Father had sent him, into the world. And like the purpose of Jesus' sending, the goal of the community's sending is that the world may be saved or believe (Jn 17.20-21). The community may even now refer to Jesus as the one who sent them, as Jesus frequently referred to the Father. In the Synoptic Gospels the disciples are also sent out, but more specifically to preach in response to Jesus' coming.[68] Their sending is not analagous to Jesus' sending as in John, and is not seen as a continuation of Jesus' sending. As with Jesus, the sending of the Johannine community defines its identity and purpose. It is a community that does not belong to this world, and is a community that exists to continue the sending of Jesus. The community exists solely to be the agent of Jesus' sending for the salvation of the world. Therefore, the Johannine community is *Christus prolongatus*. In this way, Johannine ecclesiology may also be described by the German term as a *Sendungsekklesiologie*: it is a community that has its being in the sending of Jesus.

68. Cf. Mk 6.7; 3.14; Mt. 10.5, 16; Lk. 9.2, 52; and 10.1-3. In all these references the verb ἀποστέλλω is used. In John both ἀποστέλλω and πέμπω are used in the commissioning of the disciples (cf. Jn 17.18 and 20.21).

Chapter 7

CONCLUSION

1. *Johannine Ecclesiology*

This study has highlighted the prominence and distinctiveness of ecclesiology in the Gospel of John. Ecclesiology does play an important part in John's overall theology and may have been one of the major issues for the Johannine community. The Farewell discourses place a great emphasis on the place and task of Jesus' disciples who remain in the world after Jesus' departure. And especially in John 17, the farewell prayer of Jesus, the community is the major concern. The prayer of the Johannine Jesus in John 17 serves as the Gospel's mature and final description of the Johannine community's ecclesiology. Moreover, it is probable that the composition of this prayer arose out of the community's petitionary prayers to God in their conflict with the synagogue. As such, the prayer has an apologetic and paraenetic function for the community. This fits in well with the purpose of the Gospel itself, which was to encourage or sustain the community in their attempts to continue their evangelistic mission. The Gospel is primarily not an evangelistic Gospel, that is, written for unbelievers to come to belief, but is rather a Gospel for a community with an evangelistic mission (Onuki 1984).[1]

The Johannine community has its own unique and distinctive ecclesiology. Ecclesiastical office, church order, or sacraments do not feature prominently in Johannine ecclesiology as they do in Pauline ecclesiology. It appears that the author was not concerned about these things. Instead, the Gospel places the emphasis on the community's relationship with the Johannine Jesus. The community does not exist for itself, nor is not an end in itself, but rather exists for the purpose of continuing the sending of Jesus. This again is in contrast to Pauline

---

1. See my discussion on the purpose of John in Chapter 2.

or Ephesian ecclesiology, where the church exists as the 'house of God' and has a prominent place in salvation history. In John, the community only has meaning as it continues the sending of Jesus. Therefore, the community of believers is not the new Israel, nor a new eschatological community whose existence announces the arrival of the *eschaton*. John does have a concept of salvation history, but it stops with, or is absorbed in, Jesus. The Johannine Jesus is the new Israel, or God's final act in history. The community is important only because it is *Christus prolongatus*, that is, it is one with Jesus in terms of function.

Therefore, the distinctiveness of Johannine ecclesiology consists in the close relationship between Jesus and the community. Neither Jesus nor the community belongs to this world, but are from above. And both he and they are sent to save the world. Jesus gave the glory the Father gave to him, that is, the task of saving the world, to the community. Indeed, as has been pointed out, the concept of glory is important for Johannine ecclesiology. The community exists only as it participates in the glory of Jesus, that is, in the sending of Jesus to save the world. Therefore, the purpose of Johannine ecclesiology, as with its Christology, is eminently soteriological. As Jesus was sent to give life to the world, so now the community is being sent in order that the world may believe. In fact, the community's existence and mission reflect the Johannine Jesus in almost every way, and as such continue the revelation of Jesus in the world. In this way, the history of the community plays itself out in the history of Jesus, and vice versa.[2] The Gospel, then, is not only an account of Jesus' mission and glory, but also an account of the community's mission and glory. Just as Jesus' task was to glorify God by saving the world, so too the community glorifies God by accomplishing their mission. The community not only represents Jesus on the earth (*Christus praesens*), but is *Christus prolongatus*. Therefore, this study has found, as have others, that ecclesiology and Christology are closely related in John (Minear 1982; Schnelle 1991; Gnilka 1994); in fact, these two theological categories merge into each other.

In view of this close relationship between the community and Jesus, ecclesiology and Christology, Johannine ecclesiology can be described as a *christological ecclesiology*. Therefore, though I have also referred to Johannine ecclesiology as *Herrlichkeitsekklesiologie* and *Sendungs-*

---

2.   See my discussion of Martyn's thesis in Chapter 2.

ekklesiologie, these terms describe only some aspects of Johannine ecclesiology. In the same way, Minear's *Logos* ecclesiology is too narrow to give an adequate description of Johannine ecclesiology. The expression *christological ecclesiology* is broader, and also underscores the close relationship between the Johannine community and the Johannine Jesus. It also correctly implies that Johannine ecclesiology is a function of Christology.

To clarify this expression *christological ecclesiology*, on the basis of my research, I may say that (1) a *christological ecclesiology* has as its basis or origin the revelation given by the Johannine Christ, that is, the Word, the community has been brought into being by the Word; (2) a *christological ecclesiology* emphasizes the intimate and exclusive inner life of the community as joy in the Word, unity, and love for one another; and (3) a *christological ecclesiology* emphasizes the purpose of the community which is to continue the sending of the Son into the world. Thus, John's *christological ecclesiology* describes the origin, character, and purpose of the Johannine community.

These findings suggest that the Gospel served to sustain the Johannine community in its mission, as Onuki has proposed. Onuki argues that not only the Farewell discourses serve to reaffirm the community's identity in its mission, but that the Johannine passion narrative does so as well. If this is the case, ecclesiology underlies the purpose of the Gospel, and cannot be ignored as a major topic of Johannine research.

Furthermore, I agree with Käsemann that John's ecclesiology must be seen in the wider context of the church at the end of the first century. There was a general movement away from eschatology to ecclesiology. John, however, may represent a reaction against this trend towards an institutional Christianity. If so, John calls his community back to the original vitality and mission of the early Christian movement. But instead of recalling the early emphasis on eschatology as the Montanists did, John puts the emphasis on the presence of Christ through the Spirit. John moves away from a futuristic eschatology, not to ecclesiology *per se*, but to Christology. The urgency of union with Christ and mission stems no longer from the future expectation of judgment, but from the past revelation of Christ. Therefore, there is a shift from eschatology to protology.

The present study also suggests that the Gospel of John uses traditional categories and terms that are familiar in the early Christian traditions, but that the Gospel then gives them a certain ecclesiological or missiological twist. In other words, the Gospel reinterprets traditional Christian categories, traditions, and terms (e.g. world, glory, life, sending, and so on). In John, these terms are expanded to include missiological, soteriological and ecclesiological concerns. I have also noted that John has no distinct concept of the church as the people of God, because everything has been incorporated into Christology. The Johannine Christ is the final revelation of God. Everything before and after serves only as witness to that event. The Johannine community serves the same function as the Old Testament in witnessing to Jesus, but the Johannine community is more than just a witness. The community is *Christus prolongatus*. Christology and ecclesiology overlap.

It would be interesting to apply the suggestion of the present research that John espouses a *christological ecclesiology* to the other ecclesiological motifs in the Gospel. For example, the parable of the shepherd and the sheepfold (Jn 10.1-16), and the parable of the vine (Jn 15.1-8), should be interpreted in terms of this central theological motif. It would appear that the parable of the shepherd and the sheepfold deals with the origin of the community, whereas the parable of the vine deals with the relationship between the community and Christ and also with the missiological function of the community. In addition, the role of the *Paraklete* and the sacraments should be examined afresh. And lastly, a re-examination of the Temple pericope (Jn 2.13-22) would have interesting results for assessing the Johannine view on the Temple and its relationship with the Johannine community.

2. *John's* Religionsgeschichtliche *Context*

The results of this research have also raised interesting questions regarding the Gospel's *religionsgeschichtliche* context. The research supports the view that John's immediate context is Jewish, and particularly lies in the Johannine community's conflict with the synagogue. However, having said that, the Gospel is also influenced by marginal elements in Judaism, including Essene, Samaritan and Gnostic traditions. On the one hand, concepts such as truth and glory have to be understood in terms of Old Testament thought. On the other hand, the concept of sending owes much to Gnostic thinking in the first century. The Johannine concept of life may be dependent on both Old Testament traditions and early Gnostic thought. Therefore, the interpreter has to be sensitive in dealing with each particular term or concept of the Gospel, and cannot make general statements as to the origin of Johannine theology.[3] In view of this, it must be asked whether or not a major idea controlled John's theological outlook?

The present research suggests that though John is to be seen in a Jewish context, the *crux interpretum* of the Gospel is the descent–ascent motif of the Redeemer that is found in Gnostic thought.[4] In John, the pre-existent Redeemer brings salvation to God's elected ones, and not the eschatological Son of Man who inaugurates God's kingdom as in the Synoptic Gospels and Paul. The chapter on sending has illustrated how John makes use of the Gnostic concept of the sending of the Redeemer from above into the world below, and how this gnostic concept overrides, as it were, the early Jewish and Christian ἀποστέλλω concept. This descent–ascent motif of the Redeemer or Revealer is reflected in Simon and Menander who had a considerable influence in Samaria. It may be suggested, then, that though John lies in a Jewish context, it has incorporated the dualistic paradigm of the descent–ascent of the Redeemer from a Gnostic trajectory. John, of course, has tried to find Jewish parallels for this concept as the inclusion of the Jacob/Bethel pericope shows.[5] Lattke has shown that John's soteriology reflects the dualistic Gnostic soteriology (1975a; Lattke and Franzmann 1994: 143-53).

However, this does not mean that John is a Gnostic Gospel. The idea of gnosis as the key to salvation in the Gnosticism of the second century is foreign to John. Furthermore, Onuki has shown the important difference between Gnostic and Johannine dualism. Whereas in

3. Lattke's picture of Judaism, Gnosticism and Christianity in the Greco-Roman world is helpful to understand the interaction of these traditions. 'In a simplified way, the three ancient and diverse movements within the Graeco-Roman world, i.e. Judaism, Gnosticism and Christianity, can be compared to three circles partially overlapping each other, with the circle of Judaism sitting on top of the circles of Christianity and Gnosticism which appear side by side, thus indicating the parallel origin of the latter two' (Lattke and Franzmann 1994: 150). For Lattke, the Fourth Gospel is 'the product of a Christian-Gnostic-Jewish syncretism within the late Hellenistic era and Roman empire' (Lattke and Franzmann 1994: 151).

4. Lieu writes, 'In the need to make sense of the Christian message in the hellenistic world it was necessary to make use of the thought-world of the period and to find images and analogies congenial to hearers or readers' (1979: 236).

5. *Jos. Asen.* 15.13 may also be cited as a Jewish 'precedent' for this descent–ascent Redeemer motif.

Gnosticism revelation is the function of an anticosmic dualism, in John dualism is the function of the revelation of God (1984: 39-42). Thus according to Onuki the relation between dualism and revelation is exactly the opposite in Gnosticism. Therefore, to classify John in terms of a religious tradition of the first century, neither Judaism nor Gnosticism will suffice. Instead, John has to be appreciated as a thoroughly Christian Gospel. If something is Christian when it emphasizes the historical event of Jesus, culminating in the cross and resurrection, as the way to salvation, then John certainly is (cf. Jn 14.6).[6] Again, according to Onuki the Johannine community is founded only through the revelation that came into the world through Jesus and which culminated in the cross.[7] Therefore, though the Gnostic idea of the descent–ascent of the Redeemer plays a key role in John, it should not be overlooked that this motif finds its expression in John in the historical event of Jesus. Contra Käsemann, the incarnation of the *Logos* in the historical person of Jesus is central to Johannine thought. Indeed, this study has attempted to show that John's ecclesiology, which emphasizes the community's need to be in the world though it is not of it, is rooted in its Christology.[8]

These observations, of course, raise numerous questions. If John has adopted the descent–ascent motif of the Redeemer from the Gnostic trajectory, how is the historical connection to be explained? And from where does this Gnostic motif originate? Moreover, to pick up the debate between Bultmann and Käsemann, should the author of John be regarded as a Gnostic who became a Christian, or a Christian who adopted some Gnostic ideas? The present study, however, does not attempt to answer these interesting, but difficult, questions.

6.　We may refer to Dunn's study on unity and diversity in the New Testament which sees the one unifying strand of earliest Christianity as *Jesus and faith in him* (1977: 122).

7.　'Die johanneische Gemeinde ist nach ihrem Selbverständnis allein durch die mit Jesus in die Welt gekommene Offenbarung gesammelt und begründet worden. Der Schwerpunkt liegt in diesem Selbstverständnis auf Jesu Kreuzestod, da er den Vollendungspunkt des Offenbarungsereignisses bildet' (1984: 62).

8.　Similarly, Kümmel noted that, 'It is important to see that for John too the existence of the Christian community is strictly bound to God's historical saving action in Jesus Christ' (1973: 320).

BIBLIOGRAPHY

Aalen, S.
1964.   ' "Truth", a Key Word in St John's Gospel', *SE* 2: 3-24.

Adam, A.
1959   *Die Psalmen des Thomas und das Perlenlied als Zeugnisse vorchrist-
             licher Gnosis* (BZNW, 24; Berlin: W. de Gruyter).

Agouridis, S.
1968   'The "High Priestly Prayer" of Jesus', *SE* 4: 137-43.

Albright, W.F., and C.S. Mann
1971   *Matthew: Introduction, Translation and Notes* (AB, 26; Garden City,
             NY: Doubleday).

Allen, E.L.
1955   'The Jewish Church in the Fourth Gospel', *JBL* 74: 88-92.

Anderson, P.N.
1993   *The Christology of the Fourth Gospel* (Tübingen: J.C.B. Mohr).

Appold, M.
1976   *The Oneness Motif in the Fourth Gospel: Motif Analysis and Exegeti-
             cal Probe into the Theology of John* (WUNT, 1; Tübingen: J.C.B.
             Mohr [Paul Siebeck]).
1978   'Christ Alive! Church Alive! Reflections on the Prayer of Jesus in John
             17', *CurTM* 5: 365-73).

Arens, E.
1976   *The HΛΘON—Sayings in the Synoptic Tradition: A Historical Critical
             Investigation* (ODO, 10; Freiburg: Universitätsverlag; Göttingen: Van-
             denhoeck & Ruprecht).

Arseniev, N.
1964   'Contemplation of the Glory of God in the Early Christian Message',
             SVTQ 8: 112-20.

Ashton, J.
1991   *Understanding the Fourth Gospel* (Oxford: Clarendon Press; New
             York: Oxford University Press).

Attridge, H.W.
1985   *Nag Hammadi Codex I (The Jung Codex): Notes* (The Coptic Gnostic
             Library; Leiden: E.J. Brill).

Attridge, H.W. *et al.* (eds.)
1985   *Nag Hammadi Codex I (The Jung Codex): Introductions, Texts,
             Translations, Indices* (The Coptic Gnostic Library; Leiden: E.J. Brill).

Attridge, H.W., and G.W. MacRae
1990   'The Gospel of Truth', in J.M. Robinson (ed.), *The Nag Hammadi Library in English* (San Francisco: Harper & Row, 3rd rev. edn): 38-39.

Attridge, H.W., and E.H. Pagels
1990   'The Tripartite Tractate', in J.M. Robinson (ed.), *The Nag Hammadi Library in English* (San Francisco: Harper, 3rd rev. edn): 58-60.

Augenstein, J.
1993   *Das Liebesgebot im Johannesevangelium und in den Johannesbriefen* (Stuttgart: W. Kohlhammer).

Baaren, T.P. van
1970   'Towards a Definition of Gnosticism', in *The Origins of Gnosticism: Colloquium of Messina 13–18 April 1966* (Leiden: E.J. Brill [1967]): 174-80.

Baldensperger, G.
1898   *Der Prolog des vierten Evangeliums: Sein polemisch-apologetischer Zweck* (Freiburg im Breisgau: J.C.B. Mohr).

Balz, H.
1990   'ἅγιος', *EDNT*: I, 46.
1991   'κόσμος', *EDNT*: II, 312.

Barr, J.
1988   '"Abba" isn't "Daddy"', *JTS* 39: 28-47.

Barrett, C.K.
1947   'The Old Testament in the Fourth Gospel', *JTS* 48: 155-69.
1955   *The Gospel According to St John: An Introduction with Commentary and Notes on the Greek Text* (London: SPCK).

Barth, G.
1993   'πίστις, πιστεύω', *EDNT*: III, 91-97.

Baumbach, G.
1972   'Gemeinde und Welt im Johannes-Evangelium', *Kairos* 14: 121-36.

Beasley-Murray, G.R.
1946   'The Eschatology of the Fourth Gospel', *EvQ* 18: 97-108.
1987   *John* (Dallas, TX: Word Books).

Becker, H.
1956   *Die Reden des Johannesevangeliums und der Stil der gnostischen Offenbarungsreden* (FRLANT, 68; Göttingen: Vandenhoeck & Ruprecht).

Becker, J.
1969   'Aufbau, Schichtung und theologiegeschichtliche Stellung des Gebetes in Johannes 17', *ZNW* 60: 56-83.
1970   'Die Abschiedsreden Jesu im Johannesevangelium', *ZNW* 61: 215-46.
1991   *Das Evangelium des Johannes* (2 vols.; Gütersloh: Mohn; Würzburg: Echter-Verlag, 3rd edn).

Beinert, W.
1979   'Der Einzelne und die Gemeinschaft: Ekklesiologische Aspekte zum Thema der Nachfolge', *MTZ* 30: 105-16.

Belle, G. van
1988   *Johannine Bibliography 1966–1985: A Cumulative Bibliography on the Fourth Gospel* (Leuven: Leuven University Press).

Berger, K.
1989   'Kirche II: Neues Testament', *TRE* 18: 201-18.

Bernard, A.
1977   *Pan du désert* (Leiden: E.J. Brill).

Bianchi, U.
1970   'Proposal for a Terminological and Conceptual Agreement with Regard to the Theme of the Colloquium', in *idem* (ed.), *The Origins of Gnosticism: Colloquium of Messina 13–18 April 1966* (Leiden: E.J. Brill [1967]): xxvi-xxix.

Black, D.A.
1988   'On the Style and Significance of John 17: The Gospel of John: Problems and Theology', *Criswell Theological Review* 3: 141-59.

Black, M.
1967   *An Aramaic Approach to the Gospels and Acts* (Oxford: Clarendon Press, 3rd edn).

Blank, J.
1974   'Die Sendung des Sohnes: Zur christologischen Bedeutung des Gleichnisses von den bösen Winzern Mk 12,1-2', in J. Gnilka (ed.), *Neues Testament und Kirche: Für Rudolf Schnackenburg* (Freiburg: Herder): 11-41.

Blank, S.H.
1948   'The Confessions of Jeremiah and the Meaning of Prayer', *Hebrew Union College Annual* 21: 331-54.

Boismard, M.-E.
1962   'Saint Luc et la rédaction du Quatrième Évangile', *RB* 69: 185-211.

Boccaccini, G.
1991   *Middle Judaism: Jewish Thought, 300 BCE to 200 CE* (Minneapolis: Fortress Press).

Borgen, P.
1968   'God's Agent in the Fourth Gospel', in J. Neusner (ed.), *Religions in Antiquity: Essays in Memory of Erwin Ramsdell Goodenough* (SHR, 14; Leiden: E.J. Brill): 137-48.

1983   *Logos Was the True Light and other Essays on the Fourth Gospel* (Trondheim: University of Trondheim).

Bornhäuser, K.
1928   *Das Johannesevangelium: Eine Missionsschrift für Israel* (BFChTh, 2, 15; Gütersloh: C. Bertelsmann).

Bornkamm, G.
1933   *Mythos und Legende in den apokryphen Thomasakten* (Göttingen: Vandenhoeck & Ruprecht).

1956   'Die eucharistische Rede im Johannesevangelium', *ZNW* 47: 161-69.

Bousset, W.
1905   'Der Verfasser des Johannesevangeliums', *TRU* 8: 225-44, 277-95.
1909   'Ist das vierte Evangelium eine literarische Einheit?', *TRU* 12: 1-12, 39-64.

Boyle, J.L.
1975   'The Last Discourse (Jn 13,31–16,33) and Prayer (Jn 17): Some
            Observations on Their Unity and Development', *Bib* 56: 210-22.

Braun, F.M.
1959   *Jean le Théologien et son évangile dans l'église ancienne* (Paris:
            J. Gabalda).

Brodie, T.L.
1993   *The Quest for the Historical Origin of John's Gospel: A Source-Orien-
            tated Approach* (Oxford: Oxford University Press).

Brown, R.E.
1966   *The Gospel According to St John: Introduction, Translation, and
            Notes* (AB, 29, 29a; 2 vols.; Garden City, NY: Doubleday).
1977   'The Qumran Scrolls and John: A Comparison in Thought and
            Expression', in M.J. Taylor (ed.), *A Companion to John: Readings in
            Johannine Theology* (New York: Alba House): 69-90, 274-75.
1977a   'Johannine Ecclesiology: The Community's Origins', *Int* 31: 379-93.
1978   ' "Other Sheep Not of This Fold": The Johannine Perspective on
            Christian Diversity in the Late First Century', *JBL* 97: 5-22.
1979   *The Community of the Beloved Disciple: The Life, Loves, and Hates of
            an Individual Church in New Testament Times* (New York: Paulist
            Press).
1990   'The Dead Sea Scrolls and the New Testament', in J.H. Charlesworth
            (ed.), *John and the Dead Sea Scrolls* (Christian Origins Library; New
            York: Crossroad): 1-8.
1992   'The Qumran Scrolls and the Johannine Gospel and Epistles', in
            K. Stendahl and J.H. Charlesworth (eds.), *The Scrolls and the New
            Testament* (New York: Crossroad [1957]): 183-207.

Brownlee, W.H.
1990   'Whence the Gospel According to John?', in J.H. Charlesworth (ed.),
            John and the Dead Sea Scrolls (Christian Origins Library; New York:
            Crossroad): 166-94.

Brückner, K.
1988   'A Word Study of Doxazo in the Gospel of John', *Notes on Transla-
            tion* 2: 41-46.

Buchanan, G.W.
1970   'The Samaritan Origin of the Gospel of John', in J. Neusner (ed.),
            *Religions in Antiquity: Essays in memory of Erwin Ramsdell Good-
            enough* (Leiden: E.J. Brill): 149-75.

Bühner, J.-A.
1977   *Der Gesandte und sein Weg im 4. Evangelium* (WUNT II, 2; Tübin-
            gen: J.C.B. Mohr [Paul Siebeck]).
1990   'ἀποστέλλω', *EDNT*: I, 141-42.

Bultmann, R.
1925   'Die Bedeutung der neuerschlossenen mandäischen und manichä-
            ischen Quellen für das Verständnis des Johannesevangeliums', *ZNW* 4:
            100-46.
1941   *Das Evangelium des Johannes* (Göttingen: Vandenhoeck & Ruprecht).

1951–55	*Theology of the New Testament* (2 vols.; trans. K. Grobel; New York: Charles Scribner's Sons).

Bultmann, R., and G. von Rad
1964	'ζάω–ζωή', *TDNT*: II, 832-75.
1964a.	'γινώσκω', *TDNT*: I, 689-719.
1964b	'ἀλήθεια', *TDNT*: I, 238-51.
1968	'πιστεύω', *TDNT*: VI, 174-228.
1969*l*	'The Eschatology of the Gospel of John', in R.W. Funk (ed.), *Faith and Understanding* (trans. L.P. Smith; New York: SCM Press [1928]): 165-83.
1971	*The Gospel of John: A Commentary* (trans. G.R. Beasley-Murray *et al*; Oxford: Basil Blackwell).

Burney, C.F.
1922	*The Aramaic Origin of the Fourth Gospel* (Oxford: Clarendon Press).

Burton, E.D.
1975	*A Critical and Exegetical Commentary on the Epistle to the Galatians* (Edinburgh: T. & T. Clark [1921]).
1976	*Syntax of the Moods and Tenses in New Testament Greek* (Edinburgh: T. & T. Clark, 3rd edn [1898]).

Busche, H. van den
1967	'La prière sacerdotale', in *Jean: commentaire de l'evangile spirituel* (Paris: Desclée de Brouwer): 446-62.

Caird, G.B.
1968	'The Glory of God in the Fourth Gospel: An Exercise in Biblical Semantics', *NTS* 15: 265-77.

Calvin, J.
1959	*Calvin's Commentaries: The Gospel According to St John* (ed. D.W. Torrance and T.F. Torrance; trans. T.H.L. Parker; 2 vols.; Grand Rapids, MI: Eerdmans).
1983	*Institutes of the Christian Religion* (trans. H. Beveridge; Grand Rapids, MI: Eerdmans.

Carl, K.J.
1984	'Knowing in St John: Background of the Theme', *ITS* 21: 68-82.

Carroll, K.I
1957	'The Fourth Gospel and the Exclusion of Christians from the Synagogue', *BJRL* 40: 19-32.

Carson, D.A.
1978	'Current Source Criticism of the Fourth Gospel: Some Methodological Questions', *JBL* 97: 411-29.
1987	'The Purpose of the Fourth Gospel: John 20: 31 Reconsidered', *JBL* 106: 639-51.
1991	*The Gospel According to John* (Leicester: Inter-Varsity Press; Grand Rapids, MI: Eerdmans).

Charlesworth, J.H.
1977	*The Odes of Solomon: The Syriac Texts* (SBL, Texts and Translations, 13; Pseudepigrapha Series 7; Chico, CA: Scholars Press).

1982 'A Prolegomenon to a New Study of the Jewish Background of the Hymns and Prayers in the New Testament', *Journal of Jewish Studies* 33: 265-85.

1987 'From Jewish Messianology to Christian Christology: Some Caveats and Perspectives', in J. Neusner (ed.), *Judaisms and Their Messiahs at the Turn of the Christian Era* (Cambridge: Cambridge University Press): 225-64.

1988 *Jesus within Judaism: New Light from Exciting Archaeological Discoveries* (New York: Doubleday).

1992 'Jewish Prayer in the Time of Jesus', *The Princeton Seminary Bulletin* 2: 36-55.

1992a 'From Messianology to Christology: Problems and Prospects', in J.H. Charlesworth (ed.), *The Messiah* (Minneapolis: Fortress Press): 3-35.

1993 'Prayer in the New Testament in Light of Contemporary Jewish Prayer', E.H. Lovering, Jr (ed.), *SBLSP 1993* (Chico, CA: Scholars Press): 773-86.

1995 *The Beloved Disciple: Whose Witness Validates the Gospel of John?* (Valley Forge, PA: Trinity Press International).

Charlesworth, J.H. (ed.)

1983 *The Old Testament Pseudepigrapha.* I. *Apocalyptic Literature and Testaments*; II. *Expansions of the 'Old Testament' and Legends, Wisdom and Philosophical Literature, Prayers, Psalms, and Odes, Fragments of Lost Judeo-Hellenistic Works* (Garden City, NY: Doubleday).

1985 *The Old Testament Pseudepigrapha and the New Testament: Prolegomena for the Study of Christian Origins* (SNTSMS, 54; Cambridge: Cambridge University Press).

1990 *John and the Dead Sea Scrolls* (Christian Origins Library; New York: Crossroad [1972]).

Charlesworth, J.H. *et al.*

1994 *The Dead Sea Scrolls: Hebrew, Aramaic, and Greek Texts with English Translations.* I. *Rule of the Community and Related Documents* (Tübingen: J.C.B. Mohr [Paul Siebeck]; Louisville: Westminster John Knox Press).

1994 *The Lord's Prayer and Other Prayer Texts from the Greco-Roman Era* (Valley Forge, PA: Trinity Press International).

Chazon, E. G.

1993 'Prayers from Qumran: Issues and Methods', in E.H. Lovering, Jr (ed.), *SBLSP 1993* (Chico, CA: Scholars Press): 758-72.

Cloete, G.D.

1980 *Hemelse Solidariteit: 'n Weg in die relasie tussen die christologie en soteriologie in die Vierde Evangelie* (Kampen Kok).

Coetzee, J.C.

1972 'Life (Eternal Life) In John's Writings and the Qumran Scrolls', *Neot* 6: 48-66.

Conzelmann, H.

1969 *An Outline of the Theology of the New Testament* (New York: Harper & Row).

1982   *The Theology of St Luke* (trans. G. Buswell; Philadelphia: Fortress Press).

Cook, W.R.
1984   'The "Glory" Motif in the Johannine Corpus', *JETS* 27: 291-97.

Cope, L.
1987   *The Earliest Gospel Was the 'Signs Gospel': Jesus, the Gospels, and the Church. Essays in Honor of William R. Farmer* (ed. E.P. Sanders; Macon, GA: Mercer University Press): 17-24.

Cribbs, F.L.
1970   'A Reassessment of the Date of Origin and the Destination of the Gospel of John', *JBL* 89: 38-55.

Cullmann, O.
1959   *The Christology of the New Testament* (trans. Shirley C. Guthrie and Charles A.M. Hall; Philadelphia: Westminster Press): 137-92, 270-89.

1976   *The Johannine Circle: Its Place in Judaism, among the Disciples of Jesus and in Early Christianity. A Study in the Origin of the Gospel of John* (trans. John Bowden; London: SCM Press).

Culpepper, R.A.
1975   *The Johannine School: An Evaluation of the Johannine-School Hypothesis Based on an Investigation of the Nature of Ancient Schools* (SBLDS, 26; Missoula, MT: Scholars Press).

1983   *Anatomy of the Fourth Gospel: A Study in Literary Design* (Philadelphia: Fortress Press).

Dahl, N.A.
1962.   'The Johannine Church and History', in W. Klassen and G.F. Snyder (eds.), *Current Issues in New Testament Interpretation: Essays in honor of Otto A. Piper* (New York: Harper & Brothers): 124-42.

Davies, W.D.
1966   *Invitation to the New Testament: A Guide to Its Main Witnesses* (Anchor Books; Garden City, NY: Doubleday): 398-408.

1991   *The Gospel According to Saint Matthew* (Edinburgh: T. & T. Clark).

Di Lella, A.A.
1979   'The Deuteronomic Background of the Farewell Discourse in Tob 14: 3-11', *CBQ* 41: 380-89.

Dinechin, O. de
1970   'KATHOS: La similitude dans l'évangile selon saint Jean', *RSR* 58: 195-236.

Dodd, C.H.
1953   *The Interpretation of the Fourth Gospel* (Cambridge: Cambridge University Press).

1963   *Historical Traditions in the Fourth Gospel* (Cambridge: Cambridge University Press).

Domínguez, V.
1967–68   *La Iglesia en el Ev. de S. Juan* (Urbe: Pont. Univ. a S. Thoma Aq.).

Dunn, J.D.G.
1977   *Unity and Diversity in the New Testament: An Inquiry into the Character of Earliest Christianity* (London: SCM Press).

1992. 'Messianic Ideas and Their Influence on the Jesus of History', in J.H. Charlesworth (ed.), *The Messiah: Earliest Judaism and Christianity* (Minneapolis: Fortress Press): 365-81.

Edanad, A.
1985 'Johannine Theology of the Church', *Jeevadhara* 15: 136-47.

Eicken, E., von, and H. Lindner
1975 'ἀποστέλλω', *The New International Dictionary of New Testament Theology* (ed. C. Brown; 3 vols.; Exeter: The Paternoster Press): I, 126-28.

Ellis, E.E.
1988 'Background and Christology of John's Gospel: Selected Motifs', *Southwestern Journal of Theology* 31: 24-31.

Emmel, S., *et al.* (eds.)
1984 *Nag Hammadi Codex III, 5: The Dialogue of the Savior* (The Coptic Gnostic Library; Leiden: E.J. Brill).

Fascher, E.
1968 'Christologie und Gnosis im vierten Evangelium', *TLZ* 93: 721-30.

Faulhaber, D.
1938 *Das Johannesevangelium und die Kirche* (Kassel: Johannes Stauda).

Faure, A.
1922. 'Die altestamentlichen Zitate im vierten Evangelium und die Quellenscheidungshypothese', *ZNW* 21: 99-121.

Feinberg, C.L.
1969 *The Prophecy of Ezekiel: The Glory of the Lord* (Chicago: Moody Press).

Feuillet, A.
1962. 'L'heure de Jésus et le signe de Cana', *Etudes Johanniques* (Bruges: Desclée de Brouer): 11-23.

1975 *The Priesthood of Christ and his Ministers* (trans. M.J.O. Connell; Garden City, NY: Doubleday).

Filoramo, G.
1990 *A History of Gnosticism* (trans. A. Alcock; Oxford: Basil Blackwell).

Filson, F.V.
1962. 'The Gospel of Life: A Study of the Gospel of John', in W. Klassen and G.F. Snyder (eds.), *Current Issues in New Testament Interpretation: Festschrift for Otto A. Piper* (New York: Harper & Brothers): 111-23.

Fischel, H.A.
1946 'Jewish Gnosticism in the Fourth Gospel', *JBL* 62: 157-74.

Fitzmyer, J.A.
1981, 1985 *The Gospel According to Luke* (AB, 28, 28a; 2 vols.; Garden City, NY: Doubleday).

Fortna, R.T.
1970 *The Gospel of Signs: A Reconstruction of the Narrative Source Underlying the Fourth Gospel* (SNTSMS, 11; Cambridge: Cambridge University Press).

1973 'From Christology to Soteriology: A Redaction-Critical Study of Salvation in the Fourth Gospel', *Int* 27: 31-47.

Fradua, J.L.
1991   'Eternal Life in the Johannine Writings', *Com(US)* 18: 24-34.
Freed, E.D.
1964   'Variations in the Language and Thought of John', *ZNW* 55: 167-97.
1968   'Samaritan Influence in the Gospel of John', *CBQ* 30: 580-87.
Fry, E.
1976   'Translating "Glory" in the New Testament', *Bible Translator* 27:
            421-25.
Frye, R.N.
1962   'Reitzenstein and Qumrân Revisited by an Iranian', *HTR* 55: 261-68.
Gardner-Smith, P.
1938   *Saint John and the Synoptic Gospels* (Cambridge: Cambridge University Press).
Gärtner, B.E.
1967–68   'The Pauline and Johannine Idea of the "to Know God" against the
            Hellenistic Background: The Greek Philosophical Principle "Like by
            Like" in Paul and John', *NTS* 14: 209-31.
Gaugler, E.
1924   'Die Bedeutung der Kirche in den joh. Schriften', *IKaZ* 14: 97-117,
            181-219.
Gemser, B.
1955   'The Rîb—or Controversy—Pattern in Hebrew Mentality', in M. Noth
            and D.W. Thomas (eds.), *Wisdom in Israel and in the Ancient Near
            East; presented to Professor Harold Henry Rowley by the Society for
            Old Testament Study in Association with the Editorial Board of Vetus
            Testamentum: in Celebration of his Sixtieth Birthday* (Leiden: E.J.
            Brill, 1960): 120-37.
Giverson, S. (ed.)
1963   *Apocryphon Johannis: The Coptic Text of Apocryphon Johannis in
            the Nag Hammadi Codex II with Translation, Introduction and Com-
            mentary* (Copenhagen: Prostant Apud Munksgaard).
Goguel, M.
1930–31   'Paulinisme et Johannisme', *RHPR* 10: 504-26; 11: 1-19, 120-56.
Gnilka, J.
1977   *The Origin of Christology* (Cambridge: Cambridge University Press).
1994   *Theologie des Neuen Testaments* (Freiburg: Herder).
Grant, F.C.
1953   'Modern Study of Jewish Liturgy', *ZAW* 65: 59-77.
Grant, R.M.
1950   'The Origin of the Fourth Gospel', *JBL* 69: 305-22.
1961   *Gnosticism: An Anthology* (London: Collins).
Grayston, K.
1967   'Jesus and the Church in St. John's Gospel', *London Quarterly* 36:
            106-15.
Greenberg, S.
1989   *A Treasury of Thoughts on Jewish Prayer* (Northvale, NJ; London:
            Jason Aronson).

Grese, W.C.
1979   *Corpus Hermeticum XIII and Early Christian Literature* (Studia ad
        Corpus Hellenisticum Novi Testamenti; Leiden: E.J. Brill).
Gryglewicz, F.
1959   'Der Evangelist Johannes und die Sekte von Qumran', *MTZ* 10: 226-
        28.
Haacker, K.
1973   'Jesus und die Kirche nach Johannes', *TZ* 29: 179-201.
Haenchen, E.
1962–63 'Der Vater, der mich gesandt hat', *NTS* 9: 208-16.
1984   *A Commentary on the Gospel of John* (trans. R.W. Funk; 2 vols.;
        Hermeneia; Philadelphia: Fortress Press).
Hahn, F.
1969   *The Titles of Jesus in Christology: Their History in Early Christianity.*
        (trans. H. Knight and G. Ogg; New York: World Books).
Hanson, A.T.
1974   'Hodayoth xv and John 17: A Comparison of Content and Form',
        Hermathena (Dublin) 118: 48-58.
Harnack, A.
1905   *History of Dogma*, I (trans. from the 3rd German edn; London:
        Williams & Norgate).
1923   *Erforschtes und Erlebtes* (Giessen: Alfred Töpelmann).
1958   *Geschichte der altchristlichen Literatur bis Eusebius* (II.1; Leipzig:
        J.C. Hinrichs).
Harris, R.L. (ed.)
1980   *Theological Wordbook of the Old Testament* (2 vols; Chicago: Moody
        Press).
Harrison, E.F.
1978   'A Study of John 1: 14', in R.A. Guelich (ed.), *Unity and Diversity in
        New Testament Theology: Essays in Honor of G. E. Ladd* (Grand
        Rapids, MI: Eerdmans): 23-36.
Hegermann, H.
1990   'δόξα', *EDNT*: I, 344-49.
Heinemann, J.
1977   *Prayer in the Talmud: Forms and Patterns* (trans. R.S. Sarason; Studia
        Judaica, 9; Berlin; New York: W. de Gruyter).
Hendriksen, W.
1961   *A Commentary on the Gospel of John* (Edinburgh: The Banner of
        Truth Trust [1954]).
Hengel, M.
1976   *The Son of God: The Origin of Christology and the Rise of Jewish-
        Hellenistic Religion* (Philadalphia: Fortress Press).
Hengel, M.
1989   *The Johannine Question* (London: SCM Press).
Henrix, H.H. (ed.)
1979   *Jüdische Liturgie: Geschichte-Struktur-Wesen* (Quaestiones Disputatae,
        86; Freiburg: Herder).

Higgins, A.J.B. (ed.)
1959 *New Testament Essays: Studies in Memory of Thomas Walter Manson 1893–1958* (Manchester: Manchester University Press).

Hill, D.
1967 *Greek Words and Hebrew Meanings: Studies in the Semantics of Soteriological Terms* (SNTSMS, 5; Cambridge: Cambridge University Press.

Hoffman, L.A.
1979 *The Canonization of the Synagogue Service* (Notre Dame; London: University of Notre Dame Press).

Horbury, W.
1982 'The Benediction of the Minim and Early Jewish-Christian Controversy', *JTS* 33: 19-61.

Horsley, R.A.
1992 ' "Messianic" Figures and Movements in the First-Century Palestine', in J.H. Charlesworth (ed.), *The Messiah* (Minneapolis: Fortress Press): 276-95.

Horstmann, A.
1991 'οἶδα', *EDNT*, II, 493 94.

Hoskyns, E.C.
1940 *The Fourth Gospel* (ed. F.N. Davey; London: Faber and Faber).

Hossfeld, F.-L., and van der Velden
1994 'שלח', *ThWAT*: VIII, 46-68.

Hübner, H.
1990 'ἀλήθεια', *EDNT*: I, 57-60.

Huby, J.
1937 'Un double problème de critique textuelle et d'interprétation: Saint Jean xvii 11-12', *RSR* 27: 408-21.

Ibuki, Y.
1988 'Die Doxa des Gesandten—Studie zur johanneischen Christologie', *AJBI* 14: 38-81.

Jeremias, J.
1967 *Daily Prayer in the Life of Jesus and the Primitive Church: The Prayers of Jesus* (Studies in Biblical Theology, Second Series, 6; London: SCM Press).
1972 *The Parables of Jesus* (London: SCM Press, rev. edn).

Johnson, M.D.
1985 'Life of Adam and Eve', in J.H. Charlesworth (ed.), *The Old Testament Pseudepigrapha* (Garden City, NY: Doubleday): II, 249-57.

Johnson, S.E.
1972 *A Commentary on the Gospel According to St. Mark* (London: A. & C. Black, 2nd edn).

Jonas, H.
1963 *The Gnostic Religion: The Message of the Alien God and the Beginnings of Christianity* (Boston: Beacon Press).

Jonge, M. de.
1973　　　'Jewish Expectations about the "Messiah" according to the Fourth
　　　　　Gospel', *NTS* 19: 246-70.
Käsemann, E.
1951　　　'Ketzer und Zeuge: Zum johanneischen Verfasserproblem', *ZTK* 48:
　　　　　292-311.
1964　　　*Essays on New Testament Themes* (Philadelphia: Fortress Press).
1966　　　*Jesu letzter Wille nach Johannes 17* (Tübingen: J.C.B. Mohr).
1969　　　*New Testament Questions of Today* (London: SCM Press).
1978　　　*The Testament of Jesus: A Study of the Gospel of John in the Light of
　　　　　Chapter 17* (trans. Gerhard Krodel; Philadelphia: Fortress Press).
1980　　　*Commentary on Romans* (trans. G.W. Bromiley; Grand Rapids, MI:
　　　　　Eerdmans [1973]).
Keil, C.F., and F. Delitzsch
1975　　　*A Commentary on the Old Testament* (10 vols.; Grand Rapids, MI:
　　　　　Eerdmans).
Kirby, J.C.
1968　　　*Ephesians: Baptism and Pentecost: An Inquiry into the Structure and
　　　　　Purpose of the Epistle to the Ephesians* (London: SPCK).
Kirzner, Y.
1991　　　*The Art of Jewish Prayer* (Northvale, NJ; London: Jason Aronson).
Kittel, G., and G. von Rad
1964　　　'δόξα', *TDNT*: II, 232-55.
Klauck, H.-J.
1985　　　'Gemeinde ohne Amt? Erfahrungen mit der Kirche in den johan-
　　　　　neischen Schriften', *BZ* 29: 193-220.
Koester, H.
1987　　　*Introduction to the New Testament* (2 vols; Philadelphia: Fortress
　　　　　Press).
Koester, H., and E.H. Pagels
1990　　　'The Dialogue of the Savior', in J.M. Robinson (ed.), *The Nag Ham-
　　　　　madi Library in English* (San Francisco: Harper & Row; rev. edn):
　　　　　244-46.
Koester, H., and J.M. Robinson
1971　　　*Trajectories through Early Christianity* (Philadelphia: Fortress Press).
Kolenkow, A.B.
1975　　　'The Genre Testament and Forecast of the Future in the Hellenistic
　　　　　Jewish Milieu', *JSJ* 5: 57-71.
Kotze, P.P.A.
1977　　　'Die eenheid van die kerk in die Johannesevangelie', *ThViat* 5: 111-
　　　　　14.
Kraft, R.A.
1965　　　*The Apostolic Fathers: A New Translation and Commentary*. III.
　　　　　Barnabas and the Didache (London: Thomas Nelson & Sons).
Kruijf, T.C., de
1970　　　'The Glory of the Only Son (John 1: 14)', in *Studies in John:
　　　　　Presented to Professor Dr. J.N. Sevenster on the Occasion of his
　　　　　Seventieth Birthday* (Leiden: E.J. Brill): 111-23.

Kuhl, J.
1967   *Die Sendung Jesu und der Kirche nach dem Johannes-Evangelium* (St Augustin: Steyler Verlag).
1971   'Mission nach dem Johannes-Evangelium', *VSVD* 14: 124-32.

Kuhn, H.-W.
1966   *Enderwartung und gegenwärtiges Heil: Untersuchungen zu den Gemeindeliedern von Qumran* (Studien zur Umwelt des Neues Testaments, 4; Göttingen: Vandenhoeck & Ruprecht).

Kümmel, W.G.
1966   *Introduction to the New Testament* (trans. A.J. Matil; London: SCM Press).
1973   *The New Testament: The History of the Investigation of Its Problems* (trans. S. McLean Gilmour and II.C. Kee; London: SCM Press [1972]).
1980   The Theology of the New Testament: According to Its Major Witnesses, Jesus–Paul–John (trans. J.E. Steely; London: SCM Press [1974]).

Kurz, W.
1985   'Luke 22: 14-38 and Greco-Roman and Biblical Farewell Addresses', *JBL* 104: 251-68.

Kysar, R.
1975   *The Fourth Evangelist and IIis Gospel: An Examination of Contemporary Scholarship* (Minneapolis: Augsburg).
1977   'Community and Gospel: Vectors in Fourth Gospel Criticism', *Int* 31: 355-66.
1993   *John, the Maverick Gospel* (Louisville, KY: Westminster/John Knox Press, rev. edn).

Lacomara, A.
1974   'Deuteronomy and the Farewell Discourse (Jn 13: 31–16; 33)', *CBQ* 36: 65-84.

Ladd, G.F.
1974   *A Theology of the New Testament* (Grand Rapids, MI: Eerdmans).

Lambrecht, J.
1979   'Paul's Farewell Address at Miletus (Acts 20, 17-38)', in J. Kremer (ed.), *Les Actes des Apôtres: Tradition, rédaction, théologie* (BETL, 48; Leuven: Leuven University Press): 307-37.

Lang, C.
1981   *Cornuti Theologiae Graecae Compendium* (Leipzig: B.G. Teubner).

Lattke, M.
1975   *Einheit im Wort: Die spezifische Bedeutung von ἀγάπη, ἀγαπᾶν und φιλεῖν im Johannesevangelium* (StANT, 41; Munich: Kösel Verlag).
1975a   'Sammlung durchs Wort: Erlöser, Erlösung und Erlöste im Johannesevangelium', *Bibel und Kirche* 4: 118-22.
1979–1980   *Die Oden Salomos in ihrer Bedeutung für Neues Testament und Gnosis*, Band I, Ia, II, III (Orbis biblicus et orientalis, 25; Freiburg: Universitätsverlag; Göttingen: Vandenhoeck & Ruprecht).
1985   'Heiligkeit III. Neues Testament', *TRE* 14: 703-708.

Lattke, M., and M. Franzmann
1994   'Gnostic Jesuses and the Gnostic Jesus of John', in H. Preissler *et al.*
            (eds.), *Gnosisforschung und Religionsgeschichte: Festschrift für Kurt*
            Rudolph zum 65. Geburtstag (Marburg: Diagonal-Verlag): 143-53.
Laurentin, A.
1964   'We'attah—Kai nyn: Formule charactéristique des textes juridiques et
            liturgiques (à propos de Jean 17, 5)', *Bib* 45: 168-97, 413-32.
Layton, B. (ed.)
1989   *Nag Hammadi Codex II,2-7 together with XIII,2*, Brit. Lib.*
            Or.4926(1), and P. Oxy. 1, 654, 655.: Gospel According to Thomas,
            Gospel According to Philip, Hypostasis of the Archons, and Indexes
            (The Coptic Gnostic Library; Leiden).
Leroy, H.
1968   *Rätsel und Missverständnis: Ein Beitrag zur Formgeschichte des*
            Johannesevangeliums (Bonn: Peter Hanstein).
Lieu, J.M.
1979   'Gnosticism and the Gospel of John', *ExpTim* 90: 233-37.
Lightfoot, R.H.
1956   *St. John's Gospel: A Commentary* (Oxford: Clarendon Press).
Lindars, B.
1971   *Behind the Fourth Gospel* (Studies in Creative Criticism, 3; London:
            SPCK).
1972   *The Gospel of John* (New Century Bible Commentary; Grand Rapids:
            Eerdmans).
Lindars, B., and B. Rigaux
1974.   *Témoignage de l'évangile de Jean* (Louvain: Desclée de Brouwer).
Lindemann, A.
1980   'Gemeinde und Welt im Johannesevangelium', in D. Lührmann and
            G. Strecker (eds.), *Kirche: Festschrift für Günther Bornkamm zum 75.*
            Geburtstag (Tübingen: J.C.B. Mohr [Paul Siebeck]): 133-61.
Loader, W.R.G.
1989   *The Christology of the Fourth Gospel: Structure and Issues* (Frankfurt;
            Peter Lang).
Lohse, E.
1986   *Die Texte aus Qumran: Hebräisch und Deutsch mit masoretischer*
            Punktation. Übersetzung, Einführung und Anmerkungen (München:
            Kösel Verlag; 4th edn).
Loisy, A.
1921   *Le quatrième évangile: Les épîtres dites de Jean* (Paris: Nourry, 2nd
            edn).
Luzarraga, J.
1991   'Eternal Life in the Johannine Writings', *Communio* 16: 24-34.
MacRae, G.
1970   'The Fourth Gospel and Religionsgeschichte', *CBQ* 32: 13-24.
1987   'Messiah and Gospel', in J. Neusner *et al.* (eds.), *Judaisms and their*
            Messiahs at the Turn of the Christian Era (Cambridge: Cambridge
            University Press): 169-85.

Maier, J.
1960   'Zum Begriff זחי' in den Texten von Qumran', *ZAW* 72: 148-66.
Malatesta, E.
1971   'The Literary Structure of John 17', *Bib* 52: 190-214.
Mann, C.S.
1986   *Mark: A New Translation with Introduction and Commentary* (AB, 27;
            Garden City, NY: Doubleday).
Manns, F.
1991   'La prière missionnaire de Jésus', in *idem* (ed.), *L'évangile de Jean: à
            la lumière du Judaïsme* (Studium Biblicum Franciscanum; Analecta,
            33; Jerusalem: Franciscan Printing Press): 383-400.
Marshall, I.H.
1966   'The Synoptic Son of Man Sayings in Recent Discussion', *NTS* 12:
            327-51.
1970   'The Son of Man in Contemporary Debate', *EvQ* 42: 67-87.
Martin, B.
1968   *Prayer in Judaism* (New York; London: Basic Books).
Martyn, J.L.
1977   'Glimpses into the History of the Johannine Community', in M. de
            Jonge (ed.), *L'évangile de Jean: sources, réduction, théologie*
            (Leuven: Leuven University Press): 149-75.
1978   *The Gospel of John in Christian History: Essays for Interpreters* (New
            York: Paulist Press [1968]).
1979   *History and Theology in the Fourth Gospel* (Nashville: Abingdon
            Press, 2nd rev. edn [1968]).
Marzotto, D.
1977   'Giovanni 17 e il Targum di Esodo 19-20', *RevistBib* 25: 375-88.
McPolin, J.
1969   'Mission in the Fourth Gospel', *ITQ* 36: 113-22.
Meeks, W.A.
1972   'The Man from Heaven in Johannine Sectarianism', *JBL* 91: 44-72.
Menoud, P.-H.
1947.   *L'évangile de Jean d'après les recherches récentes* (Paris: Neuchatel,
            2nd edn).
Mercer, C.
1990   'Ἀποστέλλειν and πέμπειν in John', *NTS* 36: 619-24.
1992   'Jesus the Apostle: "Sending" and the Theology of John', *JETS* 35:
            457-62.
Merrill, E.H.
1975   *Qumran and Predestination: A Theological Study of the Thanksgiving
            Hymns* (Leiden: E.J. Brill).
Metzger, B.M.
1971   *A Textual Commentary on the Greek New Testament: A Companion
            Volume to the United Bible Societies' Greek New Testament* (London;
            New York: United Bible Society, 3rd edn).
Michel, H.-J.
1973   *Die Abschiedsrede des Paulus an die Kirche Apg 20, 17-38: Motiv-
            geschichte und theologische Bedeutung* (Munich: Kösel Verlag).

Miller, E.L.
1993   'The Johannine Origins of the Johannine Logos', *JBL* 112: 445-57.
Miller, J.W.
1976   'The Concept of the Church in the Gospel according to John' (PhD
                dissertation, Princeton Theological Seminary).
Minear, P.S.
1982   'Logos Ecclesiology in John's Gospel', in R. Berkey and S. Edwards
                (eds.), *Christological Perspectives: Festschrift for H.K. MacArthur*
                (New York: The Pilgrim Press): 95-111.
1984   *The Martyr's Gospel* (New York: The Pilgrim Press).
Miranda, J.P.
1977   *Die Sendung Jesu im vierten Evangelium: Religions—und theologie-
                geschichtliche Untersuchungen zu den Sendungsformeln* (Stuttgarter
                Bibelstudien, 87; Stuttgart: Katholisches Bibelwerk).
Moloney, F.J.
1982   The Prayer of Jesus' Hour', *CleR* 67: 79-83.
Morris, L.
1971   *The Gospel According to John: The English Text with Introduction,
                Exposition and Notes* (Grand Rapids, MI: Eerdmans).
Morrison, C.D.
1965   'Mission and Ethic: An Interpretation of John 17', *Int* 19: 259-73.
Moule, C.F.D.
1975   'The Meaning of "Life" in the Gospel and Epistles of St John', *Theol*
                78: 114-25.
1995   ' "The Son of Man": Some of the Facts', *NTS* 41: 277-79.
Mowry, L.
1954   'The Dead Sea Scrolls and the Background for the Gospel of St John',
                BA 17: 78-94.
Müller, H.-P.
1986   'נָבִיא', *ThWAT*: V, 140-63.
Munck, J.
1950   'Discours d'adieu dans le Nouveau Testament et dans la littérature
                biblique', in J.J. Allmen, *et al.* (eds.), *Aux sources de la tradition
                chrétienne: Festschrift for M. Goguel* (Paris: Neuchâtel): 155-70.
Murphy-O'Connor, J., and J.H. Charlesworth (eds.)
1990   *Paul and the Dead Sea Scrolls* (Christian Origin Library; New York:
                Crossroad).
Myers, J.M.
1974   *I and II Esdras: Introduction, Translation and Commentary* (AB, 42.
                New York: Doubleday).
Neill, S., and N.T. Wright
1987   *The Interpretation of the New Testament: 1861–1986* (Oxford: Oxford
                University Press).
Nereparampil, L.
1979   'The Church in the Johannine Literature', *IJT* 28: 169-77.
Neusner, J.
1983.   *Formative Judaism: Religious, Historical, and Literary Studies* (Chico,
                CA: Scholars Press).

Nicol, W.
1972.   *The Semeia in the Fourth Gospel: Tradition and Redaction* (Leiden:
             E.J. Brill).
Noack, B.
1954   *Zur johanneischen Tradition: Beiträge zur Kritik an der literar-
             kritischen Analyse des vierten Evangeliums* (Copenhagen: Rosenkilde
             & Bagger).
Nordheim, E., van
1980   *Die Lehre der Alten. I. Das Testament als Literaturgattung im Juden-
             tum der hellenistisch-römischen Zeit* (Leiden: E.J. Brill).
North, M.
1966   *Exodus: A Commentary* (London: SCM Press).
O'Grady, J.F.
1975   'Individualism and Johannine Ecclesiology', *BTB* 5: 227-61.
1977   'Individual and Community in John' (PhD dissertation, Pontifical
             Biblical Institute).
1977a   'Johannine Ecclesiology: A Critical Evaluation', *BTB* 7: 36-44.
Odeberg, H.
1968   The Fourth Gospel: Interpreted in Its Relation to Contemporaneous
             Religious Currents in Palestine (Amsterdam: B.R. Grüner [1929]).
Oehler, W.
1936.   *Das Johannesevangelium: Eine Missionschrift für die Welt* (Gütersloh:
             Bertelsmann).
Okura, T.
1984   *Gemeinde und Welt im Johannesevangelium: Ein Beitrag zur Frage
             nach der theologischen und pragmatischen Funktion des johan-
             neischen Dualismus* (WMANT, 56; Neukirchen–Vluyn: Neukirchener
             Verlag).
1988   *The Johannine Approach to Mission. A Contextual Study of John 4:
             1-42* (WUNT, 2; Tübingen: J.C.B. Mohr [Paul Siebeck]).
Pagels, E.H.
1975   *The Gnostic Paul: Gnostic Exegesis of the Pauline Letters* (Philadel-
             phia: Fortress Press).
Painter, J.
1975   *John: Witness & Theologian* (London: SPCK).
1978   'The Church and Israel in the Gospel of John: A Response', *NTS* 25:
             103-12.
1981   'The Farewell Discourses and the History of Johannine Christianity',
             NTS 27: 525-43.
1993   *The Quest for the Messiah: The History, Literature and Theology of the
             Johannine Community* (Edinburgh: T. & T. Clark).
Pamment, M.
1983   'The Meaning of Doxa in the Fourth Gospel', *ZNW* 74: 12-16.
Pancaro, S.
1970   'People of God in St. John's Gospel?', *NThS* 16: 114-29.
1974–75   'The Relationship of the Church to Israel in the Gospel of John', *NTS*
             21: 396-405.

Parker, P.
1956   'Two Editions of John', *JBL* 75: 303-14.
Parrott, D.M.
1990   'The Sophia of Jesus Christ', in J.M. Robinson (ed.), *The Nag Ham-
              madi Library in English* (San Francisco: Harper, 3rd rev. edn): 220-
              21.
Parrott, D.M. (ed.)
1991   *Nag Hammadi Codices III,3-4 and V,1 with Papyrus Berolinensis
              8502,3 and Oxyrhynchus Papyrus 1081: Eugnostos and The Sophia
              of Jesus Christ* (The Coptic Gnostic Library; Leiden: E.J. Brill).
Pazdan, M.M.
1982   'Discipleship as the Appropriation of Eschatological Salvation in
              the Fourth Gospel' (PhD dissertation; University of St Michael's
              College [Canada]).
Percy, E.
1939   *Untersuchungen über den Ursprung der johanneischen Theologie.
              Zugleich ein Beitrag zur Frage nach der Entstehung des Gnostizismus*
              (Lund: C.W.K. Gleerup).
Pesch, R.
1986   *Die Apostelgeschichte.* II. *(Apg 13-23)* (Evangelisch-Katholischer
              Kommentar zum Neuen Testament; Zürich: Benzinger Verlag).
Petrie, F.
1908   'Aspects of Egyptian Religions', *Transactions of the Third Interna-
              tional Congress for the History of Religions* (2 vols.; Oxford: Claren-
              don Press): I, 195-98.
Poirier, P.-H.
1981   *L'hymne de la perle des Actes Thomas: Introduction, texte—traduc-
              tion, commentaire* (Homo Religiosus, 8; Louvain-La-Neuve: l'Uni-
              versité Catholique).
Pollard, T. E.
1970   *Johannine Christology and the Early Church* (Cambridge: Cambridge
              University Press).
1977   'The Father–Son and God–Believer Relationships according to St
              John: A Brief Study of John's Use of Prepositions', in *idem* (ed.),
              L'évangile de Jean: sources, rédaction, théologie (Leuven: Leuven
              University Press).
Popkes, W.
1978   'Zum Verständnis der Mission bei Johannes', *Zeitschrift für Mission* 4:
              63-69.
Potterie, I. de la
1959   'Οἶδα et γινώσκω, Les deux modes de la connaissance dans le quat-
              rième évangile', *Bib* 40: 709-25.
Quispel, G.
1975   'John and Jewish Christianity' (Gnostic Studies II; Istanbul: Neder-
              lands Historisch-Archaeologisch Instituut): 210-29.
1990   'Qumran, John and Jewish Christianity', in J.H. Charlesworth (ed.),
              John and the Dead Sea Scrolls (New York: Crossroad [1972]): 137-
              85.

Randall, J.F.
1965   'The Theme of Unity in John 17: 20-23', *ETL* 41: 373-94.
Radl, W.
1991   'καθώς', *EDNT*: II, 226.
Ray, C.A.
1983   'The Concept of Discipleship in the Johannine School' (PhD
            dissertation, New Orleans Baptist Theological Seminary).
Reicke, B.
1954–55   'Traces of Gnosticism in the Dead Sea Scrolls?', *NTS* 1: 137-41.
1992   'The Constitution of the Primitive Church in the Light of Jewish Doc-
            uments', in K. Stendahl (ed.), *The Scrolls and the New Testament*
            (Christian Origins Library; New York: Crossroad): 143-56.
Rengstorf, K.H.
1965   'ἀποστέλλω (πέμπω)', *TDNT*: I, 398-447.
Rensberger, D.
1988   *Johannine Faith and Liberating Community* (Philadelphia: Westmin-
            ster Press).
Rensburg, S.P.J.J. van
1958   'Hagios in die nieu-testamentiese voorstelling' (PhD dissertation, Uni-
            versiteit van Pretoria).
Richter, G.
1977   *Studien zum Johannesevangelium* (Biblische Untersuchungen, 13;
            Regensburg: Friedrich Pustet).
Riedl, J.
1973   'Die Funktion der Kirche nach Johannes. "Vater, wie du mich in die
            Welt gesandt hast, so habe ich auch sie in die Welt gesandt" (Joh 17,
            18)', *BiKi* 28: 12-14.
Riga, P.
1963   'Signs of Glory: The Use of "Semeion" in St John's Gospel', *Int* 17:
            402-24.
Ritt, H.
1979   *Das Gebet zum Vater: Zur Interpretation von Joh 17* (Forschung zur
            Bibel, 36; Würzburg: Echter Verlag).
1993   'πέμπω', *EDNT*: III, 68.
Robinson, J.A.T.
1959   'The New Look on the Fourth Gospel', *SE* 1: 338-50.
1959–60   'The Destination and Purpose of St. John's Gospel', *NTS* 6: 117-31.
1976   *Redating the New Testament* (London: SCM Press).
Robinson, J.M.
1959   'Recent Research in the Fourth Gospel', *JBL* 78: 242-52.
1978   'Gnosticism and the New Testament', in B. Aland (ed.), *Gnosis:
            Festschrift Hans Jonas* (Göttingen: Vandenhoeck & Ruprecht): 125-
            43.
Parrott, D.M. (ed.)
1990   *The Nag Hammadi Library in English* (San Francisco: Harper, 3rd rev.
            edn).
Roloff, J.
1993   *Die Kirche im Neuen Testament* (Grundrisse zum Neuen Testament;

Das Neue Testament Deutsch; Ergänzungsreihe, 10; Göttingen: Vandenhoeck & Ruprecht).

Rordorf, W., and A. Tuiler
1978   *La doctrine des douze apôtres (Didaché): Introduction, texte, traduction, notes, appendice et index* (Sources Chrétiennes; Paris: Cerf).

Rosenblatt, M.-E.
1988   'The Voice of One Who Prays in John 17', in C. Osiek and D. Senior (eds.), *Scripture and Prayer* (Wilmington, DE: Michael Glazier): 131-44.

Ruckstuhl, E.
1951   *Die literarische Einheit des Johannesevangeliums: Der gegenwärtige Stand der einschlägigen Erforschung* (Studia Friburgensia, 3; Freiburg in der Schweiz: Paulus-Verlag).

Rudolph, K.
1983   *Gnosis: The Nature and History of an Ancient Religion* (trans. R.M. Wilson; Edinburgh: T. & T. Clark).

Ruiz, M.R.
1987   *Der Missionsgedanke des Johannesevangeliums: Ein Beitrag zur johanneischen Soteriologie und Ekklesiologie* (Würzburg: Echter Verlag).

Sanders, E.P.
1985   *Jesus and Judaism* (London: SCM Press).

Sandmel, S.
1978   *Judaism and Christian Beginings* (New York: Oxford University Press).

Sasse, H.
1965   'κόσμος', *TDNT*: III, 868-98.

Schlatter, A.
1902   'Die Sprache und Heimat des vierten Evangelisten' (BFChTh, 6, 4; Gütersloh: C. Bertelsmann).

Schmidt, C. (ed.)
1978   *Pistis Sophia: Translation and Notes by V. Macdermot. The Coptic Gnostic Library* (The Coptic Gnostic Library; Leiden: E.J. Brill).

Schmidt, H.
1928   *Das Gebet des Angeklagten im Alten Testament* (BZAW, 49; Berlin: W. de Gruyter).

Schmithals, W.
1972   *Paul and the Gnostics* (Nashville, TX: Abingdon Press).
1978   *Zur Herkunft der gnostischen Elemente in der Sprache des Paulus. Gnosis: Festschrift für Hans Jonas* (ed. B. Aland; Göttingen: Vandenhoeck & Ruprecht): 385-414.
1992   *Johannesevangelium und Johannesbriefe: Forschungsgeschichte und Analyse* (BZNW, 64; Berlin: W. de Gruyter).

Schnackenburg, R.
1973   'Struckturanalyse von Joh 17', *BZ* 17: 67-78, 196-202.
1974   'The Church in the Johannine Writings, Including the Apocalypse', *The Church in the New Testament* (London: Burns & Oates [1965]).

1977   'Is there a Johannine Ecclesiology?', in M. Taylor (ed.), *Companion to John* (New York: Alba House [1965]): 247-56.

1984   'Der Missionsgedanke des Johannesevangeliums im heutigen Horizont', in *Das Johannesevangelium* (vol. 4; Freiburg: Herder): 58-72.

1990/[1968]   *The Gospel According to St John* (trans. K. Smyth, *et al.*; 3 vols; New York: Crossroad).

Schneider, G.

1982   'Der Missionsauftrag Jesu in der Darstellung der Evangelien', in K. Kertelge (ed.), *Mission im Neuen Testament* (Freiburg: Herder): 71-92.

1982a   *Die Apostelgeschichte*, II (Herders Theologischer Kommentar zum Neuen Testament; Freiburg: Herder).

Schnelle, U.

1991   'Johanneische Ekklesiologie', *NTS* 37: 37-50.

Schoeps, H.J.

1970   'Judenchristentum und Gnosis', in U. Bianchi (ed.), *The Origins of Gnosticism: Colloquium of Messina 13–18 April 1966* (Leiden: E.J. Brill): 528-37.

Schottroff, L.

1970   *Der Glaubende und die feindliche Welt: Beobachtungen zum gnostischen Dualismus und seine Bedeutung für Paulus und das Johannesevangelium* (WMANT, 37; Neukirchen–Vluyn: Neukirchener Verlag).

Schubert, K.

1963   'Jüdischer Hellenismus und jüdische Gnosis', *Wort und Wahrheit* 18: 455-61.

Schürer, E.

1898   *A History of the Jewish People in the Time of Jesus Christ* (2 vols.; trans. S. Taylor and P. Christie; Edinburgh: T & T. Clark).

Schwartz, E.

1907   'Aporien im vierten Evangelium', *NGWG*: 324-72.

Schweizer, E.

1939   *EGO EIMI: Die religionsgeschichtliche Herkunft und theologische Bedeutung der johanneischen Bildreden, zugleich ein Beitrag zur Quellenfrage des vierten Evangelium* (FRLANT, 56; Göttingen: Vandenhoeck & Ruprecht).

1959   'Der Kirchenbegriff im Evangelium und in den Briefen des Johannes', *SE* 1: 363-81.

1961   *Church Order in the New Testament* (trans. F. Clarke; London: SCM Press).

1966   'Zum religionsgeschichtlichen Hintergrund der "Sendungsformel" (Jn 3, 16-17)', *ZNW* 57: 199-210.

Scott, W. (ed.)

1968   *Hermetica: The Ancient Greek and Latin Writings Which Contain Religious or Philosophic Teachings Ascribed to Hermes Trismegistus* (4 vols.; London: Dawson of Pall Mall).

Scroggs, R.

1988   *Christology in Paul and John: The Reality and Revelation of God* (Philadelphia: Fortress Press).

Segovia, F.F.
1982   *Love Relationship in the Johannine Tradition: Agape/agapan in I John and the Fourth Gospel* (SBLDS, 58; Chico: Scholars Press).
1983   'John 15: 18-16: 4a: A First Addition to the Original Farewell Discourse?', *CBQ* 45: 210-30.
1985   'The Structure, Tendenz, and Sitz im Leben of John 13: 31–14: 31', *JBL* 104: 471-93.
1985a   ' "Peace I Leave with You: My Peace I Give to You": Discipleship in the Fourth Gospel', in *idem* (ed.), *Discipleship in the New Testament* (Minneapolis: Fortress Press): 76-102.
1991   *The Farewell to the World: The Johannine Call to Abide* (Minneapolis: Fortress Press).

Seynaeve, J.
1977   'Les verbes ἀποστέλλω et πέμπω dans le vocabulaire théologique de saint Jean', in M. de Jonge (ed.), *L'évangile de Jean: sources, rédaction, théologie* (Leuven: Leuven University Press): 385-89.

Smith, D.M.
1965   *The Composition and Order of the Fourth Gospel: Bultmann's Literary Theory* (New Haven: Yale University Press).
1977   'The Presentation of Jesus in the Fourth Gospel', *CBQ* 31: 367-78.
1984   *Johannine Christianity: Essays on its Setting, Sources, and Theology* (Columbia, SC: University of South Carolina Press).
1986   *John* (Philadelphia: Fortress).

Smith, D.M., and Spivey, R.A.
1989   *Anatomy of the New Testament: A Guide to its Structure and Meaning* (4th edn; New York: Macmillan).

Snaith, N.H.
1944   *The Distinctive Ideas of the Old Testament* (New York: Schocken Books): 24-50.

Stauffer, E.
1950   *Abschiedsreden: Reallexikon für Antike und Christentum* (Stuttgart: Hiersemann): I, 30-35.
1955   *New Testament Theology* (trans. J. Marsh; London: SCM Press).

Stevenson, J. (ed.)
1987   *A New Eusebius: Documents Illustrating the History of the Church to AD 337* (rev. W.H.C. Frend; London: SPCK).

Stimpfle, A.
1990   *Blinde sehen: Die Eschatologie im traditionsgeschichtlichen Prozeß des Johannesevangeliums* (Berlin: W. de Gruyter).

Tarelli, C.C.
1946   'Johannine Synonyms', *JTS* 47: 175.

Taylor, V.
1966   *The Gospel According to St. Mark: The Greek Text with Introduction, Notes, and Indexes* (2nd edn; London: Macmillan Press).

Teeple, H.M.
1974   *The Literary Origin of the Gospel of John* (Evanston, IL: Religion and Ethics Institute).

Temple, S.
 1961   'A Key to the Composition of the Fourth Gospel', *JBL* 80: 220-32.
Theobald, M.
 1988   *Die Fleischwerdung des Logos: Studien zum Verhältnis des Johannes-
             prologs zum Corpus des Evangeliums und zu 1 Joh* (Münster: Aschen-
             dorff).
Theron, S.W.
 1987   '΄INA "ΩΣIN"EN: A Multifaceted Approach to an Important Thrust
             in the Prayer of Jesus in John 17', *Neot* 21: 77-94.
Thompson, M.M.
 1989   'Eternal Life in the Gospel of John', *Ex Auditu: An Annual of the
             Frederick Neumann Symposium on Theological Interpretation of
             Scripture* 5: 35-55.
Thüsing, W.
 1975   *Herrlichkeit und Einheit. Eine Auslegung des Hohepriesterlichen
             Gebetes Jesu (Johannes 17)* (2nd edn; Münster: Aschendorff).
 1977   'Die Bitten des johanneischen Jesus in dem Gebet Joh 17 und die
             Intentionen Jesu von Nazareth', in R. Schnackenburg *et al.* (eds.),
             *Die Kirche des Anfangs: Festschrift Heinz Schürmann zum 65.
             Geburtstag* (Erfurter Theologische Studien, 38; Leipzig: St. Benno):
             307-37.
Thyen, H.
 1988   'Johannesevangelium', *TRE* 17: 200-25.
Tietze, G.
 1954   'Knowledge of God in the Fourth Gospel', *Journal of Bible and
             Religion* 22: 14-19.
Tillmann, F.
 1931   *Das Johannesevangelium* (4th edn; Bonn: Hanstein).
Torm, F.
 1931   'Die Psychologie des vierten Evangeliums: Augenzeuge oder nicht?',
             ZNW 30: 124-44.
Torrey, C.C.
 1923   'The Aramaic Origin of the Fourth Gospel', *HTR* 16: 305-44.
Turner, N.
 1976   *A Grammar of New Testament Greek*. IV. *Style* (Edinburgh: T. & T.
             Clark): 64-79.
Turner, W.
 1952–53   'Believing and Everlasting Life', *ExpTim* 64: 50-52.
Ukpong, J.S.
 1989   ' "Jesus" Prayer for his Followers (Jn 17) in Mission Perspective',
             African Theological Journal 18: 49-60.
Unnik, W.C. van
 1959   'The Purpose of St John's Gospel', *SE* 1: 382-411.
Uprichard, H.
 1984   'God's Glory in God's Son [Jn 17]', *Evangel* 2: 5-6.
Vellanickal, M.
 1977   *The Divine Sonship of the Christians in the Johannine Writings*
             (Rome: Biblical Institute Press).

| 1980 | ' "Discipleship" according to the Gospel of John', *Jeevadhara* 10: 131-47. |

Vermes, G.

1973	*Jesus the Jew: A Historian's Reading of the Gospels* (Glasgow: Fontana/Collins).
1977	*The Dead Sea Scrolls: Qumran in Perspective* (London: Collins).
1990	*The Dead Sea Scrolls in English* (3rd rev. edn; Harmondsworth: Penguin Books).
1993	*The Religion of Jesus the Jew* (Minneapolis: Fortress Press).

Viviano, B.T.

| 1984 | 'The Missionary Program of John's Gospel', *Bible Today* 22: 387-93. |

Walde, U.C. von

| 1989 | *The Earliest Version of John's Gospel: Recovering the Gospel of Signs* (Wilmington, DE: Michael Glazier). |

Waldstein, M.

| 1990 | 'The Mission of Jesus and the Disciples in John', *Com(US)* 17: 311-33. |

Walker, W.M.

| 1982 | 'The Lord's Prayer in Matthew and in John', *NTS* 28: 237-56. |

Wengst, K.

| 1981 | *Bedrängte Gemeinde und verherrlichter Christus: Der historische Ort des Johannesevangeliums als Schlüssel zu seiner Interpretation* (Biblisch-Theologische Studien, 5; Neukirchen–Vluyn: Neukirchener Verlag). |

Wenham, D. (ed.)

| 1984 | *The Jesus Tradition outside the Gospels* (Sheffield: JSOT Press). |

Wenham, J.W.

| 1965 | *The Elements of New Testament Greek* (Cambridge: Cambridge University Press). |

Westcott, B.F.

| 1955 | *The Gospel According to St John* (Grand Rapids, MI: Eerdmans). |

Wiefel, W.

| 1979 | 'Die Scheidung von Gemeinde und Welt im Johannesevangelium auf dem Hintergrund der Trennung von Kirche und Synagoge', *TZ* 35: 213-27. |

Wikenhauser, A.

| 1957 | *Das Evangelium nach Johannes* (2nd edn; Regensburg: Friedrich Pustet). |

Wilkens, W.

| 1958 | *Die Entstehungsgeschichte des vierten Evangeliums* (Zollikon: Evangelischer Verlag). |

Williams, F.E.

| 1990 | 'The Apocryphon of James', in J.M.Robinson (ed.), *The Nag Hammadi Library in English* (3rd rev. edn; San Francisco: Harper): 29-30. |

Winn, A.C.

| 1981 | *A Sense of Mission: Guidance from the Gospel of John* (Philadelphia: Westminster Press). |

Wisse, F.

1990   'The Apocryphon of John', in J.M. Robinson, *The Nag Hammadi Library in English* (3rd rev. edn; San Francisco: Harper): 104-105.

Wolf, H.

1980   'אָחַד', *TWOT*: I, 30.

Woll, D.B.

1980   'The Departure of "The Way": The First Farewell Discourse in the Gospel of John', *JBL* 99: 225-39.

Yamauchi, E.M.

1973   *Pre-Christian Gnosticism: A Survey of the Proposed Evidences* (London: Tyndale Press).

Yarbro Collins, A.

1979   'Crises and Community in John's Gospel', *Theology Digest* 27: 313-21.

Zahn, T.

1921   *Das Evangelium des Johannes* (Leipzig: A. Deichert; Erlangen: W. Scholl, 5th and 6th edn).

Zerwick, M.

1963   *Biblical Greek: Illustrated by Examples* (English edn adapted from the 4th Latin edn by Joseph Smith; Rome: Biblical Institute Press).

Zwaan, J. de

1938.   'John Wrote in Aramaic', *JBL* 57: 155-71.

INDEXES

INDEX OF REFERENCES

OLD TESTAMENT

OTHER ANCIENT SOURCES

INDEX OF AUTHORS